T0305374

Environmental Costs and Liberalization in European Air Transport

TRANSPORT ECONOMICS, MANAGEMENT AND POLICY

General Editor: Kenneth Button, *Professor of Public Policy, School of Public Policy, George Mason University, USA*

Transport is a critical input for economic development and for optimizing social and political interaction. Recent years have seen significant new developments in the way that transport is perceived by private industry and governments, and in the way academics look at it.

The aim of this series is to provide original material and up-to-date synthesis of the state of modern transport analysis. The coverage embraces all conventional modes of transport but also includes contributions from important related fields such as urban and regional planning and telecommunications where they interface with transport. The books draw from many disciplines and some cross disciplinary boundaries. They are concerned with economics, planning, sociology, geography, management science, psychology and public policy. They are intended to help improve the understanding of transport, the policy needs of the most economically advanced countries and the problems of resource-poor developing economies. The authors come from around the world and will represent some of the outstanding young scholars as well as established names.

Titles in the series include:

Analytical Transport Economics
An International Perspective
Edited by Jacob B. Polak and Arnold Heertje

Intelligent Transport Systems
Cases and Policies
Edited by Roger R. Stough

Transport and Environment
In Search of Sustainable Solutions
Edited by Eran Feitelson and Erik T. Verhoef

Environmental Costs and Liberalization in European Air Transport
A Welfare Economic Analysis
Youdi Schipper

Reforming Transport Pricing in the European Union
A Modelling Approach
Edited by Bruno De Borger and Stef Proost

Travel Behaviour
Spatial Patterns, Congestion and Modelling
Edited by Eliahu Stern, Ilan Salomon and Piet H.L. Bovy

Financing Transportation Networks
David Levinson

Environmental Costs and Liberalization in European Air Transport

A Welfare Economic Analysis

Youdi Schipper

Lecturer in Public Economics, University of Economics, Ho Chi Minh City, Vietnam

TRANSPORT ECONOMICS, MANAGEMENT AND POLICY

Edward Elgar
Cheltenham UK · Northampton, MA, USA

Published by
Edward Elgar Publishing Limited
Glensanda House
Montpellier Parade
Cheltenham
Glos GL50 1UA
UK

Edward Elgar Publishing, Inc.
136 West Street
Suite 202
Northampton
Massachusetts 01060
USA

A catalogue record for this book
is available from the British Library

Library of Congress Cataloguing in Publication Data

Schipper, Youdi, 1969–
    Environmental costs and liberalization in European air transport : a welfare economic analysis / Youdi Schipper.
        p. cm. — (Transport economics, management, and policy)
    Includes bibliographical references and index.
    1. Aeronautics, Commercial—Deregulation—European Union countries. 2. Aeronautics, Commercial—Environmental aspects. 3. Competition, Imperfect. I. Title. II. Series.

HE9842.8.Z7 E587 2001
387.7'094—dc21

00–067343

ISBN 1 84064 605 5

Printed and bound in Great Britain by MPG Books Ltd, Bodmin, Cornwall

To Elisabeth

Contents

List of figures

List of tables

Preface

What is the relation between the economic costs of environmental degradation and output in air transport markets? How does accounting for these environmental costs affect the welfare analysis of liberalization in air transport markets?

These are the main questions addressed in this book. When trying to answer these questions one has to study two distinct strands of literature regarding air transport. The first area of research concerns the estimation of environmental damages in aviation, which has received attention in the economics literature since the late 1960s. Secondly, numerous studies have addressed the welfare implications of airline liberalization since, some two decades ago, regulatory reform started to change market structures and competitive conditions in airline markets around the world. It can be argued, however, that these two areas of research have developed quite independently. As a result, the analysis of airline liberalization has largely ignored the implications for welfare through environmental degradation.

This book is an attempt to bring together these two areas of research in a welfare economic analysis of regulatory reform in European air transport markets. Such an analysis requires the estimation of environmental costs as a function of output in these markets, as well as modeling the behavior of agents in air transport markets. These two parts of the analysis are developed, respectively, in Parts I and II of the book. While uncertainties in a number of causal relations remain and the debate on many issues will continue, it is hoped that the results presented here are useful for researchers and policy makers concerned with externalities and regulation in aviation.

This book has benefitted from various kinds of support. The research has been carried out with financial support from the Netherlands Organization for Scientific Research, which is gratefully acknowledged. I would like to thank Barbara van de Kerke at RAND Europe and Anneke de Wit at the Ministry of Transport in The Hague for providing help in finding data.

I have enjoyed and learned from discussions with a number of colleagues and friends, none of whom should be held responsible for remaining errors or incongruities. I would like to thank Robin Lindsey for stimulating discussions and detailed comments. Further, I would like to thank Ken Button, Cees Dorland, Eran Feitelson, Raymond Florax, David Maddison, Jon P. Nelson, Peter Nijkamp, Eric Pels, Piet Rietveld and Erik Verhoef for their comments, advice or assistance at various stages of the research.

Youdi Schipper

Chapter 1
Introduction

1.1 Background

Competition and environmental pollution have a long tradition in aviation.[1]
At the beginning of the 'airplane age', two bicycle repairmen named Orville
and Wilbur Wright beat Samuel Langly in the attempt to make the first
successful flight, in December, 1903 on the beach at Kitty Hawk, North Carolina.
To Langly, the man whom everyone expected to be first, can, however, be
attributed the dubious honor of having created the first air transport pollution
by attempting a considerable number of test flights with experimental planes
that unfailingly plunged into the Potomac River near Washington, DC. Positive
effects were present too, as Langly's test launches were public spectacles (as well
as embarrassments), and thus created plane spotters *avant la lettre*. Ultimately,
the unfortunate attempts by Langly, who was supported by the US army,
Congress and the Smithsonian Institution, can be regarded as the first instances
of government involvement in aviation.

Aviation has changed and developed enormously since then. First of all,
technology has evolved dramatically since the take-off of the Wright Flyer (which
was, incidentally, named after a bicycle), thus allowing air transportation to
assume the crucial role it fulfills in many societies today. The development of
aviation has been one of the main factors reducing travel times and enhancing
mobility over large distances during the twentieth century. The growth of air
transportation in the past 40 years has been impressive: while global motorized
mobility (pass-km per capita) quadrupled between 1960 and 1990, the share of
air transportation in overall mobility increased from 2.6 percent to 9.4 percent
(Schafer, 1998).

The role of public authority in aviation has also been subject to considerable
change over the history of air transportation. While government involvement
through ownership and regulation has been extensive in airline markets in most
parts of the world since the 1920s, public intervention in air transport in and
between OECD countries has diminished considerably in recent years (Button,
1991; Banister and Button, 1991). The reform of government intervention in
airline markets reflects a more critical attitude among economists and policy
makers towards regulation of markets in general. This attitude resulted in
the rethinking and reforming of regulatory institutions in many industries since
the late 1970s, based on economic analyses of the working of markets and the

---

[1]   This section draws on Bryson (1994, chapter 19).

1

welfare effects of regulating markets. Critics of airline regulation argued that the regulatory structures that had been built up over the years were obsolete and inefficient, providing protection for incumbent producers while neglecting or hurting consumer interests. Such criticism paved the way for air transport policy reforms in several markets, e.g., the deregulation of the US domestic market (1978), which was followed by liberalization of the North Atlantic and European markets.

A fundamental idea in the critical evaluation of market regulation is that government intervention should be aimed at the correction of market failure. The fact that airline regulation came under critical review and was ultimately reformed in a number of cases does not imply, however, that market failure is absent in airline markets. Rather, it was felt that the types of market regulation under review were inappropriate or even counterproductive. Classic instances of market failure like externalities, information asymmetries and market power are indeed present in airline markets. This study focuses on two of these market failures, namely, market power and environmental externalities, and the way these are affected by regulatory reform.

Regulatory reform has generally aimed to reduce market power by airlines in formerly regulated markets by introducing or improving competitive conditions in airline markets. However, cost conditions in airline markets favor an imperfectly competitive market structure. Therefore, imperfect competition is likely to prevail even after reform: duopoly is a very common type of competition in aviation.

Environmental damage is present in both regulated and liberalized airline markets and thereby affects the welfare analysis of airline deregulation. Like most transportation modes, aviation contributes to pressure on the environment at various spatial levels. The contribution of aircraft emissions to climate change has been well established (FPC, 1998), and research regarding other global issues, such as the effect of aircraft emissions on atmospheric ozone depletion, is progressing (Dameris et al., 1998a,b). Furthermore, aircraft emissions affect ambient air quality and noise nuisance in communities located near to airports (Feitelson et al., 1996; Janic, 1999). Consequently, the growing importance of air transportation as a transport mode is expected to result in an increasing share in environmental damage (Archer, 1993; FPC, 1998). In particular, while airline reform may well increase output on airline markets, environmental costs are likely to increase too.

From this brief description, one can conclude that the two market failures studied here are related. Thus, policies addressing one failure may well affect the other. In other words, such policies face restrictions because they have to take account of an indirect welfare effect because of the second market failure. Therefore, the problem at hand fits into the area of second-best policy problems in which the welfare gains to consumers (passengers) from increasing output in imperfectly competitive markets have to be traded off against the welfare losses to agents who incur output-related environmental damage.

The trade-off is presented in Figure 1.1, which illustrates the welfare difference between two market equilibria $\{p_m, q_m\}$ and $\{p_c, q_c\}$, representing the standard monopoly and competitive market equilibria respectively. When the equilibrium for some reason 'moves' from the former to the latter, the welfare effect or change is represented by the triangle xyz. This is the 'deadweight loss' due to monopoly power. In the presence of output-related external costs, say $E = Q \cdot e$, the total welfare change has to be adjusted. In the case presented here, the change in external costs is represented by the area $vyzw$.

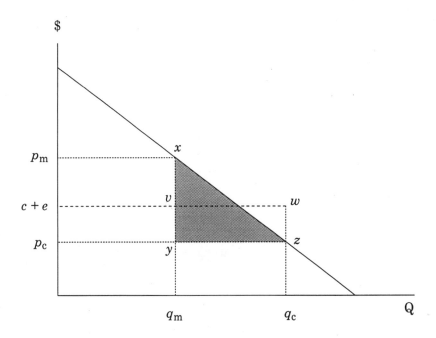

Figure 1.1: Two market imperfections

When evaluating the difference between the two equilibria, the sizes of the respective 'welfare areas' have to be compared. Clearly, the net effect depends on demand conditions and the size of the external costs in the market. When external costs are 'low' relative to the deadweight loss triangle (xyz), the introduction of competition and the subsequent expansion of output are beneficial. With 'high' external costs, a negative welfare conclusion may be obtained.

1.2 Aim and approach

This book analyzes the welfare economic effects of regulatory reform in aviation. From an economic perspective, the features of aviation described in the previous section require that attention be devoted to two general aspects. First, one should consider the welfare effects of regulatory changes within the market for air transport services. Secondly, because aviation affects the environment, the indirect welfare effect of regulatory changes through changes in the quantity (quality) of environmental goods – such as clean air, peace and quiet, safety – should be taken into account. Combining both types of effects, a welfare economic evaluation of regulatory change in aviation can be carried out.

An overview of the analytical framework is given in Figure 1.2. The effects to be considered in the analysis are represented by arrows.

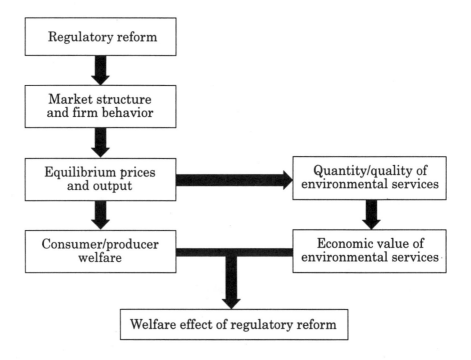

Figure 1.2: Analytical framework

The general research purpose is to offer a welfare economic evaluation of the effects of regulatory reform in aviation markets. The analysis aims to take into account a number of particular characteristics of air transport markets.

As noted above, the distinction between market internal effects and market external effects is relevant in analyses of aviation markets. Given their presence in the procurement of air transport services, environmental externalities and their relation to output in air transport markets are given separate attention in the evaluation. A considerable part of this study therefore addresses the two blocks and arrows on the right in Figure 1.2, representing the valuation of the environment by economic agents and the ways in which aviation affects the environment.

The other blocks in Figure 1.2 represent market internal changes, which are analyzed using economic models. The economic models underlying the analysis of market internal effects account for the fact that the number of suppliers in most airline markets is small. These models are based on microeconomic theory concerning imperfect competition. The form of regulatory change in airline markets considered here can be referred to as *liberalization* or *deregulation.* Such policy reform has the general characteristic that government involvement in the determination of competitive conditions is reduced.[2] Since policy reform conforming to this general description has occurred in markets in a number of regions, a.o., the United States domestic market, on the North Atlantic routes and in the European Union, the analysis has the form of an ex-post policy evaluation. The evaluation itself takes two general forms, namely, theoretical analysis combined with simulation experiments on the one hand, and empirical analysis on the other. The analysis is not concerned with regulation aimed directly at environmental themes, but the changes in environmental costs studied are a side-effect of regulatory reform in aviation.

Finally, the empirical focus in the book is on European airline markets. Therefore, empirical information, both on the market internal and external cost side, is gathered as much as possible to reflect the situation in European markets. The introduction of such a focus is necessary in order to restrict the scope of the analysis somewhat. The geographical choice is explained by the fact that regulatory reform in European aviation is of relatively recent date, and the empirical analysis of welfare effects is as yet not covered in depth. Furthermore, the choice allowed the use of specific recent information on environmental costs that has been gathered in European studies, e.g., on the effects of local air pollution.

1.3   Outline of the book

The book is divided in two parts: Part I is dedicated to environmental costs of aviation, while Part II analyzes the market internal effects as well as the evaluation

---

[2]   See Chapter 2 for a discussion of the concept of regulatory reform itself and an overview of the characteristics of regulation in a number of air transport markets.

of both types of effects combined. Thus, in terms of the framework sketched in Figure 1.1, the analysis starts with the blocks and arrows on the right-hand side. Table 1.1 presents an overview of the chapters of the book.

Table 1.1
Outline

Chapter 1	Introduction
Chapter 2	Regulation and Reform in Aviation

Part I: Environmental Costs in Air Transport Markets

Chapter 3	Evaluating Environmental Externalities
Chapter 4	Noise
Chapter 5	Emissions
Chapter 6	Environmental Costs in European Aviation

Part II: Economic Analysis of Air Transport Liberalization

Chapter 7	Frequency Choice in Air Transport Markets
Chapter 8	Frequency Choice and Liberalization: Simulation Modeling
Chapter 9	Airline Liberalization in Networks
Chapter 10	Welfare Effects of European Airline Liberalization

Chapter 11	Conclusion

Chapter 2 describes and discusses the characteristics of regulation in airline markets at the international level and, for a number of countries, in domestic markets. The economic motivation for regulation in airline markets is discussed in the context of market failure, and is compared with the arguments used to advocate the introduction of airline regulation. Furthermore, the measures taken in order to reform the system of regulation are described briefly as a background to the analysis in Part II.

Part I of the book addresses the valuation of environmental externalities. Chapter 3 discusses the concept of externalities and its relevance in the context of airline markets. Distinguishing between different types of externalities in aviation, the relative share of air transport in global externalities is discussed. Finally, the methods and format of evaluation of externalities in the subsequent chapters are addressed. The evaluation of the external effects of transportation is presented as a cause–effect chain or pathway that runs from disaggregate transport activities (individual flights in airline markets) via the contribution to ambient conditions to monetary losses. Furthermore, the difficulties in establishing the various chains in such pathways are examined.

The valuation of two types of environmental externality problems, namely, noise and emission of pollutants, is discussed in Chapters 4 and 5, respectively. In the case of noise, results of studies following one of two valuation methods used to attach monetary values to changes in ambient noise levels are reviewed. The results of a few contingent valuation studies are compared with a larger set of hedonic price valuation studies. Furthermore, the variation in estimates among the hedonic price studies is studied in a meta-analysis. The valuation results present a first part of the external costs imposed by aviation. The valuation of a number of aircraft emission types is discussed in Chapter 5. Here, valuation is indirect as the effects of increased concentrations of pollutants are valued rather than the emissions themselves. The analysis distinguishes between the valuation of the global warming effect on the one hand, and the valuation of the local effects of pollutants on human health on the other. Chapter 5 discusses the methods and assumptions used in deriving the value estimates, and presents a number of recent valuation results which are applied in European valuation studies.

The relations between individual aircraft movements and ambient environmental conditions are discussed in Chapter 6. Using information on aircraft emission and noise characteristics, the individual contribution to a deterioration in ambient environmental conditions is calculated. The damage costs per flight for a number of aircraft types are estimated by applying the monetary value attached to such environmental changes. Accident risk costs are obtained from the literature and discussed briefly. The cost estimates obtained in Chapter 6 are used as inputs to the analysis in Part II.

Part II analyzes the welfare effects of regulatory reform in aviation. Chapter 7 addresses the problem of departure frequency and price determination in the context of a model with competition between differentiated products. A number of symmetric oligopoly equilibria are derived in order to compare welfare results with the regulated solution. The symmetry assumption, implying that all firms behave identically, allows one to derive analytical solutions. The model solutions derived in Chapter 7 are then applied in Chapter 8, where parameter values are introduced using a data set for a sample of European airline markets along with the environmental cost estimates derived in Part I. Thus, the welfare effects of regulatory reform are quantified in a number of empirical simulations. Furthermore, a model of airline competition in networks with asymmetric equilibria is developed in Chapter 8, as an extension of the symmetric model. In Chapter 9, a model of airline reform in small network markets is presented as a second extension of the basic model, and numerical results are reviewed.

As a conclusion to Part II, the effects of bilateral liberalization are quantified in a statistical analysis in Chapter 10. Using the data set introduced in Chapter 9, demand and supply equations are estimated. Based on the estimation results and environmental cost estimates for the routes in the sample, the effects of liberalization on consumer welfare and on environmental costs are compared.

Finally, Chapter 11 concludes with a summary of findings of the analysis in the preceding chapters and a discussion of questions pertaining to policy makers and future research efforts.

The list of research questions connected to the general themes of regulatory reform and market failure in aviation is clearly much longer than the list presented above, and a number of potentially relevant questions and topics have not been treated in the present study. A brief list of topics not covered in the present study is presented below.

In the realm of externalities in air transport, the issues of congestion and slot allocation have not been addressed. As an external cost item, transport congestion has been valued in, e.g., Maddison et al. (1996) and Hensher (1997). The relevance of congestion in competition policy is described qualitatively in Chapter 2. Slot scarcity is, however, not considered in the welfare analysis in Part II. Market solutions with respect to slot allocation are described in Morrison and Winston (1989) and McGowan and Seabright (1989).

A potentially interesting question in the context of air transport externalities and competition is the choice of aircraft type. A numerical solution in a network scheduling context is given in Dobson and Lederer (1993). Entry deterring behavior in the airline industry involving aircraft choice is treated in Berechman et al. (1995). While this and other types of entry deterrence are interesting topics in strategic firm behavior, they are not modeled here. Other forms of strategic interaction in the airline industry not modeled are market foreclosure, e.g., through manipulation of the computer reservation system (CRS, see Chapter 2 for a qualitative discussion), and predatory behavior (e.g., Dodgson et al., 1993; Lindsey and Tomazewska, 1998).

As mentioned previously, this book presents a welfare economic evaluation of regulatory reform. However, other interesting policy-related questions are given only cursory attention. In particular, the issue of re-regulation, e.g., environmental taxation, is not taken up here. An analytical treatment of environmental taxation in airline markets is given in Nero and Black (1998), and applied studies are Bleijenberg and Wit (1997) and FPC (1998).

Numerous studies have been carried out in the field of transport externalities. A number of these studies are referred to in Part I and their results, particularly in the field of physical effects of transport emissions, are used. Valuation of general transport-related external effects has attracted much attention and valuation results have been used in applied studies, e.g., Greene et al. (1997) and Maddison et al. (1996). The valuation results are, however, mostly applied to road transport or fuel use in general. Studies aimed specifically at air transport externalities have concentrated on valuation of ambient levels of aircraft noise (see the studies used in Chapter 4) or have applied average valuation results from other studies to aircraft externalities (Perl et al., 1997; Kågeson, 1993). In this study, the results of both general and aircraft-specific externality valuations are combined with information on aircraft emissions of noise and pollutants in order to establish marginal damages in terms of transport output. To this end, a 'bottom-up' approach is followed, tracing the pathway from disaggregate aircraft contributions to ambient conditions to monetary values associated with these conditions. This allows the establishment of marginal damages in terms of individual flights for a number of aircraft types, which is needed in order to evaluate the effects of regulatory reform in Part II.

In Part II, this study contributes to the literature on airline deregulation or liberalization by adding the welfare effects associated with negative externalities to the analysis. The analysis of market internal changes applies microeconomic models of firm behavior in oligopoly to airline markets. The standard model of product differentiation in a circular market is applied to airline frequency choice. In order to capture characteristics of airline competition, the model is modified to allow for symmetric and asymmetric multi-departure equilibria, which are subsequently compared with monopoly or regulated outcomes. Another extension of the basic model concerns the application to network competition. Finally, the results in Chapter 10 add evidence concerning European airline markets to the empirical literature regarding the welfare effects of airline liberalization.

Chapter 2
Regulation and Reform in Aviation

2.1 Introduction

Regulatory reform has become a widespread trend in economic policy in OECD countries since the mid-1970s, affecting sectors such as transportation, telecommunications, banking and financial services, broadcasting and energy supply. Analyses of such policy changes, surveyed for the United States in Winston (1993), have generally concluded that the welfare effects were positive. The initiation of the reform measures has been supported by the research and predictions of (micro)economists. Although some effects were not foreseen, the predicted direction and size of results were mostly correct. Furthermore, welfare gains proved to be substantial: according to the above study, welfare improvements due to regulatory reform amounted to 7–9 percent of GNP, while an important part of these gains was the result of deregulation in transport industries.

The airline industry stands out as an important case in the recent history of policy reform: formerly an almost completely regulated sector, it has been undergoing a process of regulatory reform at both national and international levels. As a background to the analysis in the rest of the book, the next section examines the regulatory arrangements that were, until reform began, instituted in a number of airline markets. Next, the standard economic motivations for regulation in the form of market failure are analyzed. Subsequently, the arguments for airline regulation, as well as the arguments for reform, are reviewed in this context. Lastly, the reform measures are described. The focus here as well as in the rest of the book is on reform in European airline markets.

2.2 Airline regulation

In order to put the analysis of regulatory reform in context, some important developments in airline regulation are elaborated below. The discussion here is not intended to be comprehensive or detailed, but is meant to provide a background to the analysis. Detailed accounts can be found in Doganis (1991) and Button (1991).

2.2.1 International aviation

Airline regulation has generally affected economic decision making with respect to three key variables: market entry, capacity and pricing. When the signatories of the Paris Convention (1919) decided that states have sovereign rights over the air space above their territories, governments automatically controlled entry into air transport markets involving routes above their territories. As a consequence, international aviation became subject to an incomplete set of bilateral rights exchanged between governments between the wars. Attempts to reach a uniform, multilateral settlement on market entry, capacity and pricing were made at aviation conferences in Chicago (1944) and Geneva (1947). The conferences failed to reach a uniform, liberal agreement as advocated by the United States, basically because of European fears of US predominance in aviation markets given the asymmetric distribution of postwar capacity.

Only very limited agreement was reached on market access, which in aviation markets is defined in terms of so-called 'freedoms of the air'. The conference agreed on multilateral exchange of the first freedom (fly over another country's territory) and second freedom (right of an airline to make technical landings, e.g. to refuel). The important freedoms from an economic regulation point of view, i.e. those related to actual market access, were not agreed upon multilaterally. These freedoms involve the right of an airline from (registered in) country A to set down in country B passengers picked up in A (the third freedom), the right of an airline from A to pick up passengers in B for off-loading in A (the fourth freedom), and the right of an airline registered in C to carry passengers between points in A and B (the fifth freedom).

Since no multilateral agreement was reached regarding the latter three freedoms, the regulatory framework for entry, pricing and capacity decisions with respect to scheduled services was subject to conditions in so-called air service agreements (ASAs or 'bilaterals'), bilaterally negotiated between states. In terms of market structure, for many of the major international routes this implied that a collusive duopoly or joint monopoly consisting of the state-owned 'flag' carriers of the countries at the endpoints of the route prevailed. The joint monopoly in air transportation was sustained by the following general characteristics of the bilateral agreements. Market access was under the control of the states owning (large parts of) the supplying firms: in practice, multiple designation, i.e., more than one carrier from a country being licensed to operate services on a route, was exceptional. Furthermore, bilaterals specified the routes to be served between two countries; meanwhile fifth freedom rights were rarely granted. Collusive behavior consisted of the following elements. Fares had to be agreed upon by the parties signing the bilateral, while most governments explicitly adhered to fares which were set in tariff conferences organized by the International Air Transport Association (IATA). These conferences are generally considered to have functioned as cartel meetings where joint profit-maximizing or monopoly prices were fixed (Doganis, 1991). Furthermore, bilaterals often provided some kind of 'pooling' arrangement between the national carriers on the route: in many cases capacity offered on the route was limited to 50 percent per airline (capacity-sharing), while sharing of revenues was common. Clearly, such pooling arrangements remove incentives or even the possibility to compete in service levels, e.g., frequency of service.

2.2.2   Domestic aviation

In addition to the restrictions on international routes, many countries have regulated air transport on their domestic routes too. An important case is the regulation of the US domestic aviation industry from the passage of the Civil Aeronautics Act in 1938 until the formal deregulation of the industry with the Airline Deregulation Act in 1978 (Pickrell, 1991). During this period, the Civil Aeronautics Board (CAB) tightly restricted the number of carriers at the route market level for both existing and new routes,[3] thus protecting the airlines that had route authority in 1938. No new trunk airlines were allowed, mergers were controlled, and exit from routes required CAB approval. The CAB also introduced fare control, while the overall scope of control widened over the years.

Domestic aviation in Australia experienced extensive government intervention from the end of World War II until the demise of the so-called Two Airline Policy in 1990 (Forsyth, 1991). This name refers to the regulated duopoly operation of a government airline (Trans Australia Airlines) and a private carrier (Ansett) since 1957, with entry restrictions, capacity control, collusive pricing and route coordination. In Canada, regulatory policy included control of entry, both into the industry and into specific route markets, regulation of service levels and complete fare control (Oum et al., 1991; Oum and Tretheway, 1984). Air Canada, the national carrier, enjoyed monopoly rights on domestic transcontinental routes from its establishment in 1937 until 1959, and on international routes until 1948.

In Europe, domestic entry regulation and price controls were present in many countries too. Before the initiation of regulatory reforms, domestic air transport operations in OECD countries generally required licenses, the granting of which could be subject to some indication of public need for the service in case of scheduled services (OECD, 1988). Furthermore, the license usually specified which domestic routes could be served, as well as capacities and fares. The UK domestic route markets became gradually more liberalized from the 1980s onwards, when licenses were granted to new entrants on particular routes. However, domestic routes were monopolies or duopolies operated by the publicly owned national carriers in most other European countries (Button, 1991).[4]

---

[3]   During the 1950s, the CAB permitted 'local service carriers' to start 'feeder services' between small communities and cities, but these carriers were not allowed to compete with the established airlines.

[4]   Button and Swann (1989) mention that a straightforward application of the general principles of the Treaty of Rome, i.e., the elimination or harmonization of internal tariffs, quantitative restrictions and non-tariff barriers, would have had a considerable effect on this protection of domestic markets.

While the above overview of regulatory arrangements is clearly limited in its detail and geographical coverage, a common thread is discernible. It can be concluded that in the airline markets described here, regulatory arrangements stemming from the interwar or immediate postwar era have generally tended to restrict competition. The economic motivation for regulation in airline markets is examined in the next section.

2.3   Economic motivation for regulation

Economic regulation is traditionally advocated in cases where markets fail. Classic instances of market failure are the presence of externalities (see Chapter 3), information asymmetries and market power. The forms that these general types of market failure take in airline markets are presented briefly in the following (see McGowan and Seabright, 1989; Kay and Thompson, 1991; Pelkmans, 1991).

A first market failure in air transport markets is the presence of externalities or external effects. Externalities in air transport markets include noise problems, the emission of pollutants, the presence of accident risks, and congestion. The first three of these problems can be designated as environmental externalities. The concept and causes of external costs are discussed in further detail in Chapter 3. Actual intervention in many cases entails direct regulation (e.g. using noise contours) and sometimes involves charges.[5] A distinct aviation-related externality type is congestion. The market failure here is of particular concern because of the connection between the availability of airport capacity and competitive conditions in the airline market itself.

In particular, the allocation of airport slots by scheduling committees based on the 'grandfather principle' has raised considerable concern among economists, because of the inefficiency as well as the anti-competitive implications of the practice. In a nutshell, 'grandfathering' is a system that gives continued access to carriers who have previously had slots, and does not ensure that slots are allocated to those airlines that can most economically use and thus most highly value them; in other words, marginal productivity is not equalized among slots and total productivity is not maximized. If, however, the opportunity cost of airport capacity were to be reflected in the cost of using slots, this would give carriers incentives to maximize the productivity of slots. This would in turn affect the choice of aircraft and route structure. A derived concern is that limited slot availability (congestion) is a barrier to new entry (e.g. Barrett, 1992). Slot allocation based on 'grandfather rights' thus effectively protects incumbents, enabling them to earn rents because of slot scarcity. Market-based approaches to the congestion problem, either through trade or the auctioning of slot rights, have

---

[5]   E.g. aircraft noise charges in OECD (1991) and the proposed European aircraft emission charges in Bleijenberg and Wit (1997).

been proposed as more efficient solutions (see McGowan and Seabright, 1989).

Information asymmetries are present in airline markets too, with respect to safety as product quality on the one hand and availability of alternative services on the other. This information asymmetry is present because the factors which determine safety are under the control of the airline but are usually not observable by passengers. In particular, air transport services can be termed 'trust goods' as far as safety characteristics are concerned, because this quality dimension is, if all goes well, usually not apparent even after consumption. Given that safety measures are costly, adverse selection may drive out high safety standards under competitive conditions (Moses and Savage, 1990; McGowan and Seabright, 1989; Kay and Vickers, 1988). This information problem has given rise to 'non-economic' regulations on issues such as the airworthiness of the aircraft, maintenance, operating standards of airlines, crew training and (airport) infrastructure (Doganis, 1991).[6] Technical and safety standards, however, are applied to all airlines and therefore do not distort competition between individual airlines (OECD, 1988).

The other asymmetry concerns the information about competing air services available to consumers through computerized reservation systems (CRSs), which potentially affects competitive conditions in airline markets. First, investments in CRSs in the US and Europe have been made by a number of airlines and are used by travel agents when selling seats. This has raised concerns about so-called 'CRS bias', favoring the flights of the airlines owning the systems over competing services. Secondly, the CRS bias may deter entry because it substantially raises sunk costs of marketing and thus acts as a constraint on competitive conditions in airline markets (Barrett, 1992; McGowan and Seabright, 1989).

A third type of market failure concerns market power. Market or monopoly power of airline firms stems from, besides a number of factors discussed above, the technology used in air transportation. First, because it is less costly to transport three hundred passengers in one flight on a large plane than, say, in 15 flights in small jets, most air transport services are supplied in 'chunks'. Indeed, it is a general cost characteristic of air transport that unit costs decrease with aircraft size,[7] and this relation is the principal source of scale economies at the route level, generally referred to as economies of density (Tretheway and Qum, 1992; Doganis, 1991). Secondly, the 'chunks' of service on most routes are offered by a few,

---

[6]   These 'technical' requirements are generally issued by the civil aviation authorities of individual countries, while uniformity among countries is enhanced by the existence of the International Civil Aviation Organization's 'International Standards and Recommended Practices' series, which serves as a role model.

[7]   However, note that, given fixed costs per flight, costs per seat-mile decline with distance for all aircraft types. Thus, observed unit cost differences on a per seat-mile basis are partly due to differences in average route lengths of the respective aircraft types. Therefore, comparisons should rather be made between aircraft types for a particular flight distance on a per passenger basis.

often no more than two, suppliers. Although this feature can partly be explained by 'ordinary' cost characteristics, such as the sunk costs of advertising, (sunk) costs associated with entry at the route level are low in comparison with those in other industries (Beesley, 1986; McGowan and Seabright, 1989). Therefore, the presently observed number of operators may reflect other features besides the usual entry costs: one can think of the regulatory history of many markets (Pryke, 1991), the arrangements of which were only recently amended, and entry barriers, such as asymmetries in slot allocation and CRS bias discussed above.

Other entry barriers are related to the network character of aviation, particularly the operation of hub-and-spoke (HS) route systems. Without delving into the details of HS systems, one of the main advantages of operating such a system is that it allows for economies of density in the spokes by routing passengers with various destinations through the central hub (see, e.g., Oum et al., 1995; Tretheway and Oum, 1992; Brueckner and Spiller, 1991). It has, however, been observed that hubbing confers market power to the main carrier at the hub: by scheduling in a predatory way, competitors may not be able to benefit from economies of density, so that HS systems combined with strategic conduct of the incumbent operators may well act as a barrier to entry (Berechman et al., 1995). Once such a dominant position is obtained, market power can be translated into prices (Morrison and Winston, 1990; Borenstein, 1992). McGowan and Seabright (1989) thus conclude that HS networks constitute an indispensable form of vertical integration, and again, that the slot allocation process may significantly enhance the scope for maintaining dominant positions.

Closely related to the issue of market power is the concept of contestability, which defines a number of theoretical conditions[8] under which oligopoly markets are vulnerable to 'hit-and-run' entry and therefore display competitive pricing. If these conditions are fulfilled, even a small number of incumbents will be unable to exercise monopolistic power because of the threat of potential entry. The discussion bears particular relevance to the history of airline regulation, because airline markets were considered to be contestable, and contestability theory was used to advocate US domestic deregulation. However, the contestability theory has been criticized on a number of accounts, both theoretically (Schwartz, 1986; Spence, 1983) and empirically (Morrison and Winston, 1987). In particular, one of the most important postulates of the theory, price rigidity, is refuted empirically: airlines can and do change fares on a daily basis and are therefore perfectly able to use price cuts in response to entry. Therefore, it can be argued that the threat of potential entry does not actually influence incumbents' price decisions, especially when sunk costs and consumer loyalty are present. The main issue is time: time needed for a choice variable such as price to be changed, and time needed by an entrant to gain a sufficient share of the market to operate profitably. Given the

---

[8]   These conditions include a low level of unrecoverable or sunk costs for potential entrants, and slow adjustment of prices (Martin, 1993).

fact that air fares can be changed at very short notice, an incumbent can safely earn monopoly rents, even under threat of potential entry, because the entrant knows that the incumbent can engage in a price war (at least in the relevant fare classes) in the event of entry. It can thus be concluded that market power does not disappear through the threat of competitive entry and can be enhanced by the actions of incumbents.

In the area of market power, one can identify two general cases of market failure which call for regulation (Kay and Vickers, 1988). First, there is the case in which competition is desirable but is prevented by anti-competitive (predatory) behavior of incumbents. Many of the regulatory issues in liberalized markets mentioned above fall into this category, including practices such as predatory scheduling or pricing and promoting CRS bias, discussed above. In such cases, regulation with respect to the incumbent's conduct is usually proposed in order to restore or enhance competitive behavior. A quite distinct area of market power regulation concerns cases in which competition is neither feasible nor desirable from a welfare economic point of view, namely 'severe natural monopoly'. Formally, with $\Pi(n)$ denoting industry profit as a function of firm number n, 'severe' natural monopoly would imply the condition $\Pi(1) > 0 > \Pi(2)$: only a monopolist is able to earn a profit, whereas competition always results in losses for the industry (Tirole, 1988). Generally, however, public-interest arguments for monopoly provision have been phrased in terms of 'subadditivity of cost', i.e., the characteristic that costs of monopoly production are lower than aggregate industry production costs under competition (Button and Swann, 1989). The condition that competition is not feasible is more strict than subadditivity of cost only, in which case a planner would prefer monopoly production. In the case of 'severe natural monopoly', regulation with respect to price, costs, and service characteristics can be used to limit the exploitation of market power by the monopolist.

As a third, more theoretical possibility, one may identify the case in which competition is feasible but not desirable; a numerical example for airline scheduling, referred to as 'cream skimming', is given in McGowan and Seabright (1989). In such a case, total welfare decreases when competition is introduced and structure regulation to limit competition (entry) may be proposed. However, several authors stress that great care should be taken, not only in determining whether competition is really undesirable, but also in drawing policy conclusions. First, both Kay and Vickers (1988) and McGowan and Seabright (1989) believe that undesirable competition is not of great practical importance. Secondly, while the public interest in restricting competition exists in theory, the private interest in doing so is real. Firms in industries for which the restriction of competition by law is considered, e.g., by prohibiting entry, have a real incentive to argue that competition is 'wasteful and destructive', one of the classic phrases used to motivate US domestic airline regulation. Therefore, Kay and Vickers (1988, p. 305) conclude that advocates of regulation aiming to restrict 'undesirable' competition carry a 'very heavy burden of proof'.

How do common types of regulation in airline markets relate to the economic motivation for regulation discussed here? Economic arguments favoring industry (entry) regulation are often associated with the presence of market power in general and natural monopoly in particular (see, e.g., Winston, 1993; Peltzman, 1989). However, early advocates of airline regulation seem to have been less concerned with the restriction of market power than with the restriction of competition. For example, the motivation for the US domestic airline regulation established in 1938 is generally ascribed to a widespread mistrust of the efficiency and 'stability' of competitive markets during the Great Depression, and has generally been phrased in terms of undesirability of competition (Levine, 1987, 1981; Pickrell, 1991).[9]

As noted above, the qualification of competition as 'wasteful and destructive' was used in the argument against airline competition and, as such, it would fit into the 'cream skimming' or 'natural monopoly' category of arguments.[10] It should be stressed, however, that both types of argument are quite subtle and require plenty of information in order to build a case to defend the type of regulation under consideration here (McGowan and Seabright, 1989). Despite claims that competition would harm the 'public at large', many observers have outlined the private interest motives of US airline firms to seek protection from the apparently fierce competition. Notwithstanding the potential gains of entry regulation to incumbents and the possibility of influence or pressure by the industry on regulatory authorities ('regulatory capture'), however, Levine (1981) concludes that the introduction of US airline regulation was a genuine but misguided effort 'on the part of a Congress and a Roosevelt administration trying to benefit the public at large' rather than a 'widely-coordinated effort by government to transfer wealth from the general public to the airlines'. However, the refusal of European countries to liberalize controls over international air transport in 1944 (see below) is generally considered to have been inspired by protectionist motives.[11] In Canada, the national carrier Trans-Canada Airlines was created in part to ensure accessibility across the country; subsequently, however, the position of Trans-Canada Airlines had to be protected through the regulation of services and fares of other carriers (Heaver, 1991).

Whatever the initial motivation, regulatory arrangements may well result in a decrease in total economic surplus, i.e., the sum of consumer welfare and profits; in such a case, the term 'regulatory failure' applies. A clear case of regulatory

---

[9] It should be noted that the restraint of (international) competition was a common type of economic policy affecting many industries in the 1930s (Palmer and Colton, 1983).

[10] It was further argued that competition and the frequent entry and exit of carriers would impose costs of uncertainty on consumers and decrease transport safety.

[11] Analyses of strategic trade in the 1980s (e.g., Martin, 1993) show that there are circumstances in which a country's total economic surplus is increased by protection; however, it seems unlikely that such arguments were used in 1944.

failure is present when the market failure it aims to correct does not exist, e.g. suppression of competition when competitive solutions are desirable and possible. Kay and Thompson (1991) present the structural regulatory policies preventing market entry in a number of transport sectors (aviation, express coaching and local bus services) as examples of such regulatory failure. In general, however, even the existence of market failure is not a sufficient condition for a given type of intervention to be desirable: in each case, the costs and benefits of introducing regulation should be traded off. See Kay and Vickers (1988) for a discussion of the efficiency problems associated with regulation, given the different objectives and information asymmetries in the principal–agent framework.

2.4   Regulatory reform in aviation

Once regulatory failure has been identified, regulatory reform should be considered. Within the context of economics, the term 'regulatory reform' is the broad term used to indicate changes in institutional arrangements present in many industries. While the term itself is not restricted to imply a particular direction of change, in the economics literature of the last few decades it commonly refers to processes where at least some form of government control is loosened. However, the distinction between regulatory reform and deregulation should be noted. Whereas economic deregulation has been defined in the literature as 'the state's withdrawal of its legal powers to direct the economic conduct of nongovernmental bodies' (Winston, 1993, quoting Stigler), regulatory reform is a more comprehensive concept. Kay and Vickers (1988, p. 286) use regulatory reform rather than deregulation because, 'as often as not, new and generally more explicit regulatory structures are simultaneously erected' when particular regulatory arrangements are abandoned. In cases where re-regulation is present, regulatory reform seems to be the more appropriate term. Furthermore, some authors (Button and Swann, 1989) define regulatory reform in terms of changes in regulation with respect to the aforementioned economic conduct (pricing, entry and exit), while others include changes in ownership (Kay and Thompson, 1991).

A number of factors have added to the change of perception with respect to regulation in general (Button and Swann, 1989; Winston, 1993). First, whereas regulation has traditionally been considered to repair market failure in the public interest, this favorable view on regulators has been supplanted by a critical analysis of the behavior of regulators and effects of regulation, particularly since the beginning of the 1970s. The economic analysis of the behavior of regulators and interest groups has given rise to a voluminous literature on economic regulation, which will not be discussed here; see Peltzman (1989) and Winston (1993) for reviews of this literature, and Laffont and Tirole (1991) and Grossman and Helpman (1994) for more recent contributions. This research has, nevertheless, questioned the assumption that regulators' interests equal public interests.   Other academic influence has been mentioned earlier: in spite of later criticism, the theory of contestable markets has had a distinct influence on US domestic airline deregulation. An important reason for dissatisfaction with existing regulation can, however, be referred to as a 'demonstration effect': the fact that, e.g., prices or costs are lower in states or countries where markets are not regulated may well provide a stimulus for reform. The largely unregulated intrastate routes in Texas and California before US deregulation, and the US experience as a lesson for reform in Canada and in North Atlantic and European routes are but a few examples. However, the relation between US and North Atlantic and European deregulation concerns more than just a demonstration effect. This has also been referred to as a 'knock-on' effect: in the event that firms from different countries compete, deregulation in one country may compel the other country to deregulate as well (Button and Swann, 1989).

The aforementioned pressures have resulted in reform measures in a number of national and international airline markets. Detailed descriptions of institutional details and specific reform measures and effects in a variety of countries (the US, Canada and Australia) can be found in Button (1991), Banister and Button (1991) and Button and Swann (1989). Also, see Morrison and Winston (1986, 1989) and Kahn (1988) for analyses of the effects of US domestic airline deregulation. Canadian airline deregulation is described and analyzed in Oum and Tretheway (1984) and Oum et al. (1991). Doganis (1991) addresses changes in international airline markets in general. OECD (1988) gives detailed accounts of regulatory reform in OECD countries. Since the details of the regulatory arrangements and reforms are described at length in the references listed above, they will not be further described here. However, since the focus of this study is reform in European interstate airline markets, regulatory reform in these markets is reviewed in some detail in the next section.

2.4.1   European reform

Until the beginning of the 1980s, air transport on European interstate routes had been regulated by means of bilateral ASAs described in Section 2.2. Therefore, key competitive conditions in air transport markets were negotiated by states owning (large parts of) the supplying firms. The typical agreement consisted of the following elements:

- Market access: third and fourth freedom for 'flag carriers'; 'multiple designation' and 'fifth freedom rights' exceptional;
- Pricing: approval of both governments needed; fares generally agreed upon in IATA conferences;
- Pooling agreements: (50:50) capacity-sharing, revenue-sharing.

Apart from these regulatory characteristics, ownership mattered: many of the airlines on the routes received financial aid from their governments. In so far as market structure was concerned, this implied, for many of the major international routes, the prevalence of a collusive duopoly or joint monopoly consisting of the state-owned 'flag' carriers of the countries at the endpoints of the route.

A qualification should be made, however, with respect to the scope of the ASAs. Whereas the above restriction of competition applied to scheduled services only, several authors (Button and Swann, 1989; Abbott and Thompson, 1991) have pointed to the important role of charter services in particular markets. This type of service, i.e., specific flights commissioned by tour operators on particular (holiday) routes, has developed as a separate market segment over the last thirty years. On the relevant (holiday) routes, mainly in Europe and the North Atlantic, charter airlines have thus acted as a competitive force for a specific type of service at a time when scheduled services were still protected by regulation. Although charter services are subject to relatively limited regulatory conditions with respect to bookings, route access, fares and capacity, they cannot compete directly with scheduled services. Notwithstanding the large number of passengers carried by charter carriers, McGowan and Seabright (1989) argue that the importance of charter traffic competition for scheduled services should not be overstated, given the specific character and limitations of charter services.

The European regulatory system came under increasing pressure for reform after the United States deregulated its domestic aviation markets in 1978 and many of the North Atlantic and Pacific routes between 1978 and 1985. Regulatory reform in European aviation markets has taken two forms: bilaterally negotiated reform of the ASAs on the one hand and multilateral reform initiated by the European Commission on the other. This section aims to describe the main reforms in European aviation, but detailed accounts of the regulatory situation and reforms in Europe can be found in Doganis (1991), Button and Swann (1989), McGowan and Seabright (1989) and OECD (1988).

Bilateral reform

The liberalization of bilaterals has been restricted to a small number of markets, initiated by the United Kingdom. From the mid-1980s onwards, the UK signed a number of liberal bilateral agreements, starting with the UK–Netherlands agreement of 1984 (modified in 1985), which served as a model for later agreements. An important function of these bilateral reform initiatives has been to demonstrate the feasibility of airline liberalization to other member states and to the European authorities (Button, 1991). Table 2.1 sums up the main characteristics of airline bilaterals before and after liberalization (Doganis, 1991).[12]

---

[12] The term 'double disapproval' in Table 2.1 means that fares are allowed unless both governments disapprove.

Table 2.1
Bilateral reform

	Traditional bilateral	Liberalized bilateral
Operators	One (flag) carrier from each state	Multiple designation
Routes	Specified	Open route access
Capacity	Shared between designated carriers	No capacity control
Fares	Double approval needed; IATA	Double disapproval

Whereas the traditional bilaterals displayed, on average, the characteristics described in Section 2.2 and summarized in Table 2.1, the renegotiation of bilaterals aimed to introduce a more competitive framework. The overview above corresponds to what may be termed 'full liberalization', i.e., liberalization with respect to market access, capacity (frequency) and fares. In a number of cases, the UK bilaterals were renegotiated in two stages, with full liberalization arrived at only in a second agreement (e.g. as with the UK–Netherlands and the UK–Ireland bilaterals). In other cases, liberalization remained 'restricted', particularly in cases where renegotiated bilaterals allowed multiple designation but did not introduce 'double disapproval'.

Multilateral reform

At the level of the European Union, reform in airline regulation has been implemented gradually, in three packages of liberalizing measures, issued in 1987, 1990 and 1993, respectively. The tension between the protectionist quality of the airline regulation on most European interstate and intrastate markets on the one hand, and the general spirit of the Treaty of Rome on the other, is noted in Doganis (1991) and Button and Swann (1989), who discuss the political history of EU deregulation.

These authors have called attention to the difficulties in the application of the competition articles and provisions of the Treaty to the airline markets, in particular Articles 85 and 86,[13] as well as the Right of Establishment and the Freedom to Supply Services. A recurring theme is the failure of the Council of Ministers to support the Commission in its efforts towards liberalization (Button and Swann, 1989),[14] proposals for which were laid down in the Second Memorandum on Air Transport in 1984. The Council assented to the limited liberalization in the 1987 package only when it was left with almost no other option by the European Court of Justice as a result of the 1985 *Nouvelles Frontières*

---

[13]   In brief: Article 85 prohibits anti-competitive agreements and concerted practices which eliminate, reduce or distort competition (unless specific exemptions have been granted), Article 86 prohibits abuse of a dominant position within the Community (Union) so as to affect trade between member states.

[14]   E.g. by conferring adequate implementing powers with respect to the Articles in the Treaty or by removing legal loopholes which allowed authorities to refuse route access to new airlines.

case.[15]

The political resistance to liberalization is reflected in the gradual, phased introduction of competition within the three liberalization packages. The main regulation of the first package, based on the Commission's Second Memorandum of 1984, enabled the Commission to apply Articles 85 and 86 of the Treaty of Rome directly to EU interstate airline services.

The regulations of the first package, which became effective from 1 January 1988, provided for more fare flexibility, namely, the obligation of member states to approve fares if they reflect costs and approval of discounting within particular fare zones; a relaxation of capacity-sharing within minimum and maximum market share provisions per route of 45 percent and 55 percent, respectively (extended to 40–60 percent in 1989); and multiple designation of carriers per country- and city-pair. The first package further authorized fifth freedom rights (limited to 30 percent of the seats) and the right of an airline to fly to two destinations in other EU member states on one flight (Sorensen, 1991). The gradual nature of the process was emphasized by the (temporary) 'block exemption' of three categories of agreement from the application of Article 85. The exemptions pertained to agreements on technical standards, training and the definition of fare categories, to agreements with respect to joint capacity planning, revenue-sharing and fare consultations and to agreements over slot allocations and CRS arrangements. The second of these exemptions reflects the 'political horse trading' (Button and Swann, 1989, p. 274) involved in the process.

However, although the block exemptions were extended in a modified form until the end of 1992 in the second reform package of June 1990, the main achievement of this package was the fact that the member states committed themselves to 'full liberalization' by the start of 1993 through a series of measures in the third reform package. The third package covered three areas, namely, licensing of carriers, route access and air fares. First, the regulations aimed to prevent discrimination by nationality by establishing legal and economic standards and safety requirements. Secondly, the package provided for unrestricted fifth freedom rights, i.e., the freedom to operate any cross-border service in the EU. Furthermore, it eliminated capacity-sharing between airlines. Only cabotage rights, i.e., the rights of an airline established in country A to carry revenue passengers between two points in country B, remained subject to a restriction of 50 percent of the seats until April 1997. Thirdly, the package provided for freedom with respect to pricing by introducing double disapproval of fares and safeguards against predatory pricing. The exemptions of the second package elapsed at the end of 1992. Therefore, the third package lifted the structural

---

[15]   *Nouvelles Frontières*, a French travel agent offering low air fares, was charged with breaking the fare agreements among scheduled carriers (in the French Civil Aviation Code). The case turned against the French regulatory authorities when the French Competition Court referred the case to the European Court of Justice, which asked the Commission to investigate the potential breach of the Treaty of Rome by the sector's conduct.

regulation restricting entry into the industry and individual routes (including domestic routes in April 1997) on the one hand, and, on the other, eased the conduct regulation with respect to joint capacity and price determination (Marin, 1995; Stasinopoulos, 1993, 1992).

Whereas bilateral liberalization had created a division between competitive conditions in European markets, the intention of the multilateral packages was to create uniformly competitive conditions across all markets. As a result of the bilateral initiatives, two types of interstate airline markets existed when the first deregulation package was introduced in 1987 (Marin, 1995), namely, those markets still regulated by traditional ASAs and bilaterally liberalized markets.

2.5 Conclusion

Market failures in airline markets are present in the form of environmental and congestion externalities, asymmetric information with respect to safety and product alternatives, and market power. Market power stems from technology but may be enhanced by entry barriers associated with congestion, CRSs, and the strategic behavior of airlines. To address these market failures, various types of regulation have been proposed and implemented, e.g. the imposition of noise zoning and safety requirements. Although there is much variety in the details of traditional economic regulations applied in airline markets, one common thread is the restriction of competition. In bilateral air service agreements, such restriction has taken a number of forms, namely, limited designation of operators, joint capacity and price determination, and pooling of revenues.

However, while there are sound economic arguments in favor of government intervention in these cases of market failure, the arguments advanced in favor of regulation with respect to entry, pricing and capacity competition can generally not be defended in terms of market failure. Therefore, such regulation has served the interests of airlines rather than travelers. The restriction of competition in cases where competitive solutions are both feasible and desirable has been recognized as a regulatory failure and, in the case of the airline industry, has prompted regulatory reform initiatives in many OECD airline markets, both domestic and international.

The relatively high prices in European markets and the experiences with airline liberalization elsewhere gave support to reform advocates. However, although some countries liberalized their arrangements bilaterally at an early stage, many other countries refrained from any such reform. The process of multilateral liberalization under the supervision of the European Commission has been necessary in order to secure uniform competitive conditions. The discussion of market failures suggests that the mere lifting of regulatory restrictions does not guarantee perfectly competitive conditions. Therefore, complementary regulation for safeguarding the benefits of deregulation has been advocated. In particular, attention has focused on the efficient allocation of scarce airport capacity and CRS regulation.

Even though the introduction of competition in aviation is generally considered to have resulted in welfare gains for air travelers, negative environmental externalities exist in airline markets. Therefore, increases in output in air transport markets generally result in an increase in environmental costs. In order to quantify and compare both types of effects, Part I (Chapters 3 to 6) addresses the measurement of the monetary value represented by environmental effects in air transport. In Part II (Chapters 7 to 10), welfare effects for airlines, travelers and 'victims' of pollution are quantified, allowing for a comparison of positive and negative effects associated with regulatory reform.

PART I
Environmental Costs in Air Transport Markets

Chapter 3
Evaluating Environmental
Externalities

3.1 Introduction

While regulatory reform in airline markets may bring considerable direct benefits to airline passengers, other individuals or households are likely to suffer from increased environmental damage associated with air transport when output expands. The effect of market transactions on the welfare of households via the impact on the services rendered by the environment, which is present in many transport markets, is termed an external effect or externality in economic analysis. Because the effect is generally negative, the term 'external cost' is common. Although the concept of externalities is widely used in (transport) economics, a brief discussion is presented in the next section because of its importance to the analyses in this book.

3.2 Externalities

The concept of an externality is often defined in terms of its effects. A widely used definition (Myles, 1995; Baumol and Oates, 1988; Mishan, 1971) has the following general form: 'An externality is present whenever some economic agent's (Y's) welfare (utility or profit) function includes real variables whose values are chosen directly by others (X) without particular attention to the effect upon the welfare of the agent Y they affect.' Baumol and Oates (1988) underline the 'by-product' nature of externalities, thus excluding all deliberate effects of X's behavior on Y's welfare. Furthermore, Mishan (1971) emphasizes that the effect of X's behavior on Y's welfare should be *direct*, thereby distinguishing external effects from ordinary economic interdependence.[16]

A related point is the distinction between 'technological' and 'pecuniary' externalities. It is noteworthy that Baumol and Oates still devote attention to the distinction in 1988, while these 'terminological innovations', introduced by Viner (1931), are described as 'superfluous', 'possibly confusing' and 'verbal

---

[16] E.g. while smoking has a direct effect on the utility of (non-smoking) room-mates and therefore poses an externality problem, it also affects, indirectly, cigarette company profits. However, as Myles (1995) points out, the definition still depends on the institutional context: the mutual dependence in a two-person barter economy, where Robinson's utility depends directly on what Friday is willing to exchange, would normally not be considered an externality.

extravagance' by Mishan in 1971. An explanation for this attention lies in the potential confusion between real (technological) and pseudo (pecuniary) externalities in discussions about external costs and benefits in, e.g., transport markets (see, e.g., Verhoef, 1996). As explained by Baumol and Oates (1988, pp. 29–30), the fundamental, distinctive feature of a real (technological) externality is that its introduction causes a shift in output or utility as a function of the resources used, and, given a particular resource allocation, will not leave all agents in the economy indifferent. In contrast, pecuniary externalities result from mere price changes in outputs or inputs and, at a constant real resource allocation, the introduction of a pecuniary externality only redistributes income. Thus, lower production costs and consumer prices in sector A resulting from the use of a particular transport mode, i.e., an input price change in sector A, represent a pecuniary externality, not an external benefit.

The above definition may be complemented by a second definition of externalities which focuses on causes and welfare consequences of externalities (Heller and Starret, 1976): 'An externality is present whenever there is an insufficient incentive for a potential market to be created for some good and the non-existence of this market leads to a non-Pareto-optimal equilibrium.' The presence of externalities may be termed an 'instance' or manifestation of market failure, reflecting an underlying or fundamental cause of market failure (Gravelle and Rees, 1992). The term 'market failure' refers to the existence of unrealized, mutually advantageous trades or profitable production decisions: in such a situation, it is possible to make at least one person better off without making anyone else worse off, which, by definition, implies that the allocation is not Pareto efficient. The persistence of such inefficiency can be traced to the following three causes, each of which is a sufficient condition for market failure: (1) economic agents do not have sufficient control over commodities (including productive assets) to put the advantageous exchanges into effect; in other words, property rights are not fully defined; (2) individual transaction and information costs exceed the gains from trade; and (3) individuals cannot agree on the division of gains from the exchange.

Some form of insufficient control over commodities is the main cause of environmental externality problems, e.g., pollution of public goods like clean air and quiet or non-optimal use of common property resources like fishing water or grazing land. The problem and its consequences are represented in Figure 3.1.[17] On the horizontal axis the amount of pollution s is measured; s, e.g. smoke, will in many cases be a function of some other variable, e.g. the quantity q produced by a polluting firm or the amount of nicotine inhaled by a smoker. $B'(s)$ are the marginal private benefits,[18] e.g. the profits of the polluter, the satisfaction

----

[17] The problem as well as its exposition and illustration are standard; the treatment here follows Gravelle and Rees (1992).
[18] The prime (') symbol following a function – such as B(s) – denotes a first derivative.

of the smoker expressed in monetary terms, or the net consumer benefits in a competitive market; for simplicity, the benefits are written as a function of the pollution s. $ED'(s)$ are the marginal external damages imposed on victims, e.g. other firms needing clean air as an input, or individuals (non-smokers) deriving utility from clean air.

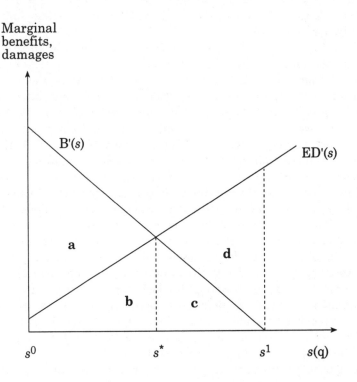

Figure 3.1: The externality problem

The welfare loss in the form of unrealized mutually advantageous trades is caused by the absence of property rights with respect to clean air and is illustrated by the figure. The adjective 'external' implies that the damages to agent Y are not taken into account by agent X, the polluter. Therefore, without any agreements or intervention with respect to the damages, X, maximizing private benefits, chooses s^1 as the amount of pollution. However, at each amount of pollution between s^* and s^1, the victim(s) Y would be willing to pay an amount equal to the marginal private benefit of X and still be better off, indicating that the 'solution' s^1 is not Pareto efficient. A maximum welfare gain, represented by d in Figure 3.1, can be obtained by inducing X to produce at or emit the welfare-maximizing amount of pollution s^*. In fact, this is the amount of pollution that would prevail in the presence of property rights with respect to clean air, be it in the hands of X or Y. Clearly, however, the division of income differs between the two cases and depends on the relative bargaining skills: if X has the property rights, the division is {X: **a** + **b** + **c** + **e**, Y: **d** − **e**}, where the 'help' variable **e**, $0 \leq$ **e** $\leq$ **d**, refers to the variable outcome of the bargaining process. If Y has the property rights, the division is {X: **a** − **f**, Y: **b** + **c** + **d** + **f**}, with the variable bargaining outcome denoted by **f**, $0 \leq$ **f** $\leq$ **a**.

In theory, agents can engage in a bargaining process in order to attain a Pareto-improved solution from any initial distribution of property rights with respect to the environmental quality in question. In other words, the above welfare-maximizing solution s^* can be reached when, e.g., the victims 'bribe' the polluter into reducing pollution. The result that the allocation of resources is efficient in a competitive economy with complete information and zero transaction costs is known as (the efficiency thesis of) the Coase theorem (Coase, 1960). However, the reasons for its limited practical relevance are as well known as the theorem itself. First of all, individual gains have to exceed transaction costs (cause 2 above). Therefore, while bargaining may be feasible in cases with small numbers of both polluters and victims, in cases with large numbers of victims, pollution reduction resulting from bargaining is likely to be a public good. Subject to free riding, incentives for individual bargaining efforts are reduced, and thus underprovision of the public good persists. In the absence of private agreements, intervention by a regulator, e.g. by means of a Pigouvian tax rate (equal to the marginal damage at s^*)[19] or a quantitative restriction, has been suggested in order to arrive at the social optimum. Even in a small-numbers case, however, the scope for bargaining solutions depends on the ability of parties to agree on the division of the gains, which is likely to be complicated by disagreements about the initial assignments of property rights in the absence of a clear legal situation.

Distinguishing between two types of economic agents, namely, consumers and producers, externalities can be categorized in four types, depending on the type of agent represented by X and Y respectively. These possibilities are summarized by means of some examples in Table 3.1.

Textbook examples of small-numbers externality problems are found in categories (a) and (d). However, Baumol and Oates (1988) argue that the major externality problems typically involve large numbers of either polluters or victims or both, thereby preventing bargaining solutions. Examples are road transport congestion and pollution, which can be found in all four categories, while air and noise pollution in sectors such as industry, aviation and railroads are typically in category (b).

---

[19]   A Pigouvian tax is an output tax which causes prices (costs) to reflect external damages.

Table 3.1
Typology of externalities

	Y is consumer
(a) X is consumer	smoking, noisy neighbors, congestion
(b) X is producer	air, noise pollution by industry or transport
	Y is producer
(c) X is consumer	bushfire started as a result of family outings
(d) X is producer	chemical plant pollutes downstream fishing water

3.3   External effects of air transport

Like many other transport sectors, air transport gives rise to externalities in the sense of the above definition. In order to analyze the problem in the context of transport markets, a number of externality types can be distinguished. A distinction can be made between positive and negative external effects, i.e., external benefits and external costs respectively.

External benefits of transport have been discussed in Rothengatter (1993) and Verhoef (1996), and in Verster (1997) with particular respect to air transport. The general conclusion is, in short, that apart from the admittedly popular activity of plane (car, train) spotting, no positive external effects in the true sense of the concept are associated with transport. There is no doubt that aviation plays an important role in present-day transport and communications, and numerous people, including environmental economists, would be seriously handicapped or temporarily jobless without it. However, the question is whether such interdependencies count as positive externalities and therefore should be balanced against negative externalities.

As Rothengatter (1993) points out, consumer and producer surpluses in transport markets are sometimes, mistakenly, presented as external benefits. Furthermore, direct and indirect 'forward and backward linkages' are typically invoked to demonstrate the presence of external benefits of transport. However, while aviation may lower costs and prices in other sectors and thereby, indirectly, stimulate production and employment, such effects take place inside, not outside, ordinary markets and therefore represent pecuniary externalities. It has already been established in the previous section that such effects do not result in any type of resource misallocation. Rietveld and Bruinsma (1998) argue that possibly positive external effects of transport infrastructure investments, e.g. image effects, should not be confused with external effects of infrastructure use itself. The overall conclusion is that transport activities themselves do not result in any significant external benefits.

External costs associated with transport have been identified in a number of categories (Freeman, 1997; Verhoef, 1996). First, there are negative external effects resulting directly from the provision of transport services itself; these effects can be represented as some function of the output, i.e., the quantity of services provided. Secondly, there are external costs in sectors related to a particular transport sector, namely, impacts associated with the production of raw materials and vehicles (upstream) or with the disposal of waste and vehicles (downstream). Thirdly, one can distinguish the external effects associated with the presence of the transport infrastructure that is used in the provision of the transport services, e.g., visual intrusion, ecosystem deterioration.

Since the external impacts of transport are complex and varied, any brief representation of such effects necessarily has its limitations. Focusing on air transportation, a possible inventory of effects, distinguishing between the above three categories, includes (Janic, 1999; Morrissette, 1996; Button, 1990, 1993):

1. External effects depending directly on output in airline markets: local air pollution, global atmospheric pollution, soil pollution and noise annoyance around airports, accident risk, and congestion.

2. Indirect external effects, upstream or downstream: pollution associated with aircraft or kerosene production, disposal of scrapped aircraft, costs associated with the 'over-exploitation' of carbon-based fuels, airport waste and environmentally harmful materials used in aircraft servicing and maintenance.

3. External effects associated with the presence of infrastructure: modification of river courses and field drainage and deterioration of ecosystems through airport construction, water and soil pollution through airport waste water and leakage from storage tanks, impacts on flora and fauna around airports.

The analysis in this book is confined to effects in category 1, i.e., those effects directly depending on output in the market for air transport services itself. In order to enhance comparability of benefits and costs resulting from regulatory reform, only effects within the airline markets themselves are considered. See Button (1993) and Maddison et al. (1996) for a discussion of the external costs resulting from upstream and downstream production and externalities associated with infrastructure.

Environmental externalities are defined here in a 'conventional' sense, and therefore the external costs associated with congestion are not included. Congestion costs have a direct, intra-sectoral effect on the actors within the transport market and only an indirect effect on the natural environment. As noted by Button (1993), congestion represents a lack of internal efficiency of the transport operations, which sets it apart from the more conventional environmental externalities. The analysis of environmental costs in the following chapters is confined to noise and the emission of air pollutants;[20] for these externality categories, data on aircraft emissions, physical impact and valuation are available. The issue of accident risk is discussed only briefly in Chapter 6. Clearly, not all costs associated with air transport accidents are external. Those accident risk costs that are imposed on 'innocent bystanders' (Moses and Savage, 1990) should surely be counted as external, while arguably not all accident costs to passengers and airlines are external.

3.3.1   Physical impact: some evidence

Estimates of the contributions to the above categories of environmental damage suggest that the share of aviation is modest, relative to both the aggregate impact of all human sources and the impact of the transport sector respectively. Without any attempt to provide a complete overview of the evidence, an impression of the contribution of air transport to some environmental issues is given in the following tables.

Table 3.2
Global emission contributions per source

Sources	CO_2	NO_x	SO_x	VOC	CO
	(Emissions in mn tonnes)				
Olivier (1995; 1990 data)					
Energy use, incl. aviation (1)	22000	82	130	27	303
Other ground sources (2)	5000	30	20	76	693
Aviation	498	1.79	0.16	0.41	0.68
Aviation as % of (1)	2.26	2.18	0.12	1.50	0.22
Aviation as % of (1)+(2)	1.84	1.60	0.11	0.40	0.07
(FPC, 1998; 1992 data)					
Land transport (3)	3600	32.64	4.90	0.76	206.90
Other human ground sources (4)	25050	67.65	143.40	319.59	766.10
Aviation (5)	453	1.84	0.13	0.40	0.99
Aviation as % of (3)	12.58	5.64	2.65	52.63	0.48
Aviation as % of (3)+(4)+(5)	1.56	1.80	0.09	0.12	0.10

As Table 3.2 shows, the relative contribution of aviation to aggregate emissions is small for all pollutants. According to both sources used, the share of aviation in total emissions only exceeds 1 percent for CO_2 and NO_x. However, the data in FPC (1998) indicate that for some pollutants, such as CO_2 and VOC, the share of aviation in the transport total is considerable. Nevertheless, the figures show

---

[20]   Thus, e.g., soil and water pollution are not addressed here.

that the various land transport modes together are responsible for considerable shares of total anthropogenic emissions, and in most cases these shares by far exceed the share of aviation. Furthermore, land transport tends to be conducted close to residential and therefore environmentally sensitive areas and is therefore particularly intrusive.

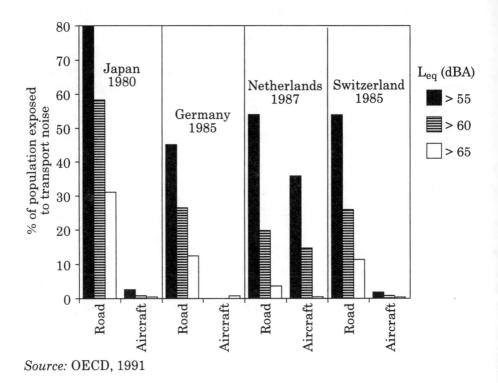

Source: OECD, 1991

Figure 3.2: Transport noise exposure

Accident statistics suggest that aviation is also a much safer mode of transport than either road or rail transport. However, such a conclusion is based on absolute yearly fatality and injury figures. As is argued in Button (1993), when statistics are given in terms of exposure time, highway travel is the safest mode of transport. Next, although general shortcomings in measurement and data collection regarding exposure to transport noise nuisance have been noted (OECD, 1991), evidence suggests that aviation contributes less than road transport in this respect too. Data from OECD country studies on the percentage of national populations exposed to particular noise levels caused by transport sources are presented in Figure 3.2. Clearly, while considerable population fractions are exposed to elevated noise levels caused by road transport, the shares of aircraft noise victims in the total population are generally much lower. Only in the Netherlands is this share impressive, with 36 percent of the population affected by an aircraft noise level of more than 55 L_{eq}.[21] For the other countries, however, the percentage of population affected by aircraft noise is lower than 5 percent for the lowest noise level considered.

Do the above statistics suggest that we should consider external costs of aviation as not much of a problem, or not consider it at all? The answer is, obviously, no. First, even if a particular external effect is 'small' compared with other problems, there is no reason not to consider its impact. The fact that an externality problem or resource misallocation is small compared with other such problems does not cancel its welfare relevance. Moreover, problems that are small globally may be very urgent locally, as is the case with a localized phenomenon like noise. Furthermore, scientific knowledge concerning some of the potentially important environmental damages of aviation is still limited, e.g. the effects of emissions at higher altitudes, where aviation may well present the main human source of pollution (Bleijenberg and Wit, 1997; Olivier, 1995; Archer, 1993).

Table 3.3
Energy use shares by mode in OECD countries

Transport mode	Energy consumption share		
	1980 (%)	1985 (%)	1995 (%)
Air	11.2	12.1	12.7
Road	79.2	80.0	80.9
Rail	3.6	2.9	2.3

Source: OECD (1997)

Another argument for giving aviation externalities close attention is presented by the high growth rates in the airline industry, which by definition affect output-related externalities. For example, output of 14 major EU airlines[22] grew, on average, 7.4 percent per year between 1980 and 1997, while annual traffic growth at 20 major European airports averaged 5.4 percent during that period. However, such average figures may hide substantial differences in local growth and thus in associated environmental effects. Since growth in aviation markets is expected, on average, to exceed economic growth in general, it is likely that the contribution of aviation to environmental problems will rise as well. Indeed, data on energy use by transport sector in OECD countries show that the share of aviation has been growing steadily; see Table 3.3. Related to this pattern, calculations in FPC

---

[21] L_{eq} is the 'equivalent sound level' (Nelson, 1978), which gives the energy equivalent of a number of separate noise events.
[22]   Scheduled international and domestic services, measured in passenger kilometers.

(1998), presented in Table 3.4, indicate a sustained increase in the share of air transport emissions of CO_2 and NO_x over the next decades.

Table 3.4
Projected emission shares

Source Emissions in 2015 from:	CO_2	NO_x
Human ground sources		
in mn tonnes	41547	134.11
increase rel. to 1992	145%	134%
Aviation		
in mn tonnes	877	3.86
increase rel. to 1992	194%	210%
share in total anthropogenic emissions in 2015 (1992)	2.07% (1.56%)	2.80% (1.80%)

Source: FPC (1998)

3.4   Evaluating external effects

In the previous section, a number of external costs associated with the output in transport markets were discussed briefly. In the next chapters, these effects will be studied in more detail, in terms of the physical impacts and, in particular, in terms of the monetary costs associated with these impacts. In this section some general observations related to the monetary evaluation of external effects are put forward.

Putting a monetary value on external effects associated with (air) transport is important for various reasons. First, it allows for a ready comparison and ordering of the various effects themselves. Furthermore, it allows for a comparison of external effects in monetary terms with other costs and benefits in projects or policies that are commonly expressed in monetary terms. It is important to realize that, in a sense, there is no escape from valuation of externalities. For example, if one for whatever reason ignores environmental goods in policy evaluation, an implicit price of zero is used. Likewise, if environmental goods are not to be sacrificed under any circumstance, the implicit price tends towards infinity. Therefore, it is possible to refrain from implicit valuation only by making valuations explicitly.

Secondly, given the brief listing of areas in which external cost problems are identified in the previous section, how should these be evaluated? As it turns out, particularly in the context of transport externalities, evaluation proceeds in an indirect manner. A general representation of the procedure is given in Figure

3.3 (Markandya, 1994; Button, 1993). As shown in the figure, the process of evaluating the external effects of transport thus makes use of a chain of separate relations, represented by the four small arrows in the figure, running from the output on transport markets to the monetary costs inflicted. A few examples are added at each stage in the pathway. Note that this is a comprehensive representation: while all links are used in the evaluation of, e.g., air pollution, this is not necessarily so for other externality types like noise or accident risk.

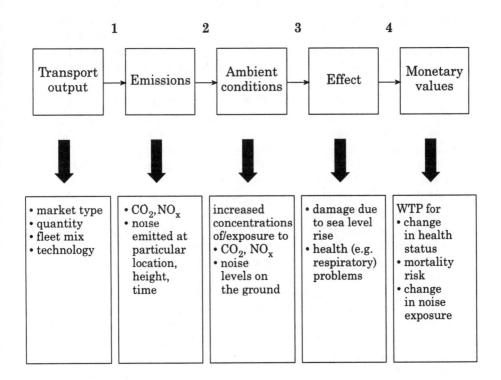

Figure 3.3: Pathway of transport externalities

Using air pollution as an example, one first needs to measure the amount of emissions. Secondly, one has to translate the total emissions emitted at the source to ambient concentrations; in the case of noise, this would mean establishing some measure of noise nuisance in residential areas. Next, a broad distinction can be made between valuing emissions directly or indirectly, depending on whether the third 'arrow' is used or not (cf. Pearce and Markandya, 1989). In the case of direct evaluation, monetary values are measured directly as a function of environmental quality, as e.g. in the studies on the relation between property values and concentrations of particulate matter (e.g. Smith and Huang, 1995) or aircraft noise property value studies (e.g. Nelson, 1978; see also Chapter 4). With indirect evaluation, two separate relations are used, namely, the effect of a change in environmental quality, e.g. on health status, and, secondly, the evaluation of such an effect (Freeman, 1993). While the valuation techniques used in both approaches may be the same, the indirect approach has the advantage that it gives more explicit and detailed insight into the processes that affect the value of services rendered by the environment. Furthermore, for some pollutants, like emissions affecting global warming, the information on physical processes added by models of global change seems indispensable to arriving at an adequate valuation. The advantage of such detail comes, however, at the cost of information. Fortunately, many recent studies evaluating the social cost of emissions (Markandya, 1994; Rowe et al., 1995; Maddison et al., 1996; Krupnick et al., 1997) use the indirect approach, drawing on a growing set of both valuation and dose–response studies. The social costs imposed by aircraft emissions are thus evaluated using the complete emission–exposure–effect–value chain depicted in Figure 3.3, which has been termed a 'pathway' in the literature (e.g. Krupnick et al., 1997; EC, 1995), while the impact to be valued is called an 'endpoint'.

Actual valuation at the endpoints thus takes place 'after' calculations in various stages of the pathway have been performed.[23] A variety of valuation techniques is used in practice. Even if there were a single preferred one, however, valuation results based on different methods usually have to be combined when studying the aggregate costs associated with several externality types and pathways. Such valuation results are presented and used in the following chapters, and therefore a brief overview of valuation methods is presented here. The discussion is not intended to be complete or detailed; comprehensive reviews of the techniques involved can be found in Freeman (1993), Palmquist (1991), Pearce and Markandya (1989) and Johansson (1987). One of many possible typologies of valuation methods is presented in Table 3.5.

The valuation methods in the table are distinguished in the first place by their use of preferences in establishing values. The non-preference methods are generally considered of little relevance as far as welfare economics is concerned, because they do not make use of information about individual preference orderings with respect to the endpoint (effect) that is to be valued. Taking a particular change in health status as an example, measuring the costs of medical treatment

---

[23] While various problems have to be confronted at all the stages of the pathway, most of the attention in this study is devoted to the last stage (arrow 4). The other stages are clearly of great importance for the final results of any cost calculation, but are typically not in the area of competence of economists. Therefore, where needed, existing information will be used without much discussion.

as 'repair' costs does not account for the welfare reduction due to the victim's pain, suffering and lost time. While in this case the total welfare loss is usually considered to be larger than the medical costs, the relation between the marginal resource costs of environmental degradation and the marginal costs of prevention or abatement programs is generally not clear. This proposition is illustrated in Figure 3.4.

Table 3.5
Valuation methods

1. Revealed preference methods	2. Expressed preference methods
• Hedonic price method	• Contingent valuation
• Travel cost method	• Contingent ranking
• Averting behavior method	• Pairwise comparison
• Production factor method	• Allocation games

3. Non-preference methods, based on:
• Prevention costs
• Actual defensive, repair or abatement costs
• Implicit valuation

The upper part of Figure 3.4 shows total abatement expenses and environmental damages as a function of environmental damage s; the lower part shows the marginal values. From a welfare economic point of view, the damages $D(s)$ represent the relevant costs to society. Therefore, at each level of pollution (production, economic activity), the value of an extra unit of pollution is equal to the marginal damage D'. As illustrated in the figure, the marginal abatement expenses are equal to marginal damages only at the socially optimal level of abatement with pollution level s^*. If the economy is not in this optimum but, e.g., in a situation represented by s^1, there is no link between abatement expenditures and welfare costs. All such policy-based valuation attempts that do not consider the damage function D are in effect instances of implicit valuation. As drawn here, the distance between true marginal costs and marginal implicit values is maximal for the extreme cases of no and complete abatement respectively. An explanation for the fact that the short-cut approaches in category 3 in Table 3.5 are used (see e.g., Bleijenberg et al., 1998; various studies cited in Bleijenberg et al., 1994) is that estimating the marginal damages is often much more time and money consuming.[24]

---

[24]   Besides, as argued in Verhoef (1996), total abatement expenditures are relevant when, from an equity point of view, one is looking for the total 'unpaid bill' by a particular sector. In such a case, however, these expenditures still have to be added to the total 'extra-sectoral' external damages imposed by the sector.

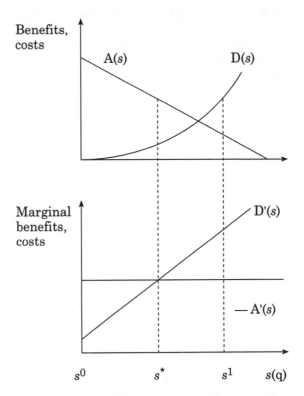

Figure 3.4: Damages and abatement

The two approaches in the 'preference' category attempt to value external effects using information on preferences of individuals. In principle, the economic or resource cost of a particular unpriced (environmental) good can be inferred from the rate at which individuals are willing to trade it for other goods. The marginal damage associated with an external effect is then equal to the resource cost at the particular level of the external effect, say pollution. If one knows the 'exchange rate' of the unpriced good, e.g. clean air, for various levels of pollution, it is possible to draw marginal damages as a function of pollution, as in Figure 3.4. In many cases, however, only the resource cost and marginal damage at a particular level of pollution can be inferred.

The remaining question is how the (opportunity) value of unpriced goods can be determined in practice. The survey methods in the expressed or stated preferences category in Table 3.5 extract information on preferences from choices in hypothetical markets. The most common form is the contingent valuation method (CVM), which tries to infer values from the stated willingness to pay (WTP) of respondents for hypothetical changes in the availability of particular environmental goods (see Hoevenagel, 1994, for a detailed study of the CVM). Strengths of the CVM are its applicability in diverse contexts and its potential to capture both use and non-use or existence values.   One of the major methodological disputes relating to the CVM is the so-called embedding effect, which occurs when respondents assign the same value to different quantities or levels of similar environmental goods.[25]   While proponents of the CVM have attributed such inconsistencies to bad survey design, critics view this as a failure of the CVM to reflect preferences properly. For example, Diamond and Hausman (1994) argue that 'contingent valuation surveys do not measure the preferences they attempt to measure', i.e. they reject the validity claim of the method. On the other hand, studies criticizing the validity of the CVM are not free from criticism themselves (Smith, 1993).[26]

Revealed preference methods make use of relations between demands for private or traded goods on the one hand and unpriced goods on the other. When such relations are present, observations on transactions in private goods markets confer information on the 'implicit' price of otherwise unpriced environmental services. The hedonic price (HP) method is based on such value inference, e.g. with respect to the implicit price of peace and quiet in markets for residential property or the implicit price of human life in labor markets.

Problems regarding the HP technique and value inference using observations for residential property markets are, however, well known. First, Pearce (1978) stresses the fact that property prices will adequately reflect preferences for localized environmental goods – e.g. noise around airports – only if people are relatively mobile. When this condition is not met, environmental costs will be present but not reflected in property prices. Starkie and Johnson's (1975) main argument against the HP approach is the fact that 'disbenefits of pollution tend to be highly and positively correlated with the benefits of increased accessibility to jobs, with the one factor partially or completely offsetting the other in their respective effect on the structuring of urban rents'.[27] Such bias in estimation, however, can in principle be prevented by proper specification of the price equation, as Pearce and Markandya (1989) observe.

Another issue affecting estimation of the implicit value is the choice of functional form. Furthermore, different households do not have identical (inverse) demand curves; only if this were so could the estimated marginal implicit price function be interpreted as the inverse demand curve for environmental goods. Given heterogeneity of households, the HP function represents a locus of equilibrium choices in the property market, not individual demand functions

---

[25]   Other 'biases' have been identified; see Hoevenagel (1994) for an overview.

[26]   E.g., Smith (1993) argues that the hypothesis, maintained by CVM critics, that larger amounts of environmental amenities would necessarily be valued more highly is questionable.

[27]   As an example, the authors cite the fact that in areas adjacent to Heathrow, 10 percent of the resident working men and 5 percent of the working women were airport employees (figures for the late 1960s).

for environmental quality. Other 'surrogate market' approaches use information on the choices made by individuals when facing costs for traveling to, e.g., a nature reserve (travel cost method) or costs associated with averting certain risks. Results of the revealed preference analyses are presented in the following chapters. In general, revealed preference techniques are only able to uncover a part of the total economic value of environmental goods,[28] and so the values obtained through the methods in this category are usually considered as lower bounds. Given this general limitation, as well as the particular issues raised above in connection with the HP method, several authors have suggested complementing revealed preference methods with stated preference research (Smith, 1993; Feitelson et al., 1996).

Two general complications associated with the valuation of externalities are mentioned briefly. First, there is a direct link between valuation, efficiency and equity. Willingness to pay for environmental quality is generally inversely related to the marginal utility of income, which should be reflected by 'correct' external cost estimates. Taking the existing distribution of income as given, 'dumping' of environmental problems in low-income countries or locations is economically efficient. Secondly, the methods described are in some cases used to value environmental externalities that will affect future generations. In such cases, current values are extrapolated, but this does not guarantee a correct reflection of the relevant preferences.

3.5   Conclusion

Summing up, it can be concluded that the relations between transport activities resulting from transactions on markets for transportation services and the external costs imposed on society are complex. Therefore, plotting an environmental cost or damage function as in Figure 3.4 using actual data, let alone finding the optimal level of abatement, may turn out to be very problematic. This can be illustrated by analyzing Figure 3.5, which presents the environmental damage pathway of Figure 3.3 in an alternative form. In quadrant IV, two environmental cost or damage functions have been drawn, one of which is convex, as in Figure 3.4. The relation between transport output Q and ambient conditions is represented in quadrant I. The relation between ambient conditions and effects (the dose–response relation) is represented in quadrant II, while the relation between effects

---

[28] The total economic value (TEV) of environmental goods to individuals is generally considered to comprise several categories of value (e.g. Markandya, 1994; Maddison et al., 1996), namely, the direct value (derived from own use of environmental services), indirect use values (from indirect benefits through use of environmental services by others), the option value (a 'premium' for the potential use of environmental services) and the existence value (an 'altruistic' value, derived from the existence of the environment itself apart from any use whatsoever). However, Markandya (1994) notes that there are difficulties in both exactly defining and measuring the latter type of value.

and total damage is represented in quadrant III.[29]

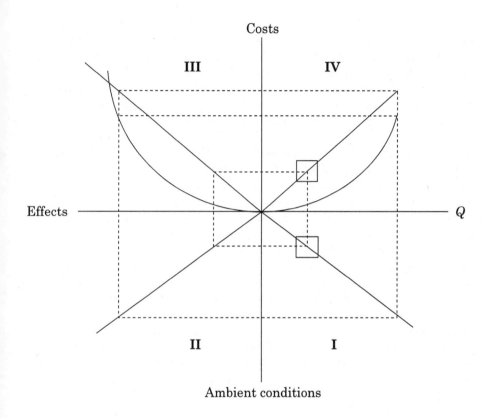

Figure 3.5: The environmental cost function

It may be noted here, and will be discussed in more detail in later chapters, that drawing each of the functions represented in the figure requires a large amount of information. In practice, it may be possible only to approximate functions or uncover parts of functions. Especially in the area of the dose–response relations (quadrant II), scientific knowledge and agreement are not complete, e.g. in the area of greenhouse gas damages and in establishing the effects of (local) air pollution. The functions in quadrants I and II are locally often assumed to be linear, as represented by the boxes in Figure 3.5. With respect to the

---

[29]   The fact that all functions pass through the origin is not necessarily realistic; Figure 3.5 is merely an illustration of the general methodological problems.

relations in quadrant I, this may be a reasonable approximation for particular aviation externalities, since the contribution of aviation to ambient conditions is very small in some cases.[30] Combined with a constant marginal valuation, this yields the linear damage function in quadrant IV, whereas an increasing marginal valuation yields the upward-sloping damage function. However, tracing out the complete functions needed for plotting the damage function is a huge task. For a complete damage function, all the functions in Figure 3.5 must be known. If only a part of or a point on one of the functions has been studied (e.g. the part in the box in quadrant I), only a limited part of the damage function in quadrant IV can be known. In many cases, only such limited knowledge is available. Finally, there is the issue of transferability. The relations represented in the graph are empirical ones, based on location- and time-specific data (with respect to non-global problems). An important question is whether, even if all the above functions were known exactly for location (time) A, these could be used when studying external transport damages in B.

Notwithstanding the above problems, it has already been argued that there is no good alternative to explicit valuation. While scientific knowledge on the diverse links in the pathway is incomplete, one can still make use of the available information. Furthermore, knowledge on many of the links has recently been advanced and is still growing. In the next two chapters, existing information will be used to value environmental impacts of air transport. Chapter 4 addresses the valuation of aircraft noise, while Chapter 5 investigates the valuation of the impact of aircraft emissions. In these two chapters, the relations depicted in quadrants II and III are investigated, so that changes in ambient conditions can be translated into monetary values. In Chapter 6, information on the relation in quadrant I is added in order to establish the effect of transport on environmental damages.

---

[30]   In other cases, however, e.g. at high altitudes, the contribution may be considerable.

Chapter 4
Noise

4.1 Introduction

Noise has been defined as 'unwanted' sound (Starkie and Johnson, 1975) and, as such, it reduces the amount of the scarce good 'peace and quiet'. As in the case of clean air, property rights with respect to peace and quiet are typically not well defined. Although in small-number cases, e.g. noise from neighbors, bargaining could theoretically occur,[31] it has been pointed out in Chapter 3 that such a solution is ruled out in large-number cases. Like transport emissions, transport noise is typically an externality with a large number of victims, and sometimes with a large number of polluters, for instance in the case of road transport.

Transport noise, which is one of the major sources of noise in the environment (Nelson, 1978; OECD, 1991), is largely produced by mobile sources in well-defined locations, such as high-density streets, highways and areas around airports. Therefore, noise pollution is not distributed uniformly over space; instead, it is a localized externality. The localized nature of the noise problem is particularly clear in the case of air transport, where only noise emitted close to the airport is considered to be pollution.

Noise may have several adverse physiological, emotional and psychological effects on human health. These effects include hearing loss, increased stress, sleep disturbance and, directly or indirectly, reduced attention and concentration (Opschoor and Jansen, 1973). While there is evidence on hearing loss caused by certain types of noise, e.g. high noise levels experienced for many years in industrial work, transport noise is generally considered not to have such effects. However, transport noise directly affects well-being through interference with communication, other auditory signals and privacy in general. In particular, the locally direct and intrusive nature of aircraft noise on human well-being is illustrated by the fact that noise nuisance has become one of the most important environmental issues associated with air transport in terms of public concern and policy attention (Janic, 1999; Feitelson et al., 1996; Button, 1993). As argued earlier, the direct effect of noise pollution on human well-being sets it apart from the more indirect effects of, e.g., greenhouse gas emissions. Therefore, valuation of noise nuisance is direct rather than indirect: the endpoint to be valued is the individual annoyance or utility loss due to 'ambient concentrations' of noise, not

---

[31] Even if bargaining solutions are being proposed in reality, they do not always seem to result in satisfactory agreements for all parties involved: in the Netherlands, 26 percent of the population claimed 'extreme discomfort' from neighborhood noise in 1987 (up from 15 percent in 1977) and 66 percent claimed 'moderate disturbance' (40 percent in 1977).

with associated (health) effects (Nelson, 1978). It should be noted, however, that this may be an underestimate of the total noise cost to the extent that there are indirect, e.g. health-related, effects too.

4.1.1 Aircraft noise valuation

Many of the earlier noise cost studies (Walters, 1975; Opschoor and Jansen, 1973) aimed to estimate the total social costs of airport expansion or relocation. To this end, a framework of the form

$$N \; > \; S + D + R \qquad (4.1)$$

$$N \; \leq \; S + D + R \qquad (4.2)$$

has been developed in order to account for the costs of both households that move as a result of increased noise levels and those who stay. N is the monetary value of the noise cost suffered by households in the latter group.[32] On the right-hand side of (4.1) the costs for the movers are represented, consisting of S, the loss of location-specific surplus, the depreciation in property value D and the costs of relocation R. If (4.1) holds, a rational noise victim (household) moves; if not, he stays. Using estimates of the number of households that stay or move, the total noise costs associated with increased noise levels can be calculated.

The aim of this chapter is to establish marginal values with respect to noise annoyance. Therefore, a number of noise valuation studies are reviewed. It should be noted, however, that these studies are primarily concerned with the left-hand sides of equations (4.1) and (4.2). That is, the studies try to establish monetary values for the utility loss associated with the noise nuisance itself, and this is the value information that is used in the present study too. The definition of N makes clear that these are the costs that represent the immediate welfare loss associated with a particular noise level, even if a household subsequently decides to move. Furthermore, in the context of a welfare analysis based on potential compensation, the presence of D on the right-hand side is questionable, since these financial losses are the gain of the next homeowner (Nelson, 1978).

Valuation studies and results are addressed in the remainder of the chapter. In Section 4.2, results of aircraft noise valuation studies using the contingent valuation method (CVM) are discussed. Results of analyses of residential property values using the hedonic price (HP) method are reviewed in Section 4.3. The large number of HP study results allows one to analyze transferability of these results in a meta-analysis, which is presented in Section 4.3.1.

---

[32] In the words of the Roskill Commission: 'The noise nuisance suffered by the householder expressed as the sum of money which would just compensate him for the nuisance suffered and make him as well off as he was before' (Opschoor and Jansen, 1973).

4.2 Survey methods

The number of survey method studies measuring willingness to pay (WTP) for a reduction in aircraft noise exposure is small relative to the number of HP property value studies. The problems of measurement and value inference in the HP studies (see below) are, however, good reasons to complement these studies with survey studies, as is argued by Smith (1993) and Feitelson et al. (1996). Aircraft noise value surveys have been conducted by, among others, Feitelson et al. (1996; hereafter FHM) and Opschoor and Jansen (1973; hereafter O&J).[33] The approaches and results of these two studies are briefly discussed and compared here.

Both surveys use the CVM, confronting respondents with a number of housing options with varying noise scenarios and asking for the WTP for each option. The noise scenarios are described qualitatively, in terms of noise type (minor/severe, occasional/frequent) in FHM and in terms of effects (percentage of people stating communication or sleep disturbance) in O&J. The studies differ in a number of details. FHM have conducted a telephone survey among communities near an airport in the US where expansion is planned; both homeowners and renters are included. Only Dutch homeowners without significant actual aircraft noise exposure are visited in the O&J survey. In FHM, zero valuations are interpreted as a sign that the respondent is not willing to consider the particular residence–noise combination at all, while this is checked separately in O&J. In FHM the noise costs are deduced from the expressed WTP for housing options, while the respondents state the compensation needed in each case specifically in O&J. Without going into specific survey design issues, the above differences between the two surveys suggest reason enough to expect differences in results. The difference in familiarity with the noise problem seems important, possibly introducing hypothetical bias (situations depicted in the questionnaire are too hypothetical to obtain valid answers) in O&J; the increased possibility of strategic bias (respondents bias their responses because of their interest in the actual noise problem) in FHM is considered of minor importance by the authors. The effect of zero bids, or unwillingness to consider a housing option, on WTP values in the respective studies is considered below.

The valuation results for homeowners are compared in Table 4.1. The comparison requires, however, a few caveats. As noted above, the noise scenarios in both CVM studies have been presented in a qualitative manner. In O&J, there is an explicit translation of these scenarios into noise contours and zones in Kosten units (Ke),[34] the Dutch measure of noise nuisance. The average level in

---

[33] Another reference is Plowden (1971), a study which inspired the survey in O&J. A recent survey for Amsterdam can be found in Baarsma (2000).

[34] The 'Kosten' unit (Ke) is the Dutch measure for aircraft noise annoyance, named after its inventor, Professor Kosten. A total of 10 percent of the population living within the 20 Ke contour experiences 'serious noise disturbance'.

these zones has been translated into the L_{eq} noise levels in the table. Because of the complex functional forms of the various national noise nuisance measures, the international translation of noise measures is only approximate.[35] The scenarios in FHM do not have an explicit translation into quantitative noise measures. Therefore, it is assumed that the four noise levels in the table (54, 63, 72 and 81 L_{eq}) correspond, respectively, to the scenarios 'occasional minor noise', 'frequent minor noise', 'occasional severe noise' and 'frequent severe noise'.[36] The noise costs or premiums in the table are expressed as the percentage of property value loss relative to the 'no-noise' scenario. Two sets of valuation results are shown: the rows titled 'Willing to buy' present the valuation results only for those respondents who indicate that they would consider living under the particular noise conditions; the alternative sets of results include the 'zero valuations', i.e., the responses of those who are not willing to consider a particular noise scenario at any price.

Table 4.1
CVM noise cost estimates

| % depreciation of house value | Average noise levels in L_{eq} | | | |
w.r.t. 'no-noise' scenario	54	63	72	81
FHM (1996)				
'Willing to buy'	1.8	1.5	1.1	1.0
Incl. 'unwilling to buy'	2.8	2.5	1.9	1.7
% unwilling	10.8	25.8	31.5	38.5
O&J (1973)				
'Willing to buy'	2.7	1.8	1.3	1.2
Incl. 'unwilling to buy'	5.6	3.4	2.6	2.1
% unwilling	37.7	48.6	58.3	64.1

Source: calculated from results in the two surveys.

The adequacy of the comparison clearly depends on the relative movement of house prices and noise prices over the years between the two studies, as well as the differences in relative scarcity between the two study locations. With these caveats in mind, the table suggests the following. First, there is a marked difference in noise valuation: the values in O&J are higher than those in FHM

---

[35] The methods and problems in (transport) noise measurement fall outside the scope of this study. Good discussions can be found in Nelson (1978) and Walters (1975). The translation of various national aircraft noise nuisance measures follows the methods proposed in OECD (1993).

[36] The 'sound-proofing' and 'overflights' scenarios in FHM are not considered. Furthermore, renters are not considered here; FHM present valuation results for homeowners and renters separately, the latter group displaying lower noise valuations than the former. The 'no-noise' scenario has been fixed at 45 L_{eq}. The latter implies that the difference between the 'frequent severe noise' and the 'no-noise' scenario is higher than in FHM; therefore the noise premium in FHM is higher.

for all table entries, part of which can be explained by the higher percentages of respondents who are unwilling to consider a particular noise-affected property. Note that this effect, central to the argument in FHM, is present in both surveys: as the noise level increases, the percentage of people who are not willing to be exposed to the particular noise level 'at any price' increases. FHM argue that these 'zero valuations' imply kinked bid curves, with WTP values for property–noise combinations falling to zero above certain noise levels, and should be included in the analysis. It may also be noted that the results in both studies indicate that marginal noise costs are decreasing: the payment required in order to compensate homeowners for higher noise exposure increases less than proportionally to the L_{eq} level.

4.3   Hedonic pricing

The HP method uses property prices as an instrument to measure the value of environmental goods or bads.[37] A considerable number of HP studies of the cost of aircraft noise have been carried out since the 1960s. HP analysis is based on the idea that a household derives utility from, among other things, the consumption of housing services. Under a hedonic price equilibrium in a competitive housing market, the change in a house price due to a change in a particular attribute equals the marginal bid of the agents in the housing market for that attribute. The HP function P_h represents the market equilibrium, and the slope of the function with respect to each of its arguments is an estimate of the marginal willingness to pay for the particular characteristic. For example, the marginal implicit or hedonic price of a particular environmental amenity–say peace and quiet or clean air–is an estimate of the marginal willingness to pay for that kind of environmental quality. It is noted again that the HP function reflects equilibrium conditions, not an implicit demand function for environmental services or quality. While such a demand function could be uncovered by a second-stage regression, most empirical studies only analyze the HP function itself.

In most aircraft noise studies, it is the relative, not the absolute, implicit price that is estimated. Often a Cobb–Douglas type of price regression equation is used, taking the form

$$P_i = \alpha e^{\beta N_i} \mathbf{X}_i^\gamma e^{u_i} \qquad (4.3)$$

where P_i is the price of property i, $\mathbf{X}_i$ is a vector containing information on physical and neighborhood characteristics of i, and N represents some measure of noise nuisance that represents the environmental (dis)amenity in this hedonic model. The model transforms to a log-linear model of the form

$$\ln P_i = \ln \alpha + \beta N_i + \gamma \ln \mathbf{X}_i + u_i \qquad (4.4)$$

---

[37]   This section draws heavily on Schipper et al. (1998b).

The natural log of price is regressed on absolute noise values and the estimate of the coefficient β represents the percentage change in a given property value associated with a decibel change in noise exposure. This quasi-elasticity has been termed the 'noise depreciation index' (NDI) in the literature. A summary of the results from 19 studies is presented in Table 4.2, while the histogram in Figure 4.1 gives the distribution of the NDI estimates.

Table 4.2
Summary of HP aircraft noise study results

No.	Study	Date of price observations	Location	NDI
1	Emerson (1969)	1967	Minneapolis	0.58
2	Dygert (1973)	1970	San Francisco	0.50
3	Dygert (1973)	1970	San Jose	0.70
4	Price (1974)	1970	Boston	0.83
5	De Vany (1976)	1970	Dallas	0.80
6	Blaylock (1977)	1970	Dallas	0.99
7	Maser et al. (1977)	1971	Rochester	0.55
8	Paik (Nelson, 1978)	1960	New York	1.90
9	Paik (Nelson, 1978)	1960	Los Angeles	1.80
10	Paik (Nelson, 1978)	1960	Dallas	2.30
11	Nelson (1978)	1970	Washington	1.06
12	Mieskowski & Saper (1978)	1971	Toronto	0.52
13	Abelson (1979)	1972	Sydney	0.40
14	Abelson (1979)	1972	Sydney	0.22
15	McMillan et al. (1980)	1975	Edmonton	0.51
16	Nelson (1981)	1970	San Francisco	0.58
17	Nelson (1981)	1970	St Louis	0.51
18	Nelson (1981)	1970	Cleveland	0.29
19	Nelson (1981)	1970	New Orleans	0.40
20	Nelson (1981)	1970	San Diego	0.75
21	Nelson (1981)	1970	Buffalo	0.52
22	O'Byrne et al. (1985)	1970	Atlanta	0.64
23	O'Byrne et al. (1985)	1980	Atlanta	0.67
24	Pennington et al. (1990)	1985	Manchester	0.15
25	Morey (1990)	1987	Coolidge	0.10
26	Uyeno et al. (1993)	1987	Vancouver	0.65
27	Uyeno et al. (1993)	1987	Vancouver	0.90
28	Levesque (1994)	1985	Winnipeg	0.58
29	Kaufman (1996)	1993	Reno	0.34
30	Yamaguchi (1996)	1996	London	3.57

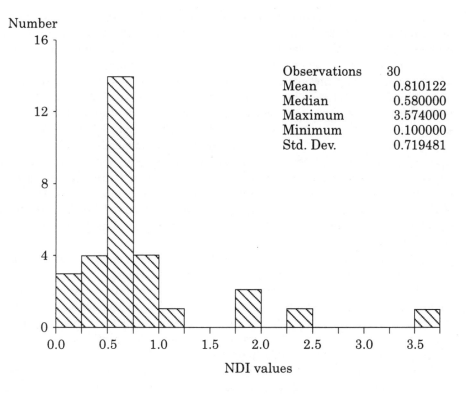

Figure 4.1: NDI estimates

The histogram suggests that the conclusion by Nelson (1980) that 'the noise discount is commonly 0.5–0.6 percent' should be adjusted slightly upward. Given such a set of HP valuation results varying in many respects, such as time, location and specific characteristics of the empirical analysis, the question of 'benefit transfer' naturally arises: i.e., are the noise depreciation estimates so homogeneous that the average can be transferred to other locations? In the next section, a meta-analysis addresses this question.

4.3.1 Meta-analysis and transfer of valuation results

Meta-analysis has been defined in the literature (e.g. Brouwer et al., 1997) as a statistical analysis of, in most cases empirical, research findings. Meta-analysis techniques have been developed and applied in the medical sciences and psychology. Clearly, when experimental contexts and formats can be controlled adequately, there is much scope for comparing the outcomes of different studies, as in meta-analysis.

Given the large amounts of empirical work on particular research questions in economics, meta-analysis seems a useful tool for economists as well. In economics, meta-analysis has been used since the mid-1980s, while most meta-analyses in environmental economics have been published in the 1990s. However, all economists using meta-analysis face the problem that economics is only a quasi-experimental science, so that study circumstances are hard to control. A typical meta-analysis in economics compares outcomes of studies that estimate a particular elasticity. Study characteristics, such as year of data collection, location, sample size, and functional form, are the independent variables that may explain differences between study outcomes. However, very often the study outcomes, e.g. the particular elasticities studied, are not directly comparable between studies, because they were not intended to be comparable at the time of the study. Clearly, meta-analysis is particularly well suited for those research questions that have been studied in comparable study formats (data definition, specification) for different locations and times.

Environmental valuation is a field in which several meta-analyses have recently been published (Smith and Kaoru, 1990; Smith and Huang, 1995; Brouwer et al., 1997). The scope for meta-analysis in environmental valuation is large: environmental policy depends on monetary values for environmental goods, but empirical valuation studies are tied to particular locations. In many cases, a policy maker will be in need of an estimate of a particular valuation result (effect size) for a location for which the particular cause–effect relation has not been studied. The costs of obtaining new valuation results for a particular site are high, which makes the use of past study results attractive. Then, however, one would like to know how transferable these results are: rather than just picking one of a number of previous estimates, one would like to test whether these estimates are similar. If so, information from different studies can be combined to obtain a pooled estimate as a predictor of the effect size; if not, one would like to see whether differences can be explained. These are the basic aims of meta-analysis, which will be discussed below for the present aircraft noise study results.

Are the estimates biased?

Before proceeding to the analysis of the noise coefficients themselves, one may take a look at the significance of the coefficients. A test for publication bias has been described by Card and Krueger (1995) for the time-series minimum-wage literature. Given a seemingly stable cause–effect relationship, such as a large number of relatively homogeneous NDI estimates, one might be concerned about the possibility that the studies give a biased view of the noise–property value relationship. Card and Krueger mention some mechanisms that may introduce such a bias: researchers may have a theoretical presumption about a particular economic relationship (in this case: 'aircraft noise has a negative influence on household welfare which translates into a noise discount'). Also, researchers may search for a specification that passes a particular, publishable, significance test, e.g., a t-ratio of 2.

The test draws on the fact that studies differ in the number of observations. Given a stable statistical relationship, according to sampling theory, the absolute value of the t-ratio should vary proportionally with the square root of the number of degrees of freedom. Another way of stating this proportional relationship is to say that a regression of the log of the t-value on the log of the square root of the degrees of freedom should theoretically return a coefficient of 1. If the t-value does not increase in the degrees of freedom, a possible explanation is that authors search for specifications that return the publishable t-ratio of about 2. Card and Krueger tested this for a set of time-series minimum-wage studies. The regression returned an insignificant negative coefficient, and the authors interpreted this as a sign of publication bias.

The same test has been applied to the above sample of HP estimates, both for a subsample containing only the published studies and for the sample as a whole. The results are presented in Table 4.3.

Table 4.3
Publication bias test results

Dependent variable: ln (t-value) of noise coefficient	Published studies	Total sample
Independent variable:		
ln (square root of DF)	0.37	0.36
t-value	8.84	5.33

Both regressions show that there is a significant positive relation between the logarithm of the t-values in the noise studies on the one hand, and the logarithm of the square root of the degrees of freedom on the other. The significance of the coefficient suggests that it is significantly different from both 0 and 1. Therefore, the conclusion that the sample of NDI estimates is plagued by publication bias, defined as the absence of a positive correlation between t-value and degrees of freedom, is not supported. One the other hand, the coefficient is admittedly well below the desired value of 1. Therefore, the data do not seem to support any strong conclusion, either positive or negative, on the issue.

Is the NDI constant?

A second meta-analytic question is whether the estimated NDIs are of similar size in a statistical sense. If so, a (weighted) average can be used as an estimate of the effect of noise on property values. Consider a set of k studies that provides a vector of unbiased effect size estimates, in this case coefficients from the original noise study regressions. As regression coefficients, the effect sizes follow a normal distribution. A test of homogeneity asks whether the studies share a common effect size, i.e., tests the hypothesis against the alternative that at least one of the effect sizes differs. Hedges and Olkin (1985) suggest a large-sample test of the form

$$Q = \sum_{i=1}^{k} \frac{(d_i - d_+)^2}{\widehat{\sigma}(d_i)} \tag{4.5}$$

where d_+ is an average of the study effect sizes weighted by the respective variances:

$$d_+ = \frac{\sum_{i=1}^{k} \frac{d_i}{\widehat{\sigma}(d_i)}}{\sum_{i=1}^{k} \frac{1}{\widehat{\sigma}(d_i)}} \tag{4.6}$$

The test statistic Q has a chi-squared distribution with $k-1$ degrees of freedom. This homogeneity test has been applied to the sample of NDI estimates, rendering a test statistic $Q = 414.25$. This value strongly rejects the null hypothesis of homogeneity of effect sizes. Therefore, it is concluded that the NDI estimates of the various aircraft noise studies display significant variation. The implication is that a valuation result from one noise study cannot be transferred to a new location without taking the variation in the results into account. In the next subsection, the variation between the NDIs is analyzed.

Can the variation in NDIs be explained?

Given a collection of k effect size estimates, such as estimated NDIs, that display significant variation, one may try to estimate a meta-model that explains the observed variation between individual effect sizes. Here a linear regression model of the form $\mathbf{d} = \mathbf{X}\boldsymbol{\beta} + \varepsilon$ is used, where $\mathbf{d}$ is a vector of individual effect sizes and the matrix $\mathbf{X}$ provides information on the individual studies and study circumstances.

A difference between the present analysis and other meta-analyses is the fact that multiple estimates per location are not used here: only the best estimates (according to the authors) for a particular location are used as dependent variables in the sample. On the one hand, this limits the number of observations, but it also precludes the problem of highly correlated or clustered observations, as indicated by Smith and Huang (1995). Furthermore, the format of presentation of results differs widely: while some authors only present the best specifications, others may give virtually all regressions leading to the best specification. Using all results presented per study may therefore lead to a very unbalanced meta-sample.

When using a linear regression model in a meta-analysis, one has to be aware that the conditions of the classical linear regression model are not likely to be satisfied. In particular, the assumption of constant variance or homoscedasticity of the error term is likely to be violated. In the present meta-analysis, it is assumed that the heteroscedasticity is caused by the differences in precision with which the original noise coefficients have been estimated. These differences are reflected by the estimated standard errors of the respective noise coefficient estimates. Therefore, the estimates of $\hat{\sigma}(d_i)$ are used as weights in a weighted least squares regression to obtain estimates for the coefficients in β.

The explanatory variables, also termed moderator variables in meta-analysis, can be roughly divided in two groups:

1. sample population characteristics: variables describing the location and/or the sample of the original noise study at the time the data for that study were collected;

2. study characteristics: specification variables, time of data collection, publication type, country.

As stated by Smith and Huang (1995), the hedonic price function is likely to be affected by the distribution of bid and offer functions over market participants. In the above model, this distribution is assumed to be affected by the category 1 variables. The lack of availability or inadequacy of this type of data has been pointed out as a common problem in meta-analysis (Brouwer et al., 1997). Obviously, the authors of the original noise studies have not taken into consideration the possibility that their study might become an object of study. Therefore, sample population characteristics that might be used as control variables in a meta-regression are often not available from the original studies, and so useful information for category 1 variables is much more difficult to obtain than for category 2 variables.

In this study, one relevant sample characteristic reported in the original studies, namely, the mean sample house price, is available. Using this sample statistic and income per capita, the meta-variable relative mean sample house price has been constructed, which is an indicator of the relative wealth of the sample population. This variable is expected to have a positive effect on the NDI: the marginal implicit price for noise damage is assumed to be higher for wealthier than for poorer communities (cf. Smith and Huang, 1995). The category 2 variables used here are: the year in which the price data were collected (last two digits); a dummy variable indicating the use of 1960 price data; a dummy indicating whether a study has been published; three dummy specification variables, indicating a log-linear specification and the inclusion of accessibility variables and neighborhood variables respectively. The sample size causes the results to be rather sensitive to individual observations. Therefore, it seemed appropriate to consider the extreme valuation result in Yamaguchi (1996), which is about four standard deviations above the sample mean, as an outlier and to exclude it from the analysis. Table 4.4 presents a summary of regression results according to two model specifications, one 'full' specification and one containing a restricted specification. The logarithm of the NDI estimate is used as the dependent variable.

Table 4.4

Meta-analysis: regression results

Dependent variable: ln (NDI)

Explanatory variables	Model 1 coeff.	(t-value)	Model 2 coeff.	(t-value)
Constant	0.11	(0.06)	136.93	(4.66)
ln (rel. mean house price)	0.45	(1.08)	1.35	(3.22)
Year of price obs.	−0.04	(−2.25)	−0.07	(−4.84)
Dummy variables				
1960	2.71	(3.03)		
Published	1.30	(4.08)		
Loglin	−0.27	(−1.15)		
Access	0.88	(2.40)		
Neighborhood	0.69	(2.03)		
Adj. R-squared		0.95		0.92
F-statistic		83.22		172.58
Included observations		29		29

In most specifications, both the year of the price observations and a publication dummy which equals 1 if the original study has been published were significant explanatory variables. The publication dummy indicates that unpublished noise studies tend to find lower NDI estimates than published ones.[38] The variable indicating the year for which the price data were collected has a negative coefficient. In other words, studies using more recent price observations are found to present lower noise cost estimates. This result contrasts with the estimate in Smith and Huang (1995). However, Smith and Huang argue that their result that more recent studies tend to obtain higher environmental valuation coefficients is not necessarily evidence of increasing 'scarcity' of the environmental good. Rather, it may reflect improved data collection and modeling. Furthermore, there is no reason why such improvements would not result in downwards adjustment of estimates, as is suggested by the present results. The dummy variable representing the use of 1960 price data has a positive effect on noise valuation. The interpretation of the 1960 effect is not clear: for aircraft noise, the difference may be due to a strong reaction of the housing market to the then new phenomenon of aircraft noise (Nelson, 1978). Otherwise, the fact that this result shows up in both the meta-analysis by Smith and Huang and the present one may indicate that it is caused by unobserved dynamics of the (US) urban housing market at

---

[38] This is true even when the unpublished 'outlying' result is included in the analysis.

the time.

Three specification dummies are present in model 1. Loglin is a dummy with a value of 1 when the estimate is based on a log-linear or semi-log. The coefficient suggests that studies using this common specification type for the HP function tend to have a lower NDI. However, the effect is not significant. Two further specification dummies indicating the presence of neighborhood and accessibility variables in the HP function have a significant positive effect on the NDI estimate. Disregarding the sign, the presence of a specification effect in these cases is to be expected. Pearce and Markandya (1989) note that in order to measure the effect of any particular factor, such as environmental quality, on property values correctly, all other factors affecting property values have to be accounted for. A standard result in econometric estimation is that the exclusion of such a relevant variable from the regression specification will result in biased estimates of the included variables. The sign of the bias depends on how included and excluded variables relate to each other and to property values.

In particular, variables describing the amenities in a particular neighborhood (parks, playgrounds) as well as the accessibility (proximity to highway, airport, city center) are relevant. Given that noise has a negative effect on property values, the exclusion of a factor which is positively correlated to both aircraft noise and property values results in a downward bias in the absolute value of the noise coefficient, because the noise variable 'picks up' the positive effects too. Clearly, the sign of the bias depends on the definition of the relevant variables. In the case of the accessibility variable, the positive sign of the dummy variable in Table 4.4 shows that accessibility in the noise studies was generally positively related to aircraft noise. The inclusion of neighborhood variables has a significant positive effect on the NDI too.

The coefficient of the (logarithm of) relative house price variable proved quite sensitive to the specification of the meta-regression. In model 1, the 'wealth effect' is positive as expected but not significantly different from zero. Only when the dummy variables are disregarded (model 2), does the effect of the relative house price on noise valuation show up significantly. However, it should be noted that the NDI measures the property value loss relative to the house price. At a constant NDI (percentage value change per unit noise increase), more expensive houses are subject to a larger absolute depreciation. Therefore, an absolute wealth effect is already present given a constant NDI. The regression results show that there is no relative wealth effect.

4.4   Conclusion

Empirical evidence regarding the cost of aircraft noise has been reviewed, using studies based on two distinct valuation methods, namely, the contingent valuation method and the hedonic price method. A comparison of the CVM and HP valuation results in terms of percentage depreciation in Tables 4.1 and 4.2 indicates that the former noise cost estimates are substantially higher than the mean of the HP cost estimates. This comparison presents additional evidence to support the conclusion that CVM noise cost estimates are significantly higher than HP estimates by Feitelson et al. (1996), who discuss the theoretical reasons to expect the discrepancy. In brief, the main reason is that the curve describing the individual willingness to pay is typically much steeper than the equilibrium hedonic price function. Therefore, with non-marginal noise changes, one would expect the WTP to be higher than the value implied by the HP estimate. Furthermore, whereas HP estimates are generally considered to uncover only 'use values', CVM estimates may uncover information on other value categories (Maddison et al., 1996). Finally, HP estimates do not use information on consumers who are not willing to consider properties because of noise nuisance, whereas this type of information was shown to further increase the CVM estimates.

The evidence with respect to aircraft noise valuation in absolute terms is summarized in Table 4.5, which presents noise costs expressed in 1995 ECU per unit L_{eq} (dBA).[39] Whereas the CVM studies give absolute noise cost values, the HP studies estimate costs relative to property values. The absolute values have been calculated as follows. The NDI value is obtained using the estimated coefficients in Table 4.4, substituting 1990 as the year of price data and setting the dummy variables for publication, accessibility and neighborhood at a value of 1. The predicted value of the NDI thus obtained is 0.48, which is below the sample mean and median values. Other choices with respect to the substituted explanatory variables are possible and obviously result in alternative predicted NDIs. However, in order to provide a wider range of results, the noise cost based on the predicted NDI is supplemented with the noise costs based on the minimum and maximum NDIs in the sample. Finally, a property value is needed as a basis to translate NDI estimates into ECU values. Two property values are used as such. A first, low, estimate of 70 000 ECU is the average of the sample mean house price in the US HP studies themselves. While this estimate is appropriate in the sense that these are properties close to airports, its relevance in a European context is questionable. A second estimate is the average of the two UK cities in the sample of 110 000 ECU, which is close to the average value of properties in the Netherlands.

---

[39] Apart from the problems concerning the translation of noise measures discussed earlier, the establishment of absolute values in terms of one common unit involves the use of price indices and exchange rates. In all cases, values in different years have been transformed to the base year (1990) and currency (ECU) using the consumer price index and exchange rates in IMF (1996, 1997) respectively.

Table 4.5
Absolute noise costs

CVM	Noise costs per household (1995 ECU/L_{eq})	
	Study	
Noise level (L_{eq})	FHM (1996)	O&J (1973)
54	3070	5620
63	2740	3400
72	2070	2560
81	1830	2060
HP	Property value	
NDI value	Low	High
Minimum NDI	70	145
Predicted: 0.48	337	530
Maximum NDI	2499	3927

Table 4.5 restates the difference in value estimates between the CVM estimates on the one hand and the HP estimates on the other. However, some overlap in noise costs according to the respective methods is present for high NDI values. Nevertheless, using the noise cost according to the 'predicted' NDI value for the high property value, a difference with the CVM noise cost estimates of a factor of 3.5 and higher can be observed. A number of arguments that explain such differences have been discussed. These arguments suggest that CVM studies should be used to complement the already large set of HP results, especially considering the present small share of CVM results in the total number of valuation results. Given the range in aircraft noise valuation estimates, no 'true' value of peace and quiet is presented here. Instead, the cost estimates available at present are used as alternatives in the evaluation: the low and high HP values, calculated using the 'predicted' NDI, are used as low and intermediate noise cost alternatives, respectively; the CVM values in the column FHM (1996) are used as 'high' value estimates.

Chapter 5
Emissions

5.1 Introduction

Aircraft engines emit a variety of pollutants when burning fuel. Important emission species are CO_2 (carbon dioxide), NO_x (nitrogen oxide), CO (carbon monoxide), SO_2 (sulfur dioxide), VOCs (volatile organic compounds) and CH_4 (methane). A number of harmful environmental impacts are associated with these emissions: e.g., some types of pollutants, alone or in combination, negatively affect human health. Because of such impacts, the emission of pollutants inflicts costs on society.

Following the approach introduced in Chapter 3 (Section 3.4), the external costs imposed by aircraft emissions are evaluated via two general pathways, one global and one local. First, one can identify the pathway relating various types of damage to the effect of emissions on changes in the earth's climate. The latter effect is usually referred to as the (enhanced) greenhouse effect. This effect can be categorized as global, since there is no direct relation between the place where the emissions occur and the resultant damage. Secondly, one can identify the effects on human health associated with aircraft emissions; this effect has a local character. Human health impacts consist of mortality and morbidity effects, the valuation of which is central in the estimation of transport accident risk costs too. Therefore, the discussion of these value estimates applies equally to the valuation of accident risk, which is treated further in Chapter 6.

Although the above two pathways, global warming and health, are generally considered to be important pathways in the establishment of environmental costs of transport emissions (Maddison et al., 1996), it should be noted that these are not the only ways in which transport emissions negatively affect welfare. Table 5.1 provides an overview of emission types and the impact pathways that have been considered in studies on ground transport externalities (cf. Eyre et al., 1997; Dorland and Olsthoorn, 1998).[40] Given these other impacts, the estimates in this study represent an underestimate of the 'true' external cost total of emissions.

Besides the above general impacts of pollutants associated with (transport) fuel use, some aviation-specific environmental effects have attracted considerable scientific attention. These aviation-specific effects are in many cases the result of the emission of pollutants during the cruise flight in chemically complex and possibly sensitive regions of the atmosphere. Environmental impacts of emissions

---

[40] Pollutants may have a direct and/or an indirect effect in a particular pathway, e.g., PM_{10} has a direct impact on health, while NO_x has both a direct effect and an indirect effect through the formation of ozone.

can occur either directly or indirectly via the formation of secondary pollutants (Veenstra et al., 1995; Archer, 1993). The direct climate effect of CO_2, CH_4 and N_2O has already been mentioned. However, other emission species are considered as indirect contributors to the enhanced greenhouse effect too, e.g., H_2O via cloud formation and NO_x, CO and VOCs via the formation of tropospheric ozone. Other aviation-specific effects include the depletion of the stratospheric ozone layer through emission at higher altitudes of NO_x (directly). Stratospheric ozone is further affected by soot and SO_x via the formation of aerosols. It has thus been established that the effect of NO_x on ozone formation depends on the altitude where emissions take place. The effects of NO_x and SO_2 on acidification and surface ozone formation are represented in Table 5.1. However, these effects on ground-level conditions depend on the altitude at which the pollutants are emitted. Although the aviation-specific impacts described here may possibly indicate serious environmental damage, much of the research in these areas is fairly recent, and in certain areas scientific understanding is far from complete (FPC, 1998).

Table 5.1
Environmental impact of transport emissions

Pollutant	Effect on
Carbon dioxide (CO_2)	climate (forests, crops)
Methane (CH_4)	climate
Nitrous oxide (N_2O)	climate
Carbon monoxide (CO)	health
Particulates (PM_{10})	health
Sulfur dioxide (SO_2)	health, crops, forests, building materials (climate)
NO_x	health, crops, forests, building materials (climate, fisheries)
VOCs	climate, health, crops (forests, building materials)
Benzene (C_6H_6)	health

Note: Items in parentheses refer to effects that have been identified but are small or difficult to estimate.

One of the areas where recent progress has been made concerns the analysis of the impact of aircraft NO_x emissions on ozone concentrations in the troposphere and lower stratosphere. In particular, these analyses have been conducted using three-dimensional chemical simulation models such as ECHAM3/CHEM (Dameris et al., 1998a,b) and MOGUNTIA (Veenstra et al., 1995). In turn, these results can be used to estimate the indirect effect of NO_x on global warming damages. This type of external cost evaluation has been conducted by Tol and Grewe (1999). Although the results of these 3D-modeling approaches are promising, the authors consider them as a first approach with considerable uncertainty in the results (Dameris et al., 1998a). In a number of other studies, the effect of NO_x on radiative forcing through the formation of ozone is assumed equal to the effect of CO_2 (FPC, 1998; Roos et al., 1997; Veenstra et al., 1995). The latter assumption has been used here in a sensitivity analysis too. Other aviation-specific impacts such as cloud formation are not considered in the analysis.

5.2   Global damage: the greenhouse effect

The 'greenhouse effect' refers to the increase in the earth's surface temperature as a result of the absorption by so-called greenhouse gases (GHGs) of radiation re-emitted by the planet. The term 'enhanced', which often precedes 'greenhouse effect', reflects the fact that the natural warming process has been accelerated by anthropogenic emissions of GHGs since the industrial revolution. The pathways associated with the (enhanced) greenhouse effect all run from aircraft emissions of GHGs via increased global warming to physical damages taking various forms.

While CO_2 is the most important GHG, CH_4, nitrous oxides ($N_2 O$) and chlorofluorocarbons (CFCs) add to global warming too. The contribution of each emission type relative to the effect of CO_2 is expressed as the global warming potential (GWP) or CO_2 equivalents. Another potentially relevant GHG is NO_x emitted in the troposphere. The larger part of NO_x emissions takes place at higher altitudes, where the amount of NO_x emitted by aircraft relative to existing concentrations is significant.[41] As mentioned above, however, scientific understanding of the processes involved is in progress but not complete.

The valuation of each unit (tonne) of CO_2 equivalent has taken the following form in the literature (Nordhaus, 1991; Maddison et al., 1996). Physical climate change effects are estimated using integrated assessment (IA) models, a whole range of which has been developed (for a critical overview and comparison of approaches see Janssen, 1996; Tol, 1997). IA models thus establish the dose–response chain. This is not the place to go into the technicalities and problems associated with IA modeling; here, reference is made only to the results of the assessments. It is appreciated, however, that IA modeling is a huge task, beset with uncertainties and methodological problems; see e.g. Maddison (1995) for a discussion of the uncertainties and contrasting views with respect to global warming mechanisms. Furthermore, many global warming damage estimates are based upon one point in the 'damage function': typically, the economic damage is calculated for the scenario in which CO_2 concentrations double, leading to an estimated long-run rise of 2.5 °C in average global temperature.[42] Given this

---

[41]   Calculations show that more than 70 percent of NO_x is emitted above an altitude of 5000 m, while the contribution of NO_x emitted by aircraft at higher altitudes 'may reach values up to 40 percent' in critical areas like the North Atlantic routes (FPC, 1998).

[42]   The Intergovernmental Panel on Climate Change (IPCC) predicts global average

temperature rise, one can estimate resulting physical effects and obtain, after valuation, so-called 2*CO_2 benchmark costs.

The field of climate change damage assessment is relatively young. Results of the studies summarized in Tol (1997) are presented, with the Nordhaus (1991) study as the earliest estimate. Several damage categories have been identified (Tol, 1997; Fankhauser, 1992), including costs associated with sea-level rises[43] (protection and loss of dryland and wetland) and the loss of biodiversity and ecosystems. Primary sector effects include effects on agricultural production (and therefore the number of people at risk of hunger, which, depending on the model used, may be positive or negative) and effects on forestry and fisheries. Furthermore, effects on other sectors (energy, water, construction, transport, tourism) are identified, as well as effects on human well-being, e.g. through the intensified spread of infectious diseases like malaria (amenity, morbidity, costs of migration) and costs associated with disasters like storms, floods, drought and hurricanes. Note that for some categories the value of the effect induced by climate change may be positive. The term 'damage assessment' for the overall effect is used to indicate that the impact summed over all categories is negative.

Table 5.2
Global warming damage estimates

Study	Warming (°C)	Damage (% GNP)
Nordhaus (1991)	3.0	1.0
Cline (1992)	2.5	1–2
Fankhauser (1992)	2.5	1.5
Maddison (1995)	2.5	1.5
Tol (1997)	2.5	2.7

The damages generally calculated in the literature are annual damage values inflicted upon present (world or national) economies by an equilibrium climate change due to a doubling of atmospheric CO_2. The different IA models may lead to differing enhanced global warming predictions and cost estimates. Results of five global warming damage cost studies (central estimates) are presented in Table 5.2. It should be stressed that the respective studies differ in comprehensiveness with respect to cost categories as well as regional coverage.[44]

---

temperatures to rise between 1.5 and 4.5 °C for a doubling of atmospheric CO_2, with 2.5 °C as a 'best guess' (Fankhauser, 1992).

[43] Fankhauser reports an estimated sea-level rise of 50 cm by the year 2100 as a result of the 2.5 °C temperature rise.

[44] Furthermore, Tol (1997) points to the absence of dynamic aspects in the damage analysis, e.g., attention to the shape of the damage function, the rate of change, adaptation to damage. Also, central estimates do not generally take into account the small chance of extreme events ('greenhouse catastrophe').

The next question is how to establish marginal values for CO_2 at a particular point in time, say t_0, given the estimated annual damages over a large number of years from t_0, which can then be used to price emissions. Marginal damage costs (MDC), taking into account damages from the present until a time horizon $t = T$, can be written (Azar and Sterner, 1996, p. 171) as

$$\text{MDC} = \int_{t_0}^{T} G(t) \frac{\partial C(m_h)}{\partial m_h} V(t) dt \qquad (5.1)$$

where $G(t)$ is the fraction of a unit CO_2 emitted at t_0 that remains in the atmosphere at time t; $\frac{\partial C(m_h)}{\partial m_h}$ is the marginal annual damage, which is based on a percentage of income loss as presented in Table 5.2; and $V(t)$ is the present-value function which determines the present value of future damage incurred at time t as a percentage of equal damage incurred at present.

Using this formulation, the authors analyze the effect of each of the three terms in the integrand on the size of the marginal values. The first term, $G(t)$, partly accounts for the difference between the marginal damage estimates in Nordhaus (1993) and Azar and Sterner (1996). Secondly, differences in the estimated annual damage $\frac{\partial C(m_h)}{\partial m_h}$ may be due to the use of different IA models, and variation in comprehensiveness and regional coverage. While the first two terms on the right-hand side of (5.1) may lead to differences in marginal damage values,[45] the huge difference between the marginal damage estimates of Azar and Sterner (1996) and, e.g., Nordhaus (1991, 1993) are due mainly to the differences in parameter values of the present-value function $V(t)$ and the fact that the former authors consider income differences explicitly.

The important parameters of the function $V(t)$ are the (negative of the) elasticity of the marginal utility of consumption, γ, the growth rate of consumption (production) g and the pure rate of social time preference ρ. These parameters determine the social discount rate as

$$r = \gamma g + \rho \qquad (5.2)$$

This general formulation of the discount rate reflects two motives for valuing present consumption higher than future consumption. First, because marginal utility is generally assumed to decrease in consumption, positive consumption growth implies that future marginal consumption has a lower value. The parameter ρ reflects impatience in individual human behavior. The establishment of a social discount rate using these two motives is the subject of debate in the literature (see Markandya, 1994, for a discussion). While $\gamma = 1$ is often used, the growth rate depends on whether or not one assumes that environmental 'carrying capacity' constraints may limit future growth. Clearly, when future growth is

---

[45]   Azar and Sterner (1996) argue that the representation of the carbon cycle in Nordhaus (1993) underestimates the retention ratio of CO_2 in the atmosphere.

limited, the discount rate decreases. Furthermore, there is a largely unresolved debate over the size of the pure rate of social time preference, which we shall not pursue here. The result is that studies usually present a range of time preference rates or social discount rates leading to a range of marginal damage values.

Another issue affecting global warming damage estimation is 'equity weighting', i.e., the weighting of losses for different income groups, which is related to decreasing marginal utility of consumption. When the utility consumers derive from consumption increases at a decreasing rate when consumption rises, the effect of changes in consumption (income) have different welfare effects for different income groups. In particular, income losses for low-income groups have larger welfare 'weights' than losses for high-income groups (see Azar and Sterner, 1996; note that potential differences in vulnerability are not taken into account). As a result, the introduction of equity weighting increases the damage estimates. Furthermore, there is a distinction between marginal values without policy intervention ('business as usual') on the one hand and, on the other, 'optimal control' values, which are the values associated with the abatement strategy in which, for the last tonne of CO_2 equivalent removed, the marginal social abatement cost equals the marginal social benefit (damage avoided). While the 'business as usual' and 'optimal control' marginal damage values need not differ much (Maddison et al., 1996), the optimal control values are lower as marginal damages are increasing. Finally, it is clear that the marginal damage value is determined by the choice of the time interval $T - t_0$ too. The sensitivity of the results in this respect, however, depends on the discount rate. For 'high' discount rates, the effect of adding a year to the time horizon will be relatively small and vice versa.

The above discussion has highlighted some of the factors that explain the differences in global warming damage estimates between studies, as presented in Table 5.2. The discussion makes clear that it would not be wise, given the current state of the global warming damage research, to make any attempt to establish one 'true' marginal damage value for each greenhouse gas. Rather, in Table 5.3, a range of estimates is presented from studies that give marginal values for three greenhouse gases separately. The table shows the relation between the marginal damage value and the discount rate, as well as a few sensitivity results. The figures are from a recent study (Tol, 1999), which applies equity weighting, and thus accounts for the differences in marginal utilities of income.[46]

The results in Tol (1999) are slightly higher than those in Maddison (1995) and Nordhaus (1991). The values in Table 5.3 are used in the calculation of environmental costs of air transport. Given the range of the estimates and

---

[46]   The values are based on calculations with the FUND 1.6 model. The baseline results, using the IPCC IS92a scenario, are presented; equity weighting is applied; emissions in 1995–2004; time horizon of damages is 2100. The values for CO_2 are in thousand ECU per tonne carbon.

keeping in mind the numerous assumptions which underlie these numbers, three
alternative estimates are used: as an intermediate value, the 'baseline' estimate
for the 3 percent discount rate is used, while the values at the 5 percent and 1
percent discount rate are used as low and high alternatives, respectively.

Table 5.3
Global warming damage estimates

Discount rate	Damage estimates (1995 ECU/tonne)		
	CO_2	CH_4	N_2O
1%	171	517	16862
3%	66	325	6005
5%	31	204	2660
	Sensitivity of CO_2 results		
	No equity weighting		
1%	73		
3%	25		
	Low (high) climate sensitivity		
1%	101 (318)		
3%	39 (123)		

Source: Tol (1999).

5.3   Local air pollution

In the damage estimation, one may distinguish several cost pathways, e.g., damage
to human health, damage to buildings, reduced visibility, damage to forests, crops
and fisheries etc. Many studies focus on the health damage pathway, which stands
out as the dominant cost effect of air pollution (Small and Kazimi, 1995; Krupnick
et al., 1997). In this study, air pollution emissions are valued using the health
damage pathway too. The health impacts to be valued are (increased) mortality
and morbidity.

5.3.1   Valuation: mortality

Mortality effects associated with both the effects of air pollution and accident
risk can be valued using the so-called 'value of statistical life' (VOSL), a value
that is derived from the value that individuals subject to risk attach to safety
improvements. Other ways to calculate the costs of mortality, such as using the
present value of future earnings, the value of life implicit in public policy, life
insurance premiums, or values of court awards, all have their shortcomings (see the
discussion in Maddison et al., 1996). Willingness-to-pay (WTP) or willingness-to-

accept (WTA) studies analyze individual preferences based on risk–money trade-offs.[47] A large number of empirical estimates of the WTP for increased safety (and the associated, implicit VOSL) can be found in the literature; see Viscusi (1993) and OECD (1994) for an overview. Risk–money trade-offs have been analyzed using three methods (Markandya, 1994). First, there is a large number of wage-risk studies, estimating the premium that is needed to induce workers to take on jobs involving higher risks.

Secondly, analyses have been made of choices in consumer markets involving a direct risk–money trade-off, such as in the case of the choice of car safety features, smoke detectors, seat belt use. Thirdly, there is research based on surveys in which respondents are asked to state their WTP for (measures that result in) risk reductions in particular situations.

The implicit VOSL estimates from the studies surveyed in Viscusi (1993) and OECD (1994) are summarized in Table 5.4. The estimates used in the table are from studies performed in both the USA and Europe, and show that results in consumer market studies are consistently low, while survey results display much more variation, providing the highest as well as the lowest VOSL estimates.

Table 5.4
Summary of VOSL estimates

	(mn 1995 ECU)			
	Mean	Sd	Max	Min
Wage–risk	5.13	4.12	14.44	0.29
Consumer market	1.27	1.10	3.57	0.53
Surveys	4.88	5.17	15.55	0.09
All	4.54	4.26	15.55	0.09

A number of issues have been raised concerning the VOSL estimation itself and the application of the VOSL estimates in the context of valuing air pollution. First, the estimation methods all have their shortcomings; see Pearce and Markandya (1989), Miller (1997) and Chapter 3 for a discussion. Markandya (1994) concludes that because of these shortcomings, study results are likely to be biased. Furthermore, the VOSL estimates are obtained in situations of voluntary risk, borne by individuals with possibly less than average risk aversion, whereas it has been suggested that the willingness to accept compensation in case of involuntary risk would be many times higher (Krupnick et al., 1997). Nevertheless, valuation studies are often in need of a single VOSL for practical use. A number of such single values have been suggested. First, reviewing the wage–risk literature, Viscusi (1993) concludes that the VOSL he places the 'greatest reliance' on is 3.65

---

[47] Note that in this case a behavioral valuation technique is used in an indirect manner: instead of using the WTP for a reduction in air pollution itself, the WTP for a change in a particular effect associated with air pollution is used in valuing the cost of pollution.

mn (1995 ECU). Markandya (1994), surveying European studies, takes an average of CVM results and arrives at 3.1 mn (1995 ECU), a value that is currently being used in externality valuation by the European Commission. Based on 'available evidence', Maddison et al. (1996) use a value of 2.56 mn (1995 ECU). It may be noted that this 2.56–3.65 mn range is 'conservative', being well below the average value in Table 5.4.

A second issue concerns the application (or transfer) of VOSL estimates. In the WTP (WTA) studies summarized above, risks with respect to 'sudden' death are typically valued by 'prime age' individuals with an unspecified health status. It has thus been proposed (EC, 1999) to use the VOSL in cases of 'sudden' deaths where the affected population is similar to the general population, e.g. when valuing fatal accidents or mortality impacts in climate change models. Therefore, these VOSL estimates may also be applied in the valuation of accident mortality costs (see, e.g., Maddison et al., 1996). However, Markandya (1994, 1998) argues that in the case of air pollution valuation, one should account for the distribution of age and health status of the victims as well as for the time lapse between exposure and impact.

First, air pollution appears to affect the elderly disproportionately. Therefore, the distribution of VOSL with respect to age is relevant. Empirical studies have come up with an inverse relationship between the VOSL and age after a particular age has been reached, e.g. the inverted U-shaped VOSL as a function of age in the CVM research in Jones-Lee (1985). Markandya (1998) observes that a behavioral model explaining such empirical results would reflect a positive income effect up to the maximum VOSL, and after that the possibly opposing forces of risk aversion and a life expectancy effect. It should be noted, however, that the empirical evidence is reportedly mixed (Maddison et al., 1996), while a practical problem is that dose–response functions generally give little information on the effects per age group.

Secondly, it can be argued that in the case of air pollution, e.g. particle pollution, it is inappropriate to apply a VOSL based on a population with an 'average' life expectancy to a population of victims with a much shortened life expectancy, such as people suffering from lung diseases. Similarly, the valuation of an increased risk of death 'now' and death in t years respectively would not be the same. In order to deal with these issues, it has been proposed to use the 'value of life years' (VOLY) approach when valuing air pollution damage. This allows one to differentiate valuation with respect to type of impact and type of victim. A distinction is made between 'acute' and 'chronic' mortality impacts, referring to the difference in life expectancies of the victims. The calculation of the costs of these mortality impacts then takes into account the VOLY, the life expectancy of the victims in the absence of air pollution, the time between the exposure and the illness, and the survival period of individuals after contracting the disease. Furthermore, the values vary with the discount rate. The estimates for acute and chronic mortality costs in Table 5.5 have been taken from EC (1999).

Table 5.5
Mortality costs (1995 ECU)

Discount rate	0%	3%	10%
Acute	73 500	116 250	234 000
Chronic	98 000	84 330	60 340

Source: EC (1999)

The values in Table 5.5 represent only a fraction of the complete VOSLs as presented in Table 5.4: e.g. the value for acute mortality is only 3.75 percent of the 'medium' 3.1 mn ECU VOSL. Therefore, taking into account the health status of victims may lead to a reduction in the valuation of air pollution damage compared with other studies. Many studies involved in pricing externalities use one single VOSL to value all mortality effects (see, e.g., Eyre et al., 1997; Maddison et al., 1996, both using a value of £2 mn), based on the VOSL estimates from the literature. Following the above considerations, three valuation alternatives are used in the evaluation of environmental costs in this study. In the calculation of the low and medium values for air pollution, the values for acute and chronic mortality in Table 5.5, at the 3 percent discount rate, are used. For the calculation of the high environmental cost estimates, the 'full' or population average VOSL of 3.1 mn ECU is used.

5.3.2   Valuation: morbidity

The welfare loss associated with non-fatal effects of air pollution has been measured in the literature too. One can distinguish three components in the valuation of health damage, namely, the value of time lost due to the illness, the utility loss due to pain and suffering, and the expenditures for treating or preventing the effects of the illness. The costs of time lost are usually valued using the wage rate and the (opportunity) cost of leisure time. The expenditures associated with a particular treatment, e.g., an emergency room visit, can be derived directly as (an average of) hospital costs. Taken together, time costs and direct expenditures are often referred to as the cost of illness (COI). The WTP to avoid pain and suffering can only be established using CVM studies. Clearly, the COI is relatively easy to establish, but presents only a part of the cost total and is not necessarily a part of the above-mentioned WTP (Markandya, 1998). As WTP values are not present for a number of morbidity endpoints, Rowe et al. (1995) have studied the relation between WTP and COI, and find that the ratio of WTP to COI is in the range of 1.3–2.4. They recommend a ratio of 2 in order to derive approximate WTP values using COI information for non-carcinogenic health effects.

In the calculation of morbidity costs, the value of the three cost components is established for a number of 'endpoints', i.e., particular events that can be linked to certain pollution types. Endpoints include 'restrictive activity days', various types of chronic illnesses, symptom days, emergency room visits, respiratory hospital admissions, etc. For an overview of the studies estimating the value of the morbidity endpoints, see Rowe et al. (1995) and Markandya (1994). As most of the morbidity valuation studies have been carried out in the United States, US results are used in the European externality studies by Markandya (1994, 1998) and EC (1999). These values represent central estimates from a limited set of mainly US WTP results. Rowe et al. (1995) conclude that the available WTP results generally range between 50 percent and 150 percent of these central estimates. Given the small number of studies, questions of transferability have not been studied and Rowe et al. assign equal probability to the low, central and upper values. However, where COI is involved in the value estimates, the value transfer could be improved by using European medical service costs, as has been done for respiratory hospital admissions. The valuation of morbidity endpoints does not vary over the three environmental cost alternatives used in the evaluation. However, the cost alternatives are calculated using differing assumptions regarding the exposure–response relations.

5.3.3   Exposure–response relations and cost estimates

Aircraft emissions contribute to ambient concentrations of pollutants that are responsible for health damage. This step in the health damage pathway can be represented by two sets of physical relations: first, the links between the concentration or dose of pollutants (in grams/m^3) and the health effects (in cases/(grams/m^3)). An overview of the health effects that are considered here is given in Table 5.6.

Table 5.6
Health effects of air pollution

Pollutant	Effect on	
	Mortality	Morbidity
Particulates (PM_{10})	D	D
Sulfur dioxide (SO_2)	D, I (SO_4)	D, I (SO_4)
Nitrogen oxide (NO_x)	I (NO_3)	D, I (NO_3)
Benzene (C_6H_6)		D
1.3 butadiene		D
Other VOCs	I (ozone)	I (ozone)
Carbon monoxide (CO)		D

D = direct effect; I = secondary effect through pollutant in parentheses

Secondly, one needs to establish the link between the amount of pollutants emitted by aircraft and the above-mentioned concentration.   The relations between ambient concentrations and health effects have been studied in the epidemiological literature. The results of such studies are reviewed in Rowe et al. (1995), Maddison et al. (1996) and EC (1998, 1999). Schwartz (1994) and Krupnick et al. (1997) analyze results in the literature on the effect of airborne particles on mortality. A general issue is, again, the transferability of the cause–effect relations. The meta-analysis by Schwartz (1994) shows a consistent relation between particle concentration and adverse health effects across mainly US longitudinal studies. Chestnut et al. (1997) compare the results of US studies with an analysis carried out in Bangkok and conclude that the effects of small-particle concentration (PM_{10}) on daily mortality are 'reasonably comparable', notwithstanding the fact that the US results have been obtained for populations, cities and climate with rather different characteristics. Therefore, there is some evidence that transfer of exposure–response relations is justified for respiratory health effects. For other effects, transferability of effect sizes is not necessarily justified.

Table 5.7
Air pollution health cost estimates
1995 ECU/(person-microgram/m^3)

Pollutant	Low	Medium	High
Particulates (PM_{10})	8.773	14.234	140.557
Sulfur dioxide (SO_2)	16.855	24.159	253.091
Nitrogen oxide (NO_x)	10.830	14.479	151.090
Benzene (C_6H_6)	0.050	0.050	0.050
1.3 butadiene	1.882	1.882	1.882
Other VOCs	1.092	1.163	18.327
Carbon monoxide (CO)	0.004	0.004	45.344

In this study, the 'base' parameters for most health effects associated with PM_{10}, SO_2, NO_x, VOCs and CO have been taken from EC (1999); only the effects of benzene and butadiene have been obtained from Rowe et al. (1995). EC (1999) applies the distinction between chronic and acute mortality, and further distinguishes between health effects that affect the entire population and those that affect the subgroups adults, children, asthmatics and elderly. Adding the monetary values corresponding to the various health effects per subgroup per pollutant, the costs per change in concentration (dose) are estimated. Clearly, the derivation of such cost estimates involves many parameter choices. While the base parameter values, which are based on recent results in European epidemiological research, appear to be a sound and relevant choice in the present analysis, air pollution costs have been calculated using two sets of alternative parameters. A 'high' estimate is obtained by using a number of additional health impacts suggested for sensitivity analysis in EC (1999), and the 'low' estimate is obtained by applying three further sensitivity analyses suggested in EC (1999).[48]

The total air pollution health cost estimates, presented in Table 5.7, provide an impression of the range of values that may be obtained using the procedures discussed here. The difference between the high cost estimates on the one hand and the low and the medium values on the other is mainly determined by the use of a single full VOSL of 3.1 million ECU for all mortality effects. The resulting cost estimates are, for the pollutants that cause mortality impacts, increased by a factor of 10; for CO, the effect is even more dramatic because the sensitivity analysis addresses a mortality impact for this pollutant. The differences clearly demonstrate the sensitivity of the cost estimates with respect to the treatment of mortality costs.

5.4   Conclusion

This chapter has addressed a number of issues in the valuation of transport emissions. The discussion has made it clear that, through its indirect nature, the establishment of cost estimates in this field necessarily relies on a number of cause–effect relations. For the estimation of both global warming and local air pollution damages, all the segments in the pathway approach have to be used. The cause–effect relations in these cases are highly complex. However, it is now well accepted that such complexities have to be dealt with in order to study the external costs of transport (Greene et al., 1997; Maddison et al., 1996). Fortunately, (transport) economists can make use of the results of research in domains other than economics in order to arrive at external cost estimates. Such results have been presented and used in the estimation of damages associated with the emission of greenhouse gases and local air pollution. Many choices have to be made before the cost of a change in ambient conditions can be established. The effect of a small number of such alternative choices is illustrated by the cost estimates in Tables 5.3 and 5.7. Although the problem of considerable variation in valuation results is clearly present, the estimates discussed here provide some measure of the economic cost associated with the emission of pollutants. As such, they respond to the need for such values, established in Chapter 3.

---

[48]   These sensitivity calculations assume no SO_2 impacts for acute mortality and respiratory hospital admissions; omission of all types of 'restricted activity days' as endpoints; and a down-scaling of exposure–response functions for chronic mortality.

Chapter 6
Environmental Costs in European Aviation

6.1 Introduction

Valuation results for noise, greenhouse warming and health effects associated with local air pollution have been examined in the previous chapters. At this point, it is useful to take another look at Figure 3.5. In terms of the graph in that figure, the relations that have been discussed are those in quadrants II and III. In the case of noise, the intermediate effects are not treated explicitly; rather, the relation between ambient concentrations and costs is direct. In contrast, the intermediate effect is of central importance in the pathways for greenhouse gas emissions and local air pollution. Thus, marginal valuations in terms of ambient concentrations have been established in Chapter 5. The relations in quadrant I are discussed briefly in this chapter.

In the next section, the relation between aircraft movements and noise annoyance is discussed, in order to establish the relation between flight frequency and noise costs. In Section 6.3, the relation between aircraft emissions and ambient concentrations is addressed, followed by a brief discussion of the treatment of accident risk costs. Using the quadrant I relations and the valuation results in the previous two chapters, environmental costs for individual flights for a number of aircraft categories are established in Section 6.4. Finally, cost information for the aircraft types flown on a sample of European interstate airline markets is used in order to estimate environmental costs on these routes.

6.2 Noise exposure

Having reviewed the evidence on the value of marginal changes in noise exposure for households in the previous chapter, the present section analyzes the relation between air transport output and household noise exposure. The absolute size of noise pollution is generally expressed in terms of the number of households exposed to a particular noise level on the ground or, rather, exposed to a noise level between two boundary levels, as illustrated using the noise data in Chapter 3. Noise contours around airports constitute such boundary levels, indicating concentric 'lines' of equal noise levels. While calculations of the number of airport noise victims are based on noise contours, these contours are not usually measured but calculated using noise models.[49] Such noise models use large data sets giving information on the size of airport traffic (the number of landings and take-offs), the distribution of this traffic over aircraft types (fleetmix) and the specific noise characteristics of each of these types, the layout of the airport, the allocation of traffic over the runways, routes used for landing and take-off, etc. Given the input data and a particular noise measure chosen, the noise model can calculate noise contours around the airport. Combining these with population figures for the relevant areas yields the number of noise victims within each contour.

This section investigates the responsibility of individual flights for the noise costs imposed on households living around airports. Using a noise model of the type mentioned above, such responsibility can be calculated in detail. However, the data and modeling requirements for such calculations fall outside the scope of the present study. Rather, noise costs per flight are calculated here using a simple statistical analysis, investigating the relation between the number of aircraft movements at a number of European airports and the annoyance experienced by individuals exposed to aircraft noise around these airports. The estimates are subsequently used to establish the marginal noise cost represented by each aircraft movement.

First, a variable measuring aggregate noise annoyance per airport has been derived using OECD data on the number of persons exposed to particular noise levels around airports (OECD, 1993, 1987). In this context, noise annoyance is defined as the difference between the noise level to which an individual is exposed and the background noise or 'no-noise' level. Next, in order to simplify the calculations, the assumption is introduced that the average of the noise levels at the boundaries of the noise zones (contours) represents the average noise level experienced by individuals living within the zones. For example, it is assumed that the average noise level experienced by individuals living between the $L_{eq}57$ and $L_{eq}62$ contours equals 59.5 L_{eq}. Using this average noise exposure, both the aggregate noise exposure and annoyance (in L_{eq}-persons) are obtained by aggregating over individuals within and over noise zones. In this manner, a measure of the aggregate noise annoyance per airport is established.

Next, the relation between this aggregate noise annoyance and the activity at the airport in terms of the number of aircraft movements is estimated using OLS. The model is formulated as

$$NA_i = f(ACM_i, t) \tag{6.1}$$

which represents the aggregate noise annoyance NA_i at airport i as a function of aggregate airport activity in terms of total aircraft movements (ACM) ACM_i and the year t of observation itself. Clearly, this is a rather stylized representation of reality, which captures only some of the factors affecting the size of the noise problem while disregarding items like the exact fleetmix and the position of the airport relative to residential areas. Nevertheless, the model does capture

---

[49]   Dutch law demands that airports calculate noise contours or zones according to specific prescriptions concerning input data and modeling. Comparable regulation is present in other countries.

two important determinants.   The motivation of the first factor is that all noise exposure measures depend in some way on the number of flights.   For example, model calculations for Schiphol airport show that the area within the 20 Ke zone increases linearly in the number of aircraft movements (Werkgroep milieuberekeningen TNLI, 1997).   The year of observation is relevant because over the last decades improvements in aircraft technology have reduced noise emissions significantly, partly as a result of increasingly stringent national and international regulation. For a given number of aircraft movements, the effect of this technological change on the number of noise victims should be negative.

Equation (6.1) has been estimated using 38 observations on noise annoyance and on aircraft movements at a number of European airports for which noise exposure data were available.[50]   Aggregate noise annoyance and the number of aircraft movements are entered in logarithms. OLS estimation results are shown in Table 6.1.

Table 6.1
Noise annoyance: OLS regression results

Dependent variable: Aggregate noise annoyance (Person-L_{eq} per airport, logarithms)	Estimated coefficient (t-value)
Independent variables:	
Constant	78.93
	(1.58)
Aircraft movements	0.92
(per airport, logarithms)	(5.16)
Year	−0.04
	(−1.63)
Adj. R-squared	0.41
F-statistic	13.59
Included observations	38

The main interest of the analysis is in the estimates of the aircraft movements coefficient, representing the effect of aircraft movements on aggregate noise

---

[50]   Observations on both noise victims and aircraft movements were available for Copenhagen, Paris, Frankfurt, Düsseldorf, Munich, Hamburg, Amsterdam, Rotterdam, Maastricht, Oslo, Geneva, Zürich, London and Manchester. The period covered by the data is 1974–1997. Data on aircraft noise exposure are from OECD (1993, 1987); data on aircraft movements per airport are from ICAO (Digest of Statistics, Airport Traffic, 1974–1997). Where data on the number of aircraft movements were not available for a particular year, the observation on the nearest available year was used.

annoyance. Because both the noise annoyance and the aircraft movements are in logarithms, the estimated coefficient is interpreted as an elasticity. In order to arrive at an estimate of the absolute change in noise annoyance per aircraft movement, the elasticity is evaluated at the sample mean values of both variables. For the complete sample, this results in a change in person-L_{eq} per aircraft movement of 6.4. An alternative estimate is obtained by evaluating the elasticity at the mean of the observations dated 1985 or later, which gives a value of 3.9 person-L_{eq} per aircraft movement. The difference between the estimates reflects the decreased ratio of noise annoyance to aircraft movements, which may be interpreted as improvements in average noise characteristics of aircraft over time. This effect is also captured by the estimated coefficient on the year variable. It is noted that the effects calculated here do not include any effects an increase in aircraft movements might have on households living outside the $L_{eq}57$ contour. In that sense, the effect on noise annoyance may be an underestimate.

The effect of aircraft movements on noise annoyance in person-L_{eq} can be evaluated in monetary terms by applying the noise costs per L_{eq} per household derived in Chapter 4. It has been shown, e.g., in Table 4.1, that the CVM noise cost estimates decrease in noise exposure. That is, a change in person-L_{eq} is valued more highly at an ambient noise level of 57 L_{eq} than at 62 L_{eq}. In order to account for this, a weighted average CVM noise cost is derived, using the average number of persons exposed to the particular noise level as weights. The HP estimates are constant over noise levels, so these can be applied directly. In the application presented here, the CVM estimates according to Feitelson et al. (1996) and the 'predicted' HP noise cost estimates for the 'low' and 'high' property value are used. For these values, the following noise costs for the average aircraft movement are obtained (Table 6.2).[51]

Table 6.2
Noise costs per aircraft movement

Person-L_{eq} change per ACM:	(1995 ECU/ACM)		
	HP low	HP high	CVM
6.4	281	1028	4771
3.9	171	626	2907

The noise conditions per aircraft movement do not differentiate with respect to aircraft type or size. Therefore, the values do not account for differences in the relative noise contribution of various aircraft types. Information regarding relative noise contributions is, however, available, and is used to derive noise costs per aircraft category in Section 6.4.

---

[51]   The noise costs in Chapter 4 are expressed in ECU per household. Therefore, the person-L_{eq} changes are transformed to household-L_{eq} changes, using an average of 3.3 persons per household (OECD, 1993).

6.3   Exposure to local air pollution

In this section the responsibility of aircraft emissions for ambient concentrations of pollutants (cf. quadrant I in Figure 3.5) and the associated damage are addressed. Unlike greenhouse gases, for which the environmental damage does not depend on where they are released, the effect of pollutants in the health damage pathway depends on their local concentrations. However, there is not a one-to-one mapping between local concentrations and the amount of pollutants emitted during, e.g., landing or take-off. Indeed, in order to establish such a mapping in a detailed manner, one would have to use so-called dispersion models. Since such simulation exercises fall outside the scope of this study, a simplified model of dispersion is used here.

First, only the emission of pollutants during the so-called landing and take-off (LTO) cycle are used in the assessment of health effects. The LTO cycle is defined as the part of the flight taking place at a height lower than 3000 feet (915 meters), and consists of four phases, namely, take-off, climb-out, approach and idling/taxiing. The LTO cycle is thus confined to the so-called atmospheric boundary layer (up to 1 kilometer), through which pollutants are being mixed back down to ground level in a few days (Olivier, 1991). The major share of CO, particles and VOCs is emitted during the LTO (Archer, 1993; NLR, 1997), but this is not true for NO_x. However, given the limited lifetime of NO_x, FPC (1998) concludes that only a small part of NO_x emissions emitted at higher altitudes will reach ground levels. Therefore, considering only LTO emissions in the assessment of the contribution of air transport to local air pollution is justifiable. Furthermore, a practical advantage of using LTO emission information is data availability, which is large compared with information on emissions during cruise.

The relation between the amount of pollutants emitted during the LTO and the concentration or dose of pollutant per person (victim) on the ground is represented by a set of parameters reported in Eyre et al. (1997). In this study, stylized relationships between emission rates and pollution doses are derived for a number of pollutants. These relationships take into account, among other factors, transformation to secondary pollutants, the range over which each pollutant is dispersed, and the average population density over that range. Applying this approach in the present study, aircraft LTO emissions are treated as electricity sector emissions, i.e., emitted from a considerable height in a few locations outside major population concentrations. Such emissions are, unlike e.g. exhaust emissions in urban centers, transported over long ranges before reaching their victims. Over such long ranges, the proposed dose calculations are valid for all sources within the boundary layer (Eyre et al., 1997).

The doses are calculated in terms of (person $\mu g/m^3$) per tonne emitted. Using these emission–dose relations, the exposure–response relations and the effect valuations discussed in Chapter 5, the marginal emission costs presented in Table 6.3 have been calculated.[52] For an overview of the marginal values for greenhouse gas emissions, see Table 5.3.

Table 6.3
Marginal air pollution damages
('000 1995 ECU/tonne emitted)

Pollutant	Low	Medium	High
Particulates (PM_{10})	5058	7463	107251
Sulfur dioxide (SO_2)	1528	2666	40968
Nitrogen oxide (NO_x)	1878	2731	38099
VOCs	718	761	13766
Carbon monoxide (CO)	3	3	34280

6.4   Accident risk

The costs associated with accident risk are treated summarily. Although aviation is generally regarded as a relatively safe transport mode, accidents do happen and thereby impose costs. When establishing the costs associated with accidents, items included in the analysis are the costs of mortality and injury (see the discussion in Chapter 5), employer and employee costs, travel delay and property damage (Miller, 1997).

The effect of an increase in output, e.g., through regulatory reform, on (external) accident costs can take two general forms: the first is the effect of increased output at a constant accident rate; the second is the effect of increased output on the accident rate itself. The effect of regulatory reform on the accident rate has received separate attention in the literature, particularly with regard to US domestic regulation. A general conclusion from this literature is that airline deregulation has not resulted in a higher accident rate (e.g., Moses and Savage, 1990; Morrison, 1994). Following this conclusion, the second type of cost is relevant here. However, it would be desirable to distinguish between internal and external accident costs in the evaluation. As mentioned in Chapter 3, those accident risk costs that are imposed on 'innocent bystanders' are external. However, it can be argued that accident risk is a quality characteristic of the product that is sold to the consumer, and that accident risk is thus not a completely unpriced good. Following the discussion on road transport externalities in Maddison et al. (1996), part of the accident (risk) costs incurred

---

[52]   The category VOCs comprises a number of substances. In the calculations, the breakdown in Olivier (1991) has been used. The weight shares of benzene and 1.3 butadiene in total (non-methane) VOC weight are thus, respectively, 2.10 percent and 1.99 percent.

by passengers and airlines could be counted as external if the accident risk were not completely reflected in the ticket price and if there were a positive relation between the number of flights and the number of accidents. In that case, the decision of an airline to schedule another flight would impose external accident risk costs.

For aviation accident costs, the analysis relies on total aviation accident cost estimates by Miller (1997) and Levinson et al. (1998). These studies present alternative estimates of total accident costs without differentiating explicitly between internal and external costs. Lacking a more precise figure, the estimated ratio of external to total accident costs in road transport, an estimated 33 percent (Miller, 1997), is applied here. This yields accident risk costs of $0.97*10^{-3}$ ECU and $0.38*10^{-3}$ ECU, respectively, per passenger kilometer. The former estimate is considered a 'medium' value, the latter a 'low' value. In the 'high' accident risk variant, 100 percent of the accident costs in Miller (1997) are treated as external costs.

6.5   Environmental cost estimates

In this section, the effect of differences in environmental costs between aircraft categories is analyzed. To this end, the noise and emission costs established in the previous section are differentiated with respect to aircraft category. This allows one to further analyze the structure of environmental costs in air transport and to estimate aggregate environmental costs for airline route markets given the aircraft used on those routes. The cost estimates per route market provide the link between Part I and Part II, as the environmental costs estimated here are used in Chapters 9 and 10 to evaluate the effects of regulatory reform.

6.5.1   Aircraft-specific environmental costs

In this subsection, environmental costs are specified for a number of aircraft categories. The classification of aircraft types has been developed at Amsterdam Airport Schiphol, and is primarily based on noise characteristics of airplanes. The classification is, however, also used in the presentation of emission costs. The method distinguishes between 12 aircraft types in 6 basic categories, running from 1 to 6/3c in ascending order of average seating capacity (see Figure 6.1). The second number in the designation refers to the ICAO 'chapter' classification: 'Chapter 2' aircraft made their first test flight before 1977, 'Chapter 3' aircraft were tested after 1977. Therefore, the environmental costs are generally higher for Chapter 2 aircraft. The calculation of emission costs for each category is based on information on one or more aircraft types belonging to the category in question.

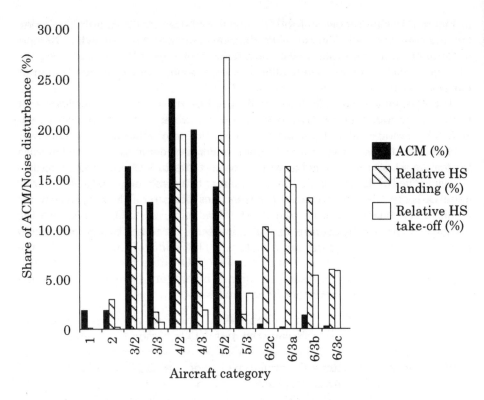

Figure 6.1: Aircraft noise categories

Specific noise contributions

Information on relative noise contributions of various aircraft types is available
in the form of so-called '*hindersommen*' (hindrance sums, HS) used for planning
purposes at Amsterdam Airport Schiphol. The methods used to calculate the
HS as well as results are described in Werkgroep LACKS (1997). The method
has been developed in order to reduce the amount of information needed in the
allocation of airport capacity given the constraint of noise zone regulation. In a
nutshell, the method specifies the relative noise contribution at a particular noise
contour[53] for a number of aircraft categories during landing and take-off. While
the noise contribution of a particular aircraft movement or operation depends on
a large number of factors, such as routing, procedures for climb and descent, and
flight distance, a standard distribution of operations with respect to these factors
is assumed in the method.[54] The relative HS per aircraft category are presented

---

[53]   The 35 Ke zone has been used in the calculation of results used here.

[54]   Again, note that the method and information discussed here concern *calculation*, not

in Figure 6.1 as percentages of the HS aggregated over the 12 aircraft categories. Furthermore, the figure shows the distribution of aircraft movements for a sample of European interstate routes over the aircraft categories.

The calculated HS are used to allocate the noise annoyance changes per aircraft movement derived in Section 6.2 to the 12 aircraft categories. To this end, noise contribution indices are calculated, indicating the HS value of a movement for a particular aircraft type relative to the HS of an average aircraft movement, say $\overline{HS}$. This average value depends on the distribution of aircraft movements over aircraft noise types in the area or location under consideration; here, the average HS for the set of international intra-European routes in 1990 is used as a basis.

Using the HS data, weighted by the number of aircraft movements by aircraft noise category, the relative noise contributions per aircraft noise category for landings and take-offs can be calculated. Combining this information with the marginal values for the average aircraft movement, the noise costs per movement for various aircraft categories are calculated. The results of this exercise for the noise costs of aircraft landings and take-offs (LTO) are presented in Table 6.4. (Here and in the following, results for aircraft in category 1 are omitted, because they are not involved any further in the analysis.)

Table 6.4
Noise cost per LTO
(1995 ECU)

Category	Representative type	Low	Medium	High
2	Dass. Falcon 20	58	212	985
3/2	B737-100	338	1235	5731
3/3	B757-200	41	150	697
4/2	DC9-50	563	2056	9545
4/3	B737-300	152	555	2577
5/2	B727-200	767	2805	13019
5/3	B767-300	81	297	1380
6/2c	DC10-30	332	1212	5626
6/3a	B747-200	516	1886	8754
6/3b	B747-400	320	1170	5430
6/3c	Lockh. Tristar 200	196	716	3322

The figures have been calculated using the average HS for the EU routes; the 'low', 'medium' and 'high' values are based on the marginal value estimates in Table 4.5; furthermore, the lower effect of aircraft movements on noise annoyance in Table 6.2 (3.9 person-L_{eq}/ACM), has been used. The noise valuation according to the minimum and 'predicted' NDI in combination with the high (European) property value are presented as the low and medium value respectively; the high

---

measurement, of noise levels.

value is based on the CVM results in the study by Feitelson et al. (1996). The difference in noise performance between the Chapter 2 and 3 aircraft is clearly illustrated in Table 6.4, as well as the effect of size (weight) on noise characteristics. However, because of the age effect, the relation between size and noise costs is not monotonic.

Specific emission contributions

In this section, emission costs are specified for a number of aircraft categories. The emission costs are based on published emission data for a set of 21 aircraft types belonging to the categories introduced in Table 6.4 (Archer, 1993; Woodmansey and Patterson, 1994). Clearly, the presentation given here is not complete as far as aircraft types are concerned, and the analysis can no doubt be refined and extended in terms of aircraft types and technical detail. However, using the data at hand, emission costs could be calculated for a number of frequently used aircraft types of various size categories. In cases where data on more than one aircraft type are available for a category, the average cost for the category has been calculated.

Table 6.5
Emission costs for LTO (cruise)
1995 ECU (1995 ECU/km)

Category	Representative type	Low		Medium		High	
2	Dass. Falcon 20	16	(n.a.)	27	(n.a.)	1110	(n.a.)
3/2	B737-100	40	(0.09)	73	(0.19)	965	(0.50)
3/3	B757-200	56	(0.08)	99	(0.18)	1184	(0.45)
4/2	DC9-50	55	(0.07)	93	(0.14)	1783	(0.36)
4/3	B737-300	41	(0.07)	75	(0.15)	939	(0.39)
5/2	B727-200	134	(0.12)	209	(0.26)	5161	(0.69)
5/3	B767-300	104	(0.12)	180	(0.25)	2602	(0.64)
6/2c	DC10-30	160	(0.19)	271	(0.40)	4297	(1.04)
6/3a	B747-200	248	(0.24)	417	(0.50)	7980	(1.30)
6/3b	B747-400	191	(0.27)	341	(0.58)	3618	(1.51)
6/3c	Lockh. Tristar 200	182	(0.20)	302	(0.42)	5480	(1.09)

Three values are presented for each aircraft category, corresponding to two sets of emission valuations presented in Chapter 5. The low, medium and high values in Table 6.5 are, on the one hand, based on the three 'main' greenhouse gas valuation results in Table 5.3 for a 5 percent, 3 percent and 1 percent discount rate respectively.[55] The three emission cost estimates represent, on the other

---

[55] It should be noted, however, that the costs for methane (CH_4) are not represented, because no emission data were available for this pollutant.

hand, the respective valuation results for the health effects of local air pollution presented in Table 5.7.

As discussed in Chapter 5, one of the main effects in the sensitivity analysis with respect to the local air pollution values was the huge positive change in CO valuation in the high estimate. This effect is illustrated by the relatively large 'high' value for the category 2 aircraft, which emit a relatively large amount of CO. A comparison of the values in Tables 6.4 and 6.5 shows that LTO emission costs are lower than LTO noise costs when the medium valuation results are used. However, the uniform treatment of mortality effects and the mortality effect of CO has a large positive effect on emission valuation in the 'high' estimate. Therefore, the emission costs are in some cases higher than noise costs when the high estimates are compared.

6.5.2   Environmental costs in European airline markets

As a final step in the estimation of the environmental costs in air transport markets, environmental costs for individual flights are now linked to observations on output in a series of airline markets. To this end, and given the empirical interest in regulatory reform in European markets, the scope of the analysis is now narrowed to a set of 36 European interstate airline markets.[56] Characteristics of these markets relevant to the calculation of environmental costs as well as environmental costs per passenger are presented in Table 6.6, for the year 1990. Environmental costs presented in the table are the sum of noise, emission and accident risk costs according to the medium valuation results presented in the previous sections. In the calculation of the average environmental costs per flight per route, the valuation results per aircraft category have been weighted by the share of flights per aircraft category used on each route on a representative week (OAG *World Airways Guide*). The average environmental costs per passenger are obtained by dividing costs per flight by the average number of passengers per flight on the route.[57]

---

[56]   These routes are also studied in Part II; therefore, the environmental cost estimates derived here can be applied directly in the welfare analysis in the following chapters. The sample has been selected in order to represent various traffic densities, stage lengths and regulatory status in European interstate aviation.

[57]   Passenger data are from ICAO, *Digest of Statistics* 1990, Traffic by Flight Stage series. Environmental cost estimates are based on the 'medium' valuation results for noise, emissions and accident risk presented in the previous sections of this chapter.

Table 6.6
Environmental costs in EU airline markets (1990)

	Route	Dist. (km)	No. of flights	Aircraft most freq. used	Cat.	Env. cost/ pass. (ECU)
1	Athens–Brussels	2092	1683	B727-200	5/2	29
2	Athens–Frankfurt	1807	2398	Airbus A310	5/3	19
3	Athens–Lisbon	2850	237	B737-300	4/3	14
4	Athens–London	2413	2658	Airbus A300	5/3	6
5	Barcelona–Brussels	1081	2328	B737-200	3/2	30
6	Barcelona–Frankfurt	1092	2749	DC9	4/2	21
7	Barcelona–Lisbon	994	681	B737-200	3/2	19
8	Barcelona–London	1145	4092	B727-200	5/2	23
9	Madrid–Brussels	1315	2787	DC9	4/2	36
10	Madrid–Frankfurt	1422	2876	DC9	4/2	28
11	Madrid–Lisbon	513	3757	DC9	4/2	26
12	Madrid–London	1244	7311	B737-200	3/2	15
13	Milan–Brussels	703	3892	MD82	4/3	11
14	Milan–Frankfurt	512	5601	DC9	4/2	19
15	Milan–Lisbon	1683	1016	MD82	4/3	11
16	Milan–London	979	6361	MD82	4/3	10
17	Paris–Brussels	284	7577	B737-300	4/3	15
18	Paris–Frankfurt	471	8009	Airbus A320	3/3	15
19	Paris–Lisbon	1470	2034	Airbus A300	5/3	10
20	Paris–London	365	15857	B767-300	5/3	4
21	Stockholm–Brussels	1287	1866	DC9	4/2	30
22	Stockholm–Frankfurt	1222	2781	DC9	4/2	26
23	Stockholm–Lisbon	2996	169	B737-300	4/3	13
24	Stockholm–London	1474	6221	B737-200	3/2	15
25	Vienna–Brussels	922	1332	MD82	4/3	24
26	Vienna–Frankfurt	619	6239	MD82	4/3	20
27	Vienna–Lisbon	3080	126	MD82	4/3	20
28	Vienna–London	1272	4162	B737-200	3/2	17
29	Liverpool–Dublin	223	1595	Bae atp	2	22
30	London–Amsterdam	372	19277	DC9	4/2	14
31	London–Brussels	350	13379	B737-200	3/2	10
32	London–Dublin	450	10155	B737-300	4/3	19
33	Manchester–Amsterdam	484	3613	Bac 111	4/2	23
34	Manchester–Brussels	536	2660	Bac 111	4/2	35
35	Manchester–Dublin	264	60	B737-300	4/3	23
36	Tees-side–Amsterdam	476	578	Bae 146	3/3	6

In Table 6.6, only the aircraft types that represent the largest share of aircraft movements are presented. It is noted, however, that on most routes, and particularly on the more dense routes such as Paris–London or London–Amsterdam, aircraft types belonging to several categories are used.

Variation in average environmental costs over routes is explained by a number of factors. First, the environmental characteristics of the aircraft categories differ between routes. Secondly, environmental costs per passenger increase with stage length because of CO_2 emissions during cruise. However, the results presented in Sections 6.2 and 6.3 suggest that for all aircraft types the environmental costs consist of a large fixed component, due to the noise and emission costs during landing and take-off, and a relatively small cost per kilometer flown. This implies that when environmental costs are expressed on a per kilometer basis, average environmental costs are lower for longer routes. Another scale characteristic concerns aircraft size. Using the environmental cost estimates for the set of 21 aircraft mentioned in the previous section, a scatter plot of environmental costs per kilogram versus weight (maximum take-off weight, MTOW) is presented in Figure 6.2.

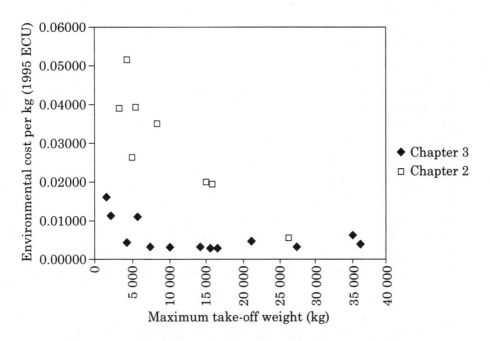

Figure 6.2: Average environmental costs vs MTOW

The plot distinguishes between Chapter 2 and Chapter 3 aircraft and suggests a difference in 'returns to scale' between the two groups. Whereas environmental costs per unit (kilogram) seem to decrease over a considerable range for Chapter 2 aircraft, this effect is present only for Chapter 3 aircraft of less than 75 000 kilograms MTOW. The plot suggests that for the heavier Chapter 3 aircraft, the effect of size on unit environmental costs is absent or even slightly positive. Considering both aircraft groups at the same time, however, the plot indicates that, for an average fleet, environmental costs per kilogram are decreasing in aircraft weight. Aircraft size or weight is related to distances flown in the sense that, whereas large aircraft are used on short distances, there are technical limits on the sector length for smaller aircraft (Doganis, 1991). Given the relation between distance and aircraft size, and the decreasing unit environmental costs, both in distance and in aircraft size, one obtains decreasing environmental costs per passenger-kilometer. The relation between environmental costs per passenger-kilometer and distance is presented in the scatter plot in Figure 6.3.

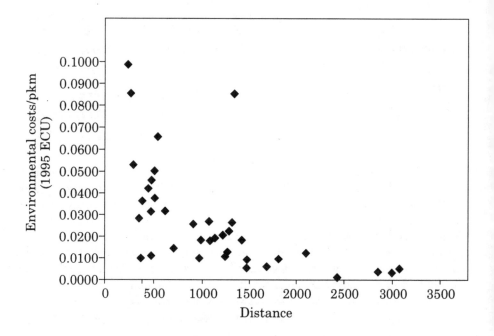

Figure 6.3: Environmental costs per passenger-kilometer

Finally, results for some subsets of the sample are presented, as a prelude to the evaluation of regulatory reform in Part II. Two types of routes can be distinguished in the sample, namely, those routes for which restrictive air service agreements had been renegotiated bilaterally, and those for which restrictive conditions had been only affected marginally by the first (1987) multilateral reform package. In the first group, one can differentiate further between the degree of liberalization that had been introduced bilaterally, distinguishing between bilaterals subject to 'full' and 'restricted' liberalization respectively (see Chapter 2).

Environmental cost estimates are presented in Table 6.7 for these groups of routes separately. The columns heads LIBFULL and LIBRESTR refer to the routes between countries that had signed bilaterals introducing 'full' and 'restricted' liberalization respectively, and REG refers to the routes for which bilaterals had not been renegotiated bilaterally.

Table 6.7
Environmental costs and liberalization status

	All routes	LIBFULL	LIBRESTR	REG
	Liberalization status			
Avg. pass./flight	93	74	130	79
Avg. distance/route	1124	394	960	1457
Avg. share Chap. 2 ACM	0.42	0.37	0.53	0.41
Environmental costs		(1995 ECU)		
Env. cost per pass. km	0.018	0.038	0.015	0.015
Env. cost per pass.	13.99	14.99	10.27	18.01
Env. cost per flight	1301	1117	1331	1431

A few observations with respect to the table are in order. First, average distances for LIBFULL routes are short relative to the other two groups. This is reflected in both the lower costs per flight, and the relatively high cost per passenger-kilometer. As discussed above, relatively high costs per passenger-kilometer on shorter distances can also be explained by the use of smaller aircraft on these routes. LIBRESTR routes are, on average, shorter than REG routes, but have an equal cost per passenger-kilometer because their much higher average density allows for the use of larger aircraft. Differences in unit environmental costs are of course also influenced by the share of Chapter 2 aircraft in total aircraft movements. However, the differences in this respect are quite small on average, and they are not reflected in the environmental costs per passenger-kilometer.

6.6   Conclusion

The relation between external costs and output on air transport markets has been addressed in order to establish aggregate environmental damages. In particular, the results of the analysis in this chapter and the discussion of noise and emission valuation in Chapters 4 and 5 have been used to estimate environmental costs for a set of European airline markets. In order to establish the relation between individual aircraft movements and noise and emission costs, two sets of data have been used. First, OECD data have been used to estimate the aggregate noise annoyance around European airports as a function of airport activity in terms of aircraft movements. Data on aircraft emissions have been obtained from the literature, where detailed figures on emissions per aircraft type are available, particularly for the LTO cycle. Furthermore, parameters in Eyre et al. (1997) have been used to translate aircraft emissions into ambient concentrations. Using the relative noise contributions of different aircraft categories and emission data per aircraft type, the environmental costs for 11 aircraft categories are estimated.

Results are presented for three alternative estimates of marginal values. The three alternatives correspond to the medium, low and high valuation alternatives for noise and emissions presented in Chapters 4 and 5. For noise costs, differences between alternatives are the result of differences in valuation techniques, whereas for emissions, differences are mainly due to alternative assumptions about the discount rate (greenhouse gases) and mortality valuation (local air pollution).

The results show that for the LTO cycle, emission costs are generally lower than noise costs. This conclusion is in line with the results in Levinson et al. (1998). Environmental costs per passenger-kilometer have been shown to decline with distance: this effect is due to the fixed environmental cost for the LTO cycle and the decrease of average environmental costs with aircraft size.

Finally, environmental costs have been calculated for a series of European interstate airline markets. Differentiating between the regulatory status of routes, average environmental cost figures show that the highest costs per flight are incurred on the relatively long regulated routes. Because distances of fully liberalized routes are relatively short, costs per passenger-kilometer are relatively high. Differences between the three groups in the share of Chapter 2 aircraft are present, but not large.

The marginal environmental damage values for air transport output presented here are based on information concerning different parts of the cause–effect chain between individual flights and environmental costs. Apart from the difficulties in establishing the complete chain, discussed in the previous chapter, a problem is posed by the variation in endpoint valuations, whereas insight into the relative confidence with respect to alternative valuations is scarce. Therefore, alternative endpoint valuation results have been presented in the previous chapters and applied in the present chapter, while the decisions made in the derivation of results have been highlighted. In this way, some insight has been given into the way the alternative estimates have been established. Using these insights, the choice for particular environmental values can be defended. For example, the 'high' estimates represent an undifferentiated treatment of mortality effects, a practice which may be questioned but which has been used in many applications. Furthermore, it can be argued that the noise cost estimates underlying the medium values are relatively low; however, the empirical evidence for the higher cost estimates is scarce. Therefore, the medium values are used as a baseline valuation result in Part II, where the welfare effects of regulatory reform in aviation are evaluated.

PART II
Economic Analysis of Air Transport Liberalization

The second part of this book concerns the changes in airline behavior following regulatory reform. In order to analyze such changes and study their welfare implications for airline firms, travelers and the environment, models of the airline market are developed in the following chapters. In Chapter 7, the basic modeling framework for an airline city-pair market is established and the effects of regulatory reform are studied analytically. Chapter 8 provides a number of extensions to the basic framework and offers numerical solutions: changes in frequencies, prices and welfare are calculated using empirically derived parameters. The analysis proceeds by modeling airline behavior in small networks in Chapter 9. Chapter 10 concludes Part II, estimating an econometric model of European interstate airline markets and calculating the welfare effects of bilateral liberalization.

Chapter 7
Frequency Choice in Air Transport Markets

7.1 Introduction

Firm behavior in airline markets has been amply analyzed in the literature, both theoretically and empirically. The theoretical analysis has in many cases been based on homogeneous product Cournot or Bertrand oligopoly models: in such models, airline firms are assumed to offer a homogeneous product and compete in quantities (see e.g. Nero, 1996; Oum et al. 1993). Using such models, equilibria can be computed in terms of quantities and prices for airline seats and the welfare effects of reform can be computed.

The nature of the competition to be modeled depends on the structure of preferences that is assumed. In the case of the Cournot model, consumer preferences in the airline market are (implicitly) modeled as 'one dimensional': in the model, utility of a potential consumer depends on price only. If the price is 'right', i.e., below a particular threshold for this consumer, he buys the ticket. With different types of consumers, the number of tickets sold is a function of price. In (air) transport markets, consumer preferences are often considered as 'two dimensional': travelers pay for the ticket and allocate valuable time to the trip. This basic difference in the way consumer preferences are viewed turns out to make an important difference in the modeling of the transport market and the calculation of equilibria. In particular, the presence of a time variable in the utility and demand functions implies that some service variable affecting time costs of travelers may be included in the profit functions of the transport firms. Consequently, market equilibria can be computed in two dimensions, namely, prices and time costs or service. Given a particular routing and aircraft technology, departure frequency is commonly considered as the service variable of interest; the relevant type of time affected by frequency is the so-called schedule delay time, not the travel time itself. The welfare relevance of considering such a variable has been demonstrated empirically in Morrison and Winston (1986).

Departure frequency has, however, another significant impact on welfare. As discussed in Part I of this book, the environmental costs of aviation can be expressed in monetary terms. These monetary costs are calculated per flight of a particular aircraft type rather than per passenger. Thus, modeling of the frequency equilibrium allows one to apply directly the environmental costs associated with flights.

As mentioned above, explicit modeling of the frequency decision is not present in the Cournot model. Equilibria in both departure frequencies and prices in transport markets have, however, been derived using models of spatial competition (see Evans, 1987, for a model of bus competition; Panzar, 1979, and Greenhut et al., 1991, for airline competition). Such models have also been used to analyze the economic effects of (air) transport regulatory reform or deregulation. In this chapter, the basic spatial demand structure in these models is used. A standard model in the spatial competition literature, due to Salop (1979), serves as a starting point to analyze the welfare implications of regulatory reform in aviation. The assumptions of the standard model are discussed and modifications are analyzed. A number of possible equilibria are compared with a regulated equilibrium, and parameter conditions with respect to the sign of the welfare change are derived. It should be noted that only efficiency of the equilibria is considered, while no equity considerations are taken into account: consumer surplus is not considered to be socially more desirable than profit.

In the following section, the basic model structure is specified. Then, assuming inelastic demand, properties of a number of equilibria are discussed. Using the monopoly solution as a reference case in Section 7.3, a few competitive solutions are analyzed, namely, the symmetric mono-departure equilibrium (where each firm offers only one flight) in Section 7.4, and the symmetric multi-departure equilibrium (where each firm can offer more than one flight) in Section 7.5. Welfare properties of the different equilibria are discussed in Section 7.6; using these differences, the effect of regulatory reform is evaluated.

7.2   A model of airline competition

7.2.1   The demand model

A city-pair market for air transport is considered, in which carriers offer flights from some origin A to some destination B. A potential traveler derives gross utility $\bar{v}$ from taking this trip, and faces a price p. Furthermore, the traveler has an optimal departure time t_{pref}. If a flight departs later or earlier than t_{pref}, the traveler incurs a schedule delay cost. It is noted that other time costs, e.g. due to flight time, are not considered: it is assumed that these do not differ between flights. Schedule delay costs are linear: a traveler on flight i suffers a utility loss of θx when flight i leaves at a time distance $x = |t_i - t_{pref}|$ from his or her preferred departure time.[58] This traveler thus derives utility

$$v_i = \bar{v} - p_i - \theta x \qquad (7.1)$$

from flight i, where $\bar{v}$ is gross utility. When the gross utility $\bar{v}$ exceeds the sum of price and schedule delay cost, the net (consumer) surplus is positive and the traveler buys a ticket. Consequently, demand for flight i is derived by counting all travelers for whom (7.1) is positive.

Utility in (7.1) is modeled as a function of two variables, namely, price and distance with respect to a consumer-specific optimal departure time. It is noted that this type of utility specification is general, and has been applied to other dimensions than departure time. The consumer-specific optimum is often referred to as the consumer's 'address', and the model type is generally referred to as an 'address model'. In address models, the preferences of consumers are distributed in a particular manner. In order to keep the analysis tractable, the widely used uniform distribution of addresses is chosen here.

Potential travelers are distributed uniformly with respect to desired departure time on a circular market of time length L and density D; in the rest of the chapter, notation is simplified by setting $L = 1$. The departure times of various flights on offer are also located on this circle. In particular, the departure times of flights i and $i + 1$, t_i and t_{i+1} respectively, separated by a headway H, are considered.

Potential passengers who are 'located' at some preferred departure time $t_{pref} \in (t_i, t_{i+1})$ face a time distance $x = t_{pref} - t_i$ with respect to the departure time t_i and a distance $H - x = t_{i+1} - t_{pref}$ with respect to t_{i+1}. These potential passengers derive the following net utilities or consumer surplus from the two options:

$$
\begin{aligned}
v_i &= \bar{v} - p_i - \theta x \qquad &(7.2)\\
v_{i+1} &= \bar{v} - p_{i+1} - \theta(H - x)
\end{aligned}
$$

Clearly, a consumer will choose the flight belonging to the larger of the above expressions and buy a ticket if the net utility is positive.

If one defines t_+ as the address of the consumer for whom $v_i = v_{i+1}$, the consumers choosing flight i are located in an area of size

$$x_+ = t_+ - t_i = \frac{p_{i+1} - p_i + \theta H}{2\theta} \qquad (7.3)$$

All potential passengers located between t_i and t_+ will take flight i, if they fly

---

[58]   We thus make the assumption that the utility loss caused by taking a flight at a time distance x *earlier* than the preferred departure time is equal to the utility loss caused by taking a flight at x *later* than the preferred departure time. The term 'schedule delay cost' is meant to capture both types of utility loss.

at all, and those located between t_+ and t_{i+1} will choose flight $i + 1$, again, if they fly at all.[59] Similarly, there exists an address t_- which marks the boundary between the market areas of flight i and an earlier flight $i - 1$.

In the present model, consumer heterogeneity can be present in two forms. First and standard in address models, the preferred product varieties (departure times) differ between consumers. Secondly, at a given address, consumers may have different gross valuations $\bar{v}$. In other words, $\bar{v}$ may be consumer specific.[60] If gross valuations differ over consumers, demand is said to be elastic. In contrast, if there is no heterogeneity in gross valuations, all consumers at a particular address behave identically; in this case, demand may be inelastic.

Let $s(t)$ be the share of potential passengers D at a particular address t with a positive net utility v_i. The number of passengers with preferred departure time t is thus $D \cdot s(t)$. Aggregate demand for flight i is then obtained by adding passengers over all preferred departure times t between t_- and t_+, giving

$$q_i = D \int_{t_-}^{t_+} s(x)dx \qquad (7.4)$$

The difference between the elastic and inelastic demand is determined by the form of $s(x)$ in (7.4). With elastic demand, gross valuations at each t are distributed in a particular manner, giving rise to, for instance, linear or exponential demand functions (see, e.g., Greenhut et al., 1987).

Throughout this chapter, gross valuations $\bar{v}$ are assumed homogeneous across consumers. If no heterogeneity is present, $s(x)$ is either zero or one. Consider a marginal consumer located at t_+; if his net utility $v_i = v_{i+1} < 0$, then, under homogeneity, no consumer at t_+ buys a ticket. As a result, flight i is not in direct competition with flight $i + 1$ under these conditions. In analyses of competition (e.g. Bensaid and de Palma, 1994) it is often assumed that gross valuations $\bar{v}$ are so high as to never be binding. Under this assumption, all consumers located between t_i and t_{i+1} buy a ticket and therefore aggregate demand is inelastic.

7.2.2   Cost and profit

Air transport services are offered by $n \geq 1$ airline firms in the market. Total costs C for each airline l on the route AB consist, for each period considered, of a fixed cost F plus operating costs. Operating costs consist of costs per flight denoted c^f times the flight frequency and marginal costs c^p per passenger times the passenger number.[61] Denoting f_l as the number of flights operated and q_l as

---

[59]   It is assumed that $x_+ > 0$ or, in general, $|p_{i+1} - p_i| < \theta H$.

[60]   Subscripts referring to individual consumers have been omitted for notational simplicity.

[61]   Fixed flight costs depend on aircraft capacity (type) k. Aircraft choice is mainly determined by the distance flown. Given the stage length of the city-pair market under consideration, k may be assumed constant.

the total number of passengers carried by airline l, costs are

$$C_l = F + f_l c^f + q_l c^p \tag{7.5}$$

Revenues are pq, so that profits for the airline firm can be represented by

$$\pi_l = p_l q_l - C_l \tag{7.6}$$

Airlines do not differentiate prices, e.g. with respect to classes or flights; prices p_l are therefore firm specific, not flight specific. It is assumed that airlines are completely identical: they have identical cost functions, and passengers do not have idiosyncratic preferences for any of the airlines. Therefore, the airlines face identical demand functions. Finally, all n airlines should earn a non-negative profit in equilibrium.

In the next section, market solutions in terms of prices and frequencies are derived using alternative assumptions concerning the market structure. Subsequently, the solutions can be compared in terms of welfare. The welfare analyses in this book are all concerned with the difference between solutions under different economic regimes. As discussed in Chapter 2, the welfare effect due to regulatory reform can be analyzed as the welfare difference between a competitive and a collusive market solution. In the context of regulatory reform in aviation, the latter is modeled as a monopoly solution, whereas the former is some type of oligopoly solution. In the following subsections, the monopoly and oligopoly solutions are derived.

7.3   Monopoly

The analysis starts by considering the monopoly price decision for a single flight i departing at t_i. By definition, the monopolist can charge a price without paying attention to competition, and therefore demand is derived by solving $v_i = 0$ for x using (7.1). In this case, marginal consumers at t_+ and t_- are indifferent between buying and not buying a ticket. Therefore

$$x_+ = t_+ = -t_- = \frac{\bar{v} - p_i}{\theta} \tag{7.7}$$

Given homogeneity and using (7.4), demand for flight i is

$$q_i = D \int_{t_-}^{t_+} 1 dx = 2D \left(\frac{\bar{v} - p_i}{\theta} \right) \tag{7.8}$$

Substituting (7.8) in (7.6), the profit-maximizing monopoly price is

$$p^m = \frac{\bar{v} + c^p}{2} \tag{7.9}$$

which gives equilibrium demand for flight i

$$q_i^m = D\left(x_- + x_+\right) = D\left(\frac{\bar{v} - c^p}{\theta}\right) \qquad (7.10)$$

Assuming that the profit for flight i is positive (or at least non-negative), total profit for the monopolist can be increased by operating another flight at a headway $H^m = 2 \cdot x_+$. In general, profit can be increased as long as parts of the circular market length $L = 1$ are not covered.[62] Profit is thus maximized by operating

$$f^m = \frac{1}{H^m} = \frac{\theta}{\bar{v} - c^p} \qquad (7.11)$$

flights. At this frequency and the monopoly price, profit per flight is maximized, and the complete market is covered: the heads and tails of the respective market areas touch, and the consumers at the boundaries are indifferent between buying and not buying the ticket.

In order to compare the market outcomes under a collusive and a competitive regime, respectively, competitive solutions are analyzed in the following sections. In the next subsection, a standard model in the spatial competition literature is discussed.

7.4   Single-departure competition

Salop (1979) analyzes a model in which n single-product firms play a two-stage game: in the first stage, potential entrants simultaneously decide whether to enter, while those who have entered simultaneously choose prices in the second stage. Brand or location choice is not considered explicitly in the model: instead, maximal differentiation or equal spacing around the circle is exogenously imposed. While realism might be added by introducing an extra stage, letting firms choose their locations before the price game, the model in Salop (1979) avoids this extra complexity in order to focus in a simple and tractable way on the number of firms in the symmetric zero-profit equilibrium (SZPE). This equilibrium is characterized by a number n of equally spaced firms (brands) such that each earns zero profit at the profit-maximizing Nash price p charged by all firms. The Salop model distinguishes between monopoly, kinked and competitive equilibria. At the monopoly equilibria, consumers buying from a particular firm would not obtain a positive surplus from any other firm: market areas do not 'overlap'. It should be noted, however, that profits are still zero in these equilibria, which thus generally differ from the monopoly equilibrium as derived in the previous section. In contrast, in competitive equilibria, firms attract consumers who would otherwise buy from competing firms at other locations. At a kinked equilibrium,

---

[62]   It is assumed that the frequency solution is not necessarily an integer value.

monopoly markets just touch.

The Salop model has been applied to transport frequency modeling: see, e.g., Panzar (1979) and Greenhut et al. (1991) for aviation and Evans (1987) for bus competition. These studies have used the SZPE concept for the case of competitive equilibria. The use of the single-departure (single-product) model has been justified by assuming that there are no increasing returns to departure frequency or product variety (e.g., in Panzar, 1979). With a positive fixed cost of route operation F, however, increasing returns to departure frequency are present: costs per departure decrease, because fixed costs, say indirect operating costs associated with administration or maintenance, are spread over more departures as frequency increases. In contrast, the single-departure model assumes that these fixed route costs are negligible so that increasing returns in product variety or departure frequency are not present. Therefore, fixed costs of route operation F are equal to zero in this case.

In the following exposition of the model and its solution, the simple case of homogeneous consumers in a competitive equilibrium is analyzed. Thus, all consumers buy from some firm so that aggregate demand is inelastic and there are no 'gaps' in demand on the circle. Furthermore, it should be noted that in the single-departure (product, brand) case described here, the aggregate number of flights is equal to the number of firms. Therefore, $f^{SZPE} = n^{SZPE}$.

The competitive price equilibrium is derived using (7.3). Given two competing neighboring departures charging a price p_{-l}, airline l faces the profit maximization problem

$$\max_{p_l} \ \pi_l = D\left(p_l - c^p\right) \frac{p_{-l} - p_l + \theta H^{SZPE}}{\theta} - c^f \tag{7.12}$$

It is noted that with equal spacing, $H^{SZPE} = \frac{1}{f^{SZPE}}$. Solving (7.12) for p_l, one obtains the best-response function p_l^* as a function of the competitors' price p_{-l}.[63] Imposing symmetry, the profit-maximizing price solution is obtained as a function of the number of firms (departures). Simultaneously, the equilibrium market frequency is derived using the zero-profit condition. Using the price equation and the zero-profit condition, the SZPE equilibrium can be solved for the two unknowns, price and frequency. The frequency solution is

$$f^{SZPE} = n^{SZPE} = \sqrt{\frac{D\theta}{c^f}} \tag{7.13}$$

$$p^{SZPE} = c^p + \frac{\theta}{n^{SZPE}} = c^p + \sqrt{\frac{\theta c^f}{D}} \tag{7.14}$$

The existence of a competitive price equilibrium should be checked for the above

---

[63] Since $\frac{\partial^2 \pi_l}{\partial p_l} = -\frac{2}{\theta} < 0$, the second-order condition is satisfied.

equilibrium solutions to hold. As pointed out by Salop (1979), the equilibrium configuration (competitive, kinked or monopoly) is determined by the parameters of the model. The assumption of a competitive price equilibrium implies that all consumers buy a ticket (inelastic aggregate demand) so that net utility is non-negative for all consumers in equilibrium. In particular, this should be checked for the consumers at the boundaries of market areas, who incur the highest schedule delay costs. Substituting the equilibrium solutions in the utility function for these consumers, the parameter condition

$$v\left(x_b\right) = \bar{v} - c^p - \frac{3}{2}\sqrt{\frac{\theta c^f}{D}} \geq 0 \tag{7.15}$$

is obtained. If this restriction on the parameter values is satisfied, the competitive price equilibrium holds.[64]

Comparative static properties for the above solutions are as follows: the number of firms (departures) increases in demand density D and the value of schedule delay time θ, and falls in the fixed flight cost c^f. Prices decrease in the number of firms, but increase in the schedule delay cost. The combined effect causes prices to increase in θ. As Salop (1979) points out, $\bar{v}$ dces not affect prices in the competitive configuration.

7.5 Symmetric multi-departure competition

One of the assumptions underlying the SZPE solution is that each firm represents one product in the circular market. As discussed in the previous section, such mono-product competition can be justified when there are no advantages associated with the provision of multiple products, e.g., in cases when there are no fixed costs associated with market presence apart from the costs associated with the production of a particular product, outlet or brand. While such an assumption may represent conditions in some markets, it is questionable in the context of frequency determination in transport markets. Like most transport markets, air transport markets are oligopolies in which firms offer multiple departures. Economies of product variety are present indeed: the operation of a particular route involves both costs associated with the operation of flights and costs associated with general route operation.[65] Therefore, air transport markets do not entirely conform to the assumptions of the standard spatial competition

---

[64] Further, demand is discontinuous at a price p_l which is so low that consumers located *at* the address of a competitor $-l$ switch to the flight of l; this may imply non-existence of the SZPE. However, Salop (1979) points out that, for constant marginal cost, choosing such a price results in losses, so that this 'supercompetitive' type of behavior is ruled out.

[65] In particular, airlines distinguish between indirect operating costs and direct operating costs. This distinction and its relation to the model are discussed further in Chapter 8 and Appendix B.

model. Rather, firms offering (air) transport services can be viewed as multi-product firms, offering a range of products that are differentiated with respect to time.

A number of assumptions, however, is retained, and a few others are introduced. First, the equal spacing assumption from the SZPE solution is retained here: in the context of transport markets, this means that the time distance between successive departures (the 'headway') equals the total time span considered divided by the number of departures and is thus maximized by assumption. This is not to say that the choice of headway is not interesting or relevant. However, abstracting from this problem reduces complexity and allows one to focus on the main question of interest, the determination of frequencies and prices (cf. Norman and Thisse, 1996). Also, the assumption of inelastic aggregate demand is retained. The number of firms is assumed constant in the short run, whereas it is endogenous in the long run.

Furthermore, in order to derive a tractable solution, an additional symmetry condition with respect to the equilibrium and an assumption on the configuration of flights are introduced. The first condition is that the frequency equilibrium is symmetric, i.e., all firms operate the same number of departures in equilibrium. Given a symmetric frequency equilibrium, however, one may consider various price equilibria. In the single-product SZPE equilibrium, pricing is 'competitive' because consumers choose between flights operated by competing airlines. However, when airlines operate multiple flights, this is no longer automatically the case. The configuration may be more or less competitive, depending on the assumptions made. Two extreme configurations are presented in Figure 7.1.

The first configuration in Figure 7.1 depicts a situation in which all flights have neighboring departures operated by a competitor. Such a configuration is labeled 'interlaced', and results in competitive price equilibria. The second configuration is non-interlaced, so some consumers are 'located' between non-competing flights. Following Norman and Strandenes (1994), the assumption adopted in this chapter is that the configuration of flights is 'interlaced', implying that for all flights, the two neighboring flights are operated by competitors. With an interlaced configuration, the neighboring flights are always in price competition. Whereas the assumption of symmetry is quite common in oligopoly models, the assumption on the configuration may seem rather specific. Admittedly, one may object that oligopolists would seek a less competitive configuration than the interlaced one if the choice were theirs. In particular, a profit-maximizing configuration would minimize the number of competing neighbors. However, given that configuration choice is not part of the model, some assumption has to be made. Interlacing may be interpreted as a competition-enhancing configuration as would be chosen by competition authorities. The fact that this would be a good choice from a competition policy point of view is suggested by empirical evidence in Nero (1998). Furthermore, the interlacing assumption reduces complexity and allows one to

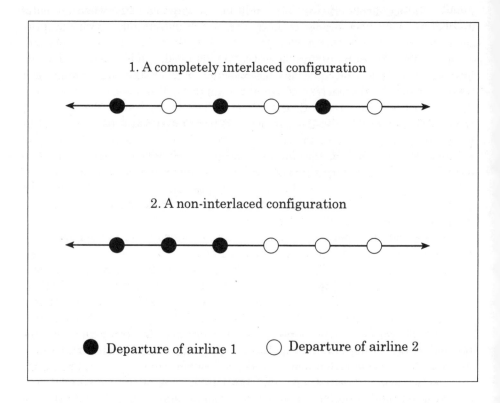

Figure 7.1: Interlaced vs non-interlaced departure configurations

focus on the frequency decision. The implications of loosening the symmetry and interlacing assumptions are investigated in Chapter 8.

The solution in frequencies and prices can now be arrived at in two alternative ways, depending on an assumption about the flexibility of the decisions to be made. First, one may assume that both frequencies and prices are flexible, so that both can be changed in the short run. In that case, one can consider the decisions about prices and frequencies as being taken simultaneously, giving rise to a simultaneous frequency–price game as in, e.g., Norman and Strandenes (1994). Alternatively, one may consider a game with frequency (scheduling) choices being less flexible than pricing decisions. In this case, frequency decisions are taken before price decisions. Then, having observed the frequency decisions, airlines decide on prices. In such a game, the airlines take price decisions into account when choosing frequencies.

Both types of solutions are discussed below. It should be noted that the 'simultaneous frequency–price game' is in fact a dynamic game when the entry decision is taken into account. Therefore, the 'simultaneous' frequency–price game is actually a two-stage game, where the entry decision is taken in stage one. Similarly, the 'dynamic' frequency–price game is a three-stage game. However, since our main concern here is the frequency and price decisions, reference will be made to simultaneous and dynamic frequency–price games.

7.5.1   Simultaneous frequency–price competition

The game under consideration is solved using the assumptions made earlier in this section. The general problem to be solved by the airlines is

$$\max_{p_l, f_l} \ \pi_l = f_l D \left(p_l - c^p \right) \frac{p_{-l} - p_l + \theta H}{\theta} - f_l c^f - F \qquad (7.16)$$

Given equal spacing, headway H is calculated as the length of the market $L = 1$ divided by the total number of flights offered. Thus,

$$H = \frac{1}{\sum_{l=1}^{n} f_l} = \frac{1}{f_l + \sum_{-l=1}^{n-1} f_{-l}} \qquad (7.17)$$

Because of the assumption of an interlaced configuration, the price solution has the form of the SZPE solution. Since all flights are equally spaced and in competition, the price best-response function is found by solving equation (7.12) as in the previous section. At the same time, the frequency best-response function is derived using the first-order condition. The equilibrium frequency and price are derived as the best responses in a symmetric equilibrium.[66] Referring to the equilibrium as the simultaneous symmetric multi-departure equilibrium (SSME), aggregate flight frequency and price are:

$$f^{SSME} = \sqrt{\frac{(n-1)}{n} \frac{D\theta}{c^f}}, \quad n \geq 2 \qquad (7.18)$$

$$p^{SSME} = c^p + \sqrt{\frac{n}{(n-1)} \frac{\theta c^f}{D}}, \quad n \geq 2 \qquad (7.19)$$

Finally, the equilibrium solutions are functions of the number of airlines n. Therefore, at a given n, it should be checked that the symmetric equilibrium profit is non-negative. The analysis in Norman and Strandenes (1994) assumes that the number of airlines n is determined exogenously. Alternatively, one can assume that the number of firms is determined endogenously by a zero-profit condition.

---

[66]   The second-order conditions, both on the own second derivatives, i.e. $(\pi_{pp})_l < 0$ and $(\pi_{ff})_l < 0$, and on the cross derivative, $(\pi_{pp}\pi_{ff})_l - (\pi_{pf})_l^2 > 0$, are satisfied in the symmetric equilibrium.

As in the SZPE case, the profit condition is then automatically satisfied. The endogenous firm number n^* is found as the solution to

$$\frac{1}{n^*}\left(\frac{1}{D^2(n^*-1)}-\frac{1}{n^*}+\frac{1}{(n^*)^2}\right)=\frac{F^2}{D\theta c^f} \tag{7.20}$$

The left-hand side of this expression decreases in n. Therefore, a decrease in F causes an increase in the number of firms. In principle, two cases may be distinguished for the SSME regime, namely, a short-run equilibrium and a long-run equilibrium. In the short run, e.g., shortly after entry is permitted by regulatory reform, the number of firms can be assumed fixed. In the long run, the number of firms is endogenously determined as in (7.20).

7.5.2 Dynamic frequency–price competition

An alternative assumption about airline competition is that frequency decisions are less flexible than price decisions. Such a time structure has some empirical relevance: while prices may vary daily in the airline industry, departure frequencies of scheduled airlines are much less flexible. Therefore, one can formulate airline competition as a dynamic game: after entry, airlines simultaneously choose frequencies first, and then, having observed the chosen schedules, they simultaneously choose prices. The solution is then derived backwards by calculating the price solution first and using this solution in the calculation of the subgame perfect frequency equilibrium.

Using the symmetry of the price solution as before, the profit-maximizing price of carrier l is a function of all flights offered, including those operated by l.

$$p_l^*\left(f_l,f_{-l}\right)=c^p+\frac{\theta}{\sum_{l=1}^n f_l} \tag{7.21}$$

Substituting the symmetric price solution (7.21) in the airlines' profit function (7.6), the frequency game can be solved. Holding the standard Nash conjecture, i.e., a change in own frequency does not affect the frequency choice of competitors, each airline solves the frequency choice problem. The derivative of profit with respect to frequency for airline l is then

$$\frac{\partial \pi_l}{\partial f_l}=p_l^*\frac{\partial q_l}{\partial f_l}+\frac{\partial p_l^*}{\partial f_l}q_l-\frac{\partial C_l}{\partial f_l} \tag{7.22}$$

Substituting the profit-maximizing price p_l^* and using symmetry of the frequency equilibrium ($f_l=f_{-l}$, all l), the dynamic symmetric multi-departure equilibrium (DSME) aggregate frequency and price are

$$f^{DSME}=\sqrt{\frac{(n-2)D\theta}{n}\frac{}{c^f}},\quad n\geq 3 \tag{7.23}$$

$$p^{DSME} \;=\; c^p + \sqrt{\frac{n}{(n-2)}\frac{\theta c^f}{D}}, \quad n \geq 3 \qquad (7.24)$$

The DSME solution appears subject to a rather restrictive condition, namely, $n \geq 3$. This type of condition is, in the less restrictive form $n \geq 2$, present in the simultaneous frequency–price game too; in that case, however, it does not appear to impose any restriction, given that one is modeling a competitive situation. The restrictions, however, reflect the fact that the effect of individual marginal changes on own profit decrease in the number of firms present. Furthermore, an increase in frequency has a number of effects on profit (see 7.22): apart from a cost effect, there is an effect on demand, and, in the dynamic game, an effect on price, some of which may well conflict. For instance, the addition of a departure in the present model increases firm demand on the one hand, while at the same time the extra flight has a 'cannibalization effect' on the demand of the existing flight; see, e.g., Raubitschek (1987) for a comparable effect in a different multi-product model. Clearly, the larger the number of firms, the smaller the cannibalization with respect to the own demand. In the dynamic frequency–price game, there is a further negative effect on the profit-maximizing price that the firm has to take into account when making the frequency choice. Again, the larger the number of competitors, the smaller this effect. In particular, for $n < 3$, the negative effect dominates, so that the derivative of profit with respect to own frequency is always negative.[67]

For $n \geq 3$, the equilibria SSME and DSME can be compared. As the above discussion already suggests, the flight frequencies and prices under SSME are higher and lower respectively than under DSME. It is concluded that the backwards induction present in the dynamic frequency–price game causes firms to schedule less competitively.

7.5.3   Comparative statics analysis

Because of the imposed symmetry, all airlines have the same flight frequency in equilibrium, which is the proportional share of the total number of flights. Both the total number of flights and the number of flights per airline are functions of the number of airlines n, the schedule inconvenience costs θ and the fixed cost per flight c^f. The following comparative static results hold for both the simultaneous and the dynamic frequency–price game: $\frac{\partial f^{SME}}{\partial \theta} > 0, \frac{\partial f^{SME}}{\partial D} > 0$, and $\frac{\partial f^{SME}}{\partial c^f} < 0$, stating respectively that the equilibrium flight frequency increases in both the

---

[67]   When the schedule delay costs are quadratic, the effect is even stronger and the condition is $n \geq 4$. It should be pointed out that these results are specific; with a more general model – e.g. allowing for elastic demand – the negative frequency effect on profit is likely to be reduced (see Chapters 8 and 9).

schedule inconvenience cost θ and the demand density D, while it decreases in the fixed flight cost c^f. Furthermore, the number of departures is a function of the number of firms: $\frac{\partial f^{SME}}{\partial n} < 0$, $\frac{\partial n f^{SME}}{\partial n} > 0$. An increase in the number of firms causes a decrease in the number of departures per firm, but results in an increase in the total number of flights.[68]

Comparative static results for the equilibrium price are: $\frac{\partial p^{SME}}{\partial \theta} > 0$, $\frac{\partial p^{SME}}{\partial c^f} >$ 0 and $\frac{\partial p^{SME}}{\partial n} < 0$, $\frac{\partial p^{SME}}{\partial D} < 0$. The equilibrium price increases in the schedule inconvenience cost θ. A high schedule inconvenience cost implies a high willingness to pay for a flight at a convenient time. This reduces price competition between neighboring flights and thus enables airlines to set higher prices. Increases in the number of airlines and the demand density have a depressing effect on price, while a rise in fixed flight costs has a positive effect.

7.6   Welfare analysis

Welfare is the sum of three components: aggregate consumer surplus, industry profits and external costs. Aggregate consumer welfare or consumer surplus is the sum of the individual utilities derived by airline passengers. As shown in the expression for utility (7.1), consumer welfare is affected by two variables determined in the market, namely, price and schedule delay cost. Schedule delay costs are determined by the equilibrium frequency due to the assumption of equal spacing; they increase linearly from zero, for consumers located exactly at the departure time, to $\theta x_b = \frac{\theta H}{2}$, for consumers located at a market boundary. Aggregate schedule delay costs can therefore conveniently be evaluated at the average schedule delay:

$$\theta \overline{x} = \frac{\theta H}{4} = \frac{\theta}{4f} \tag{7.25}$$

Given that the gross valuations $\overline{v}$ are uniform and that the price equilibria are symmetric, aggregate consumer surplus can be expressed as

$$CS = D\left(\overline{v} - p^* - \frac{\theta}{4f^*}\right) \tag{7.26}$$

where the asterisks indicate (aggregate) equilibrium values. Profits are

$$\Pi = D(p^* - c^p) - C_l \tag{7.27}$$

Thirdly, welfare depends on external costs E which are assumed to depend only on total flight frequency in the market. Conforming to the analysis in Part I of

---

[68]   It is noted that these results are qualitatively similar to those derived by Raubitschek (1987).

this book, environmental costs are a linear function of the total number of flights, given the flight distance and the aircraft type used. The (constant) marginal environmental flight cost is ε. Therefore, aggregate environmental costs are

$$E = f^* \cdot \varepsilon \qquad (7.28)$$

Aggregate welfare, the sum of (7.26) and (7.27) minus (7.28), is then

$$W = D\left(\overline{v} - c^p - \frac{\theta}{4f^*}\right) - f^*\left(c^f + \varepsilon\right) - nF \qquad (7.29)$$

It should be noted that the equilibrium price is not present in the above welfare sum. This is due to the fact that in all symmetric equilibria, all consumers fly and pay the same price. Therefore, deadweight losses are not present.[69]

In order to evaluate the differences between the respective regimes, the welfare components consumer surplus, profit and external costs are first analyzed separately. In the following analysis, the simultaneous frequency–price competition results are used in the discussion of the symmetric multi-departure equilibrium. Although the dynamic game is less 'competitive', the characteristics of both equilibria are quite similar. Since no reduced-form expression has been derived for the number of firms n, the SSME results are not expressed in reduced form for the long-run equilibrium. Welfare results per component for the monopoly, SZPE and SSME regime are presented in Table 7.1.

Equation (7.26) shows that consumer welfare consists of two parts: the difference between gross valuation and price on the one hand, and schedule delay costs, determined by frequency, on the other; the sum of these two parts is presented in the table. Profits are maximal under monopoly and zero for the SZPE regime. For the SSME regime, two cases are distinguished. The first, $SSME_{SR}$, is the fixed-number oligopoly case: this situation is considered to represent a short-run equilibrium, e.g., shortly after regulatory reform has taken place. In the second case, $SSME_{LR}$, entry may take place as long as post-entry profits are positive; in the long run, entry causes profits to decline to zero.

7.6.1   Evaluation

Some conclusions can be drawn with respect to absolute differences between the regimes studied. Since profits are maximized under monopoly, the difference between monopoly profit and $SSME_{SR}$ profit is positive. Using this fact allows one to derive that the difference between the frequency choices under $SSME_{SR}$ and monopoly respectively is positive too (see Appendix A for a proof):

---

[69]   See the next chapter for results based on an analysis with non-homogeneous demand in which such losses are present.

Table 7.1
Welfare components

CS	Π	E
Monopoly $\frac{1}{4}D(\bar{v}-c^p)$	$\frac{1}{2}D(\bar{v}-c^p) - \frac{\theta c^f}{(\bar{v}-c^p)} - n_{coll}F$	$\frac{\theta\varepsilon}{\bar{v}-c}$
SZPE $D(\bar{v}-c^p) - \frac{5}{4}\sqrt{D\theta c^f}$	0	$\sqrt{\frac{D\theta}{c^f}}\,\varepsilon$
SSME$_{SR}$ $D(\bar{v}-c^p) - \frac{5}{4}\sqrt{\frac{n}{n-1}D\theta c^f}$	$\sqrt{D\theta c^f}\left(\sqrt{\frac{n}{n-1}} - \sqrt{\frac{n-1}{n}}\right) - nF$	$\sqrt{\frac{(n-1)}{n}\frac{D\theta}{c^f}}\,\varepsilon$
SSME$_{LR}$ $D(\bar{v}-c^p) - \frac{5}{4}\sqrt{\frac{n^*}{n^*-1}D\theta c^f}$	0	$\sqrt{\frac{(n^*-1)}{n^*}\frac{D\theta}{c^f}}\,\varepsilon$

Table 7.2
Frequency results

	Frequency	Fixed costs
Optimum	$\frac{1}{2}\sqrt{\frac{D\theta}{c^f+\varepsilon}}$	F
SZPE	$\sqrt{\frac{D\theta}{c^f}}$	0
SSME$_{SR/LR}$	$\sqrt{\frac{(n-1)}{n}\frac{D\theta}{c^f}}$	$nF \geq 2F$
Monopoly	$\frac{\theta}{\bar{v}-c^p}$	$n_{coll}F$

$$\Pi^m - \Pi^{SSME} > 0 \Rightarrow f^{SSME} - f^m > 0 \qquad (7.30)$$

As a consequence, environmental costs are lower under monopoly than under competition. For the other relevant effects, such a general conclusion cannot be drawn. Further analytical conclusions therefore have to be phrased in terms of conditions on the parameters. For example, the sign of the difference in consumer surplus between monopoly and $SSME_{SR}$ depends on the parameters as follows:

$$D > \overline{D}_1 = \frac{25}{9} \frac{n\theta c^f}{(n-1)(\overline{v} - c^p)^2} \Rightarrow CS^{SSME} - CS^m > 0 \qquad (7.31)$$

Secondly, the relation between monopoly prices and competitive prices can be represented as follows:

$$D > \overline{D}_2 = 4 \frac{n\theta c^f}{(n-1)(\overline{v} - c^p)^2} \Rightarrow p^{SSME} - p^m < 0 \qquad (7.32)$$

The conditions (7.31) and (7.32) illustrate that the effect of introducing competition in airline markets on consumer surplus and price depends on the parameter combination. It can, however, be concluded that condition (7.32) is more strict than (7.31) as $\overline{D}_2 > \overline{D}_1$. Thus, given values for the other parameters, (7.31) is satisfied if (7.32) is, but not vice versa. In other words, a liberalized airline market may experience an increase in consumer surplus despite an increase in fares; however, if a fare decrease is present, an increase in consumer welfare is certain.

Comparable conclusions can be drawn for the SZPE case. Profits are zero under SZPE, and the equilibrium frequency in this case is higher than under SSME, so that $f^{SZPE} - f^m > 0$. Furthermore, prices are lower under SZPE than under SSME, while the results in Table 7.1 show that consumer surplus under SZPE is higher than under SSME. Therefore, if conditions (7.31) and (7.32) hold, consumer surplus and price are higher and lower, respectively, under SZPE compared with the monopoly situation.

In order to assess the overall social desirability of regulatory reform in aviation, the welfare components in Table 7.1 can be added and compared between competition and monopoly. However, the analytical expression representing the difference between aggregate welfare sums does not have an unambiguous sign. Therefore, absolute aggregate welfare sums are compared numerically in the next chapter. In the next section, the relative welfare properties of the aggregate welfare solutions are compared with the socially optimal solution.

7.6.2   Optimal versus market solutions

Expression (7.29) shows that the welfare sum under the respective regimes is a concave function of the aggregate number of flights and decreases in the number of firms. The socially optimal solution can therefore be formulated in terms of these variables. Given the fact that a new firm in the market incurs entry or set-up costs F, a welfare optimum requires minimization of the number of firms. The socially optimal frequency is found by maximizing the welfare expression over aggregate frequency f^a, which is the same as minimizing schedule inconvenience costs and fixed flight costs. The first-order condition for the problem is

$$\frac{\partial W}{\partial f^a} = \frac{D\theta}{(2f^a)^2} - \left(c^f + \varepsilon\right) = 0 \tag{7.33}$$

The solution is given by

$$\left(f^a\right)^{opt} = \frac{1}{2}\sqrt{\frac{D\theta}{c^f + \varepsilon}} \tag{7.34}$$

The market solutions derived in the previous sections can now be compared with the socially optimal solution using the frequency solutions, which are summarized in Table 7.2. Care should be taken when comparing the welfare results of the SZPE. Since the SZPE is based on the assumption that fixed costs are absent, one should use $F = 0$ when comparing the aggregate welfare sum with the monopoly result. In order to make meaningful comparisons, a distinction has to be made between cases with $F = 0$ and cases with $F > 0$. Therefore, comparisons involving the SZPE regime, for which fixed route costs have been assumed zero, are based on the respective frequency solutions only.

Table 7.2 shows that the optimum frequency is smaller than both the SZPE frequency and the SSME frequency, even when environmental costs are zero. As mentioned earlier, the SZPE frequency is higher than the SSME frequency. When environmental costs increase, the frequency difference between the two competitive solutions and the optimum solution widens. Further, fixed costs are minimized in an optimal solution, and therefore are lower than in the SSME solution. When there is only one operator in a monopoly market, i.e. $n_{coll} = 1$, fixed costs of operation are minimized too. In cartel solutions, fixed costs are higher than in the optimum.

It has been concluded that the monopoly frequency is lower than the competitive frequency solutions. The relation between the monopoly frequency solution and the optimal condition takes the form of a condition on the environmental cost parameter ε. The monopoly frequency is lower (higher) than the optimal frequency for

$$\varepsilon < (>) \frac{D\left(\bar{v} - c^p\right)^2}{4\theta} - c^f \qquad (7.35)$$

It can thus be concluded that the monopoly frequency solution lies between the optimal and the competitive solution if ε is larger than the right-hand side of (7.35). In that case, disregarding entry, aggregate welfare decreases when competition is introduced. On the other hand, if the 'smaller than' sign in (7.35) applies, departure frequency is suboptimal, e.g., where environmental costs would not be present at all ($\varepsilon = 0$).

7.7   Conclusion

In this chapter, the problem of frequency and price determination in airline markets has been analyzed in an 'address' model. In such a model, consumers are identified by their most preferred product variety which represents their address in product space. In the context of (air) transport modeling, the preferred departure time of the consumer is a natural application of the address concept.

In order to assess the welfare effects of airline liberalization, a number of competitive solutions in the address framework are compared with a regulated or monopoly solution. The symmetric zero-profit equilibrium (SZPE) due to Salop (1979) was first analyzed. The mono-product or mono-departure assumption in the SZPE model is replaced by the assumption of a fixed number of competitors in the symmetric oligopoly equilibrium (SME).

The main results in the symmetric oligopoly model are that departure frequencies per firm decrease and aggregate frequency increases in the number of (symmetric) firms. Furthermore, the number of departures per firm increases in demand density and schedule inconvenience costs, and decreases in the fixed cost per flight. In oligopoly equilibrium, the number of departures is larger than the socially optimal one, while it is smaller than the free-entry mono-product frequency. Further, the number of firms under competition decreases in the fixed entry costs.

Using the fact that profits are lower under competition than under monopoly, it has been concluded that a change from monopoly to a competitive regime results in an increase in departure frequency and therefore in an increase in environmental costs. Furthermore, parameter conditions under which consumer welfare and prices are higher and lower, respectively, under competition than under monopoly were established. It was concluded that the conditions for a price decrease after liberalization are more strict than those for an increase in consumer welfare. Finally, a condition in which aggregate welfare under monopoly is higher than under competition was derived. In order to obtain further insights into the welfare effect of liberalization and more quantitative welfare conclusions, it is necessary to establish parameter values and derive numerical results. Such simulations are carried out in the next chapter.

Chapter 8
Frequency Choice and Liberalization: Simulation Modeling

8.1 Introduction

The present chapter carries the analysis further by addressing empirical results based on the theory introduced in the previous chapter. The general spatial model of product differentiation applies, while a number of assumptions of the model are varied in the course of this chapter. Given this continuity, the reader is referred to Chapter 7 for the theoretical background of the analysis in the cases for which no new theoretical analysis is required.

Observations on prices, frequencies, passengers and costs are used to derive parameter values for a number of regulated European airline markets. The discussion of data, sample and the derivation of parameters is presented in Appendix B. Using the parameters, the effect of regulatory reform with symmetric frequency competition is analyzed in the next section. In Section 8.3, the model is extended by allowing for asymmetric frequency competition.

8.2 Symmetric solutions

This section presents and discusses numerical solutions to the models presented in Chapter 7. Two cases are distinguished: first, the assumption of inelastic aggregate demand (consumer homogeneity and complete coverage of the circular market) is used to derive results; thus, the numerical solutions conform to the reduced-form solutions presented in Chapter 7. The other assumptions used in the derivation of these solutions apply, i.e., interlaced and equally spaced scheduling in a circular market. Numerical results are compared for the monopoly regime, representing a regulated market with collusive behavior, and the simultaneous symmetric multi-departure oligopoly equilibrium (SSME). Results for the mono-departure symmetric zero-profit equilibrium (SZPE) are referred to only briefly; the emphasis is put on firms offering more than one flight since this is considered the more realistic model. The dynamic symmetric multi-departure oligopoly equilibrium (DSME) will not be analyzed; however, dynamic strategic interaction is taken up in the next section when asymmetric solutions are analyzed.

Secondly, the assumption of consumer homogeneity is relaxed, implying that gross valuations with respect to flights differ between consumers with identical preferred departure times, while the other assumptions are maintained. This alteration causes aggregate demand to become elastic, so that the number of passengers may change when moving from one economic regime to the other. Here, numerical results are compared for the monopoly and the SSME regime.

In the following, the homogeneous and heterogeneous consumer cases are referred to as models with inelastic and elastic demand respectively. Further, in both the inelastic and the elastic demand case, SSME results are calculated for the one-stage 'long-run' variant of the equilibrium. This implies that the number of symmetric firms is determined endogenously, as the maximum number of firms under which firm profits are positive. As the number of firms is an integer, the SSME equilibrium profit is not necessarily equal to zero.

8.2.1   Results: inelastic demand

In this subsection, the long-run SSME equilibrium is compared with the monopoly equilibrium. Numerical results for the effects of airline liberalization on individual routes are shown in Table 8.1; in order to illustrate some of the results in Chapter 7, the effects for mono-departure competition (SZPE) are given in the last three columns of the table. The effects for the variables price, frequency and loadfactor (Lf) are given in percentage changes with respect to the monopoly case. The change in firm number (for SSME) is given as an absolute value.

The third column in Table 8.1 shows the effect of replacing the monopoly equilibrium with the long-run SSME on the number of firms. The results show that in ten of the twenty-one markets studied, no change in the number of operators takes place according to the simulation. These ten markets represent, however, the smaller markets in terms of pre-liberalization density. In the denser markets, more entry is observed, as well as the exit of an operator in two markets. In markets where operators ceased to operate, the symmetric competitive equilibrium at the pre-liberalization number of firms was not profitable. In the four markets with the lowest densities, namely, Athens–Lisbon, Barcelona–Lisbon, Stockholm–Lisbon and Vienna–Lisbon, the two-firm SSME is not 'sustainable': it turns out that in these markets, SSME profits are negative at the minimum of two operators. Interestingly, these markets were operated by one carrier only in 1990. Apparently, even with the possibility of profit sharing, these markets did not attract a second operator. Therefore, the single-operator monopoly equilibrium is not altered by reform for these markets. In the remaining seventeen markets, a competitive solution is 'sustainable'.

When competition is sustainable, a frequency increase is observed, as was discussed in the previous chapter. Given the assumption of inelastic demand, loadfactors decrease in all these cases. The results illustrate the result derived in Chapter 7 that $f^{SZPE} > f^{SSME}$. Prices are shown to decrease in almost all cases.

Only for two markets does a price increase prevail after liberalization: for these low-density markets (Stockholm–Brussels and Vienna–Brussels), competition is sustainable but the condition for a price decrease derived in Chapter 7 is not satisfied. Finally, the price effects for the SZPE regime are all negative and, conforming with the analysis in Chapter 7, SZPE prices are lower than SSME prices.

Table 8.1
Airline liberalization in EU markets:
simulation results: inelastic demand, symmetric equilibria, LR

Regime:		SSME			SZPE		
Change in:	Firms	Price	Freq.	Lf	Price	Freq.	Lf
Market	(#)	(%)	(%)	(%)	(%)	(%)	(%)
1 Athens–Brussels	0	-2	104	-51	-29	189	-65
2 Athens–Frankfurt	0	-12	129	-56	-28	181	-64
3 Athens–Lisbon	0	0	0	0	-8	120	-54
4 Athens–London	2	-22	158	-61	-29	188	-65
5 Barcelona–Brussels	0	-7	114	-53	-33	203	-67
6 Barcelona–Lisbon	0	0	0	0	-30	193	-66
7 Madrid–Brussels	1	-17	141	-59	-31	196	-66
8 Madrid–Lisbon	-1	-11	126	-56	-36	219	-69
9 Milan–Brussels	1	-33	201	-67	-45	269	-73
10 Milan–Frankfurt	1	-40	235	-70	-50	311	-76
11 Milan–Lisbon	0	-4	110	-52	-31	197	-66
12 Paris–Brussels	-1	-30	188	-65	-50	307	-75
13 Paris–Lisbon	2	-28	180	-64	-37	223	-69
14 Stockh.–Brussels	0	15	73	-42	-17	145	-59
15 Stockh.–Frankfurt	1	-9	120	-54	-24	169	-63
16 Stockh.–Lisbon	0	0	0	0	-28	184	-65
17 Stockh.–London	2	-20	152	-60	-28	182	-65
18 Vienna–Brussels	0	5	90	-47	-24	168	-63
19 Vienna–Frankfurt	1	-25	168	-63	-34	210	-68
20 Vienna–Lisbon	0	0	0	0	0	100	-50
21 Vienna–London	1	-29	187	-65	-38	231	-70
Average		-13	118	-47	-30	199	-66
Average: competition		-16	146	-58			

Two averages per variable are presented in the last two rows of Table 8.1: the first is the average result over all markets; the second excludes, for the SSME regime, the markets where competition was not sustainable. It can be concluded that on average, according to the model, airline liberalization causes fares to decrease by some 13 percent, departures to increase by more than 100 percent and loadfactors to decrease by some 50 percent. Clearly, where only the markets with 'sustainable competition' are considered, the average change increases in magnitude.

Welfare changes are given in Table 8.2 for the SSME solution. The pattern of welfare changes is not surprising, given the previous results. As the analysis in Chapter 7 has shown, consumer welfare decreases in price and decreases in average rescheduling costs, i.e., increases in departure frequency. Therefore, consumer welfare under SSME is superior to monopoly in the markets where a competitive solution prevails; likewise, consumer surplus is higher under SZPE than under SSME. SSME profits are lower than monopoly profits for all markets. Finally, the pattern of effects for the environmental costs follows the frequency change. Therefore, SSME environmental costs in competitive markets are higher than environmental costs under monopoly, while environmental costs per passenger under SZPE are higher than under SSME for all markets. It should be noted, however, that only the values for the 'medium' valuation results are presented in Table 8.2.

The relative desirability of the three regimes in terms of welfare can now be established using the three components of consumer welfare, profits and environmental costs. Given the stable pattern of change, the assessment is based on the average of the results for the individual routes. The results indicate that, in most airline markets under consideration, a substantial gain in consumer welfare is obtained due to the introduction of competition. Only in a few cases does the small demand density preclude the presence of more than one airline in the market, in which case the monopoly equilibrium prevails after liberalization takes place.

According to the SSME results, which are arguably based on the more realistic model, a welfare gain of 199 ECU (weighted average) to airline passengers has to be traded off against a loss to other consumers in terms of environmental goods worth 27 ECU. Therefore, as far as consumers are concerned, the net welfare effects of airline liberalization are positive. Competition further results in a considerable reduction in monopoly profit. The SZPE effects are similar but larger. This leads to a remarkable conclusion, namely, the profit loss renders the overall welfare result negative in both the SSME and the SZPE case. Clearly, regulatory reform implies a redistribution between producers, consumers and externality victims. It should be noted, however, that consumer gains are understated with inelastic demand. Therefore, results for a model with elastic demand (consumer heterogeneity) are calculated in the next subsection.

Table 8.2

Airline liberalization in EU markets:

welfare results: inelastic demand, symmetric equilibria, LR

Regime:	SSME				
Change in:	Consumer surplus		Profits		Env. costs
		(ECU/		(ECU/	(med. val.,
Market	(%)	pass.)	(%)	pass.)	ECU/pass.)
1 Athens–Brussels	55	119	–50	–117	30
2 Athens–Frankfurt	82	159	–81	–177	25
3 Athens–Lisbon	0	0	0	0	0
4 Athens–London	106	256	–99	–321	10
5 Barcelona–Brussels	67	138	–61	–130	34
6 Barcelona–Lisbon	0	0	0	0	0
7 Madrid–Brussels	93	228	–95	–283	51
8 Madrid–Lisbon	79	80	–52	–53	33
9 Milan–Brussels	134	283	–94	–291	21
10 Milan–Frankfurt	151	210	–96	–205	46
11 Milan–Lisbon	62	160	–59	–154	13
12 Paris–Brussels	126	123	–72	–87	28
13 Paris–Lisbon	121	331	–100	–392	17
14 Stockholm–Brussels	12	29	–25	–45	22
15 Stockholm–Frankfurt	72	161	–90	–224	31
16 Stockholm–Lisbon	0	0	0	0	0
17 Stockholm–London	102	240	–98	–305	23
18 Vienna–Brussels	36	86	–65	–92	22
19 Vienna–Frankfurt	113	180	–98	–205	33
20 Vienna–Lisbon	0	0	0	0	0
21 Vienna–London	126	320	–96	–347	33
Average	73	148	–63	–163	22
Average: competition	90	183	–78	–202	28
Weighted average	103	199	–84	–221	27

8.2.2   Results: elastic demand

This subsection explores the effects of introducing SSME competition when the assumption of homogeneous consumers or inelastic aggregate demand is relaxed. A linear demand model, based on Greenhut et al. (1987), is used here.[70] The

---

[70]   The demand specification ultimately depends on the assumed distribution of gross valuations $\bar{v}$. A well-known alternative to linear demand is the negative exponential distribution, as used in e.g. Evans (1987). However, that specification does not allow one to solve the calibration equations for the parameters of the model.

general form is

$$q = 2Dx \left(\alpha - p - \frac{\theta x}{2} \right) \tag{8.1}$$

where α is a demand parameter, representing the maximum gross valuation among consumers. A problem is that, even using simple specifications of elastic demand, analytical equilibrium solutions are hard to trace (Evans, 1987; Norman and Thisse, 1996; Greenhut et al., 1987, 1991). Therefore, the presentation of results for the elastic demand case is restricted to numerical solutions.

The calibrating procedure is similar to that used by Norman and Strandenes (1994), which has also been used for the case of inelastic demand described in Appendix B. Using the above demand structure and the cost data introduced earlier, the monopoly profit function is obtained. Then, first-order conditions for profit maximization with respect to price and frequency for a monopolist are derived. Using these two conditions, the demand function and the data in Table 8A.1, the three unknown demand parameters α, θ and D can be solved for each market. The elastic demand function and the parameters obtained are then used to replace the homogeneous consumer demand model in Chapter 7. Subsequently, the profit function is derived and symmetric Nash equilibria (SSME) in frequencies and prices are computed. In the computation of the frequency equilibrium, only integer departure frequencies are considered. At each symmetric frequency choice, the marginal profitability of flight frequency is computed and the equilibrium departure frequency determined as the maximum number of flights at which marginal profitability is positive (cf. Norman and Strandenes, 1994). In the computation of the price equilibrium, prices are restricted not to be negative. Profit-maximizing prices are calculated for each airline given the profit-maximizing price of competitors in an iterative procedure until successive price changes fall below a threshold value. At that point, the iteration stops and the final prices are considered the Nash equilibrium prices.

Simulation results are presented in Table 8.3. Note that a column for changes in passenger numbers has been added here. There are broad similarities between the respective results for elastic and inelastic demand. First, the same four low-density markets as in the previous section remain a monopoly when demand is elastic. However, the Vienna–Brussels market, the smallest market in terms of pre-liberalization demand, turns out not to be profitable at the competitive duopoly equilibrium, and therefore becomes a single-operator monopoly. In all competitive markets, frequencies increase and prices decrease. It may be noted, however, that the price decreases are much more pronounced than in the inelastic demand case, while the frequency increases are much smaller: the average changes are –45 percent and +61 percent respectively. The possibility of attracting new passengers by lowering prices results, in all competitive markets, in a much lower equilibrium price. At the same time, the equilibrium frequencies are smaller than in the inelastic demand case, as the (average) schedule delay costs can be higher in equilibrium because of the lower equilibrium prices. The column with the percentage changes in passengers shows that the passenger increase is considerable for all competitive markets, averaging some 51 percent over all markets. The combination of higher departure frequencies and higher passenger numbers has an effect on loadfactors that varies substantially over markets; on average, loadfactors decrease slightly.

Table 8.3
Airline liberalization in EU markets:
simulation results: elastic demand, symmetric equilibria, LR

Change in: Market	Firms (#)	Price (%)	Freq. (%)	Pass. (%)	Lf (%)
1 Athens–Brussels	0	−51	63	58	7
2 Athens–Frankfurt	0	−55	96	67	−8
3 Athens–Lisbon	0	0	0	0	0
4 Athens–London	1	−58	100	69	−10
5 Barcelona–Brussels	0	−56	73	65	3
6 Barcelona–Lisbon	0	0	0	0	0
7 Madrid–Brussels	0	−54	63	62	4
8 Madrid–Lisbon	−1	−60	72	69	2
9 Milan–Brussels	0	−69	78	76	3
10 Milan–Frankfurt	0	−75	81	81	2
11 Milan–Lisbon	0	−53	60	58	10
12 Paris–Brussels	−1	−75	84	81	0
13 Paris–Lisbon	2	−65	100	73	−6
14 Stockh.–Brussels	0	−36	44	43	7
15 Stockh.–Frankfurt	0	−45	56	55	4
16 Stockh.–Lisbon	0	0	0	0	0
17 Stockh.–London	1	−58	107	72	−15
18 Vienna–Brussels	−1	0	0	0	0
19 Vienna–Frankfurt	0	−63	100	74	−11
20 Vienna–Lisbon	0	0	0	0	0
21 Vienna–London	0	−67	103	77	−9
Average		−45	61	51	−1
Average: competition		−59	80	68	−1

The welfare effects, presented in Table 8.4, have again broadly the same characteristics as in the inelastic demand case. In all markets where competition prevails after liberalization, consumer surplus has increased relative to the monopoly equilibrium, whereas profits are lower and environmental costs are higher. The relative size of the changes in the various welfare components is, however, quite different. The effect of introducing elastic demand has a particular effect on the consumer welfare change, which amounts to 119 percent (simple average) or even a weighted average of 164 percent. The percentage profit change of –60 percent is comparable to the profit change in the inelastic demand case.

Table 8.4
Airline liberalization in EU markets:
welfare results: elastic demand, symmetric equilibria, LR

Change in:	Consumer surplus		Profits		Env. costs
		(ECU/		(ECU/	(med. val.,
Market	(%)	pass.)	(%)	pass.)	ECU/pass.)
1 Athens–Brussels	132	224	–71	–106	11
2 Athens–Frankfurt	148	215	–93	–121	11
3 Athens–Lisbon	0	0	0	0	0
4 Athens–London	156	278	–89	–169	11
5 Barcelona–Brussels	148	224	–87	–114	13
6 Barcelona–Lisbon	0	0	0	0	0
7 Madrid–Brussels	139	258	–68	–125	14
8 Madrid–Lisbon	158	115	–78	–48	11
9 Milan–Brussels	187	256	–81	–142	5
10 Milan–Frankfurt	206	176	–87	–102	9
11 Milan–Lisbon	137	280	–82	–135	4
12 Paris–Brussels	206	124	–95	–63	7
13 Paris–Lisbon	177	333	–99	–223	6
14 Stockh.–Brussels	89	208	–63	–78	9
15 Stockh.–Frankfurt	115	212	–59	–94	10
16 Stockh.–Lisbon	0	0	0	0	0
17 Stockh.–London	156	268	–92	–166	9
18 Vienna–Brussels	0	0	71	100	0
19 Vienna–Frankfurt	169	186	–89	–107	11
20 Vienna–Lisbon	0	0	0	0	0
21 Vienna–London	181	310	–89	–182	10
Average	119	175	–60	–89	7
Average: competition	154	226	–81	–121	9
Weighted average	164	220	–84	–124	9

The absolute changes (in ECU/pass.) are expressed relative to the passenger number under competition, and are therefore not readily comparable with the inelastic demand case. These figures show that, both on average and for each individual market, airline liberalization results in considerable net benefits according to the simulation results: even when profit losses and increased environmental costs are taken into account, a welfare gain of some 80 ECU per passenger is obtained. It should be noted that only the medium valuation results are taken into account in this assessment. However, the calculated changes in environmental costs according to the high valuation estimates are, on average, 39 ECU (all markets) and 50 ECU (competitive markets only). Clearly, applying these higher environmental cost estimates diminishes the calculated net welfare gains, but the positive conclusion is not altered qualitatively.

8.3   Asymmetric frequency competition

The present section investigates an extension of the symmetric frequency model by modeling airline competition as a two-stage game in frequency and prices, while allowing for asymmetric equilibria. The assumption of exogenous maximal product differentiation, as in Salop (1979), is retained, however. In the context of transport markets, this means that the time distance between successive departures (the 'headway') is assumed constant and equals the total time span considered divided by the number of departures. Furthermore, the imposed interlaced configuration is replaced by the assumption of exogenous maximal interlacing, which takes away the product positioning decision. Again, abstracting from this problem reduces complexity and allows one to focus on the main question of interest here, i.e., the determination of frequencies and prices. In particular, the effect of non-interlacing on the equilibrium price is studied. The relevance of the configuration of flights to the determination of the average price per airline firm has been demonstrated empirically by Nero (1998). In the analysis that follows, the basic demand and cost structure presented in Section 8.2 applies. The next subsection, however, analyzes configuration types that may result from allowing asymmetry in the frequency equilibrium. Finally, the analysis in this section is restricted to duopoly competition.

8.3.1   Configurations

The configuration of products in the circular 'time' market is considered here. Where one allows for asymmetric frequency equilibria, non-interlaced configurations may emerge. In particular, at an asymmetric duopoly frequency equilibrium the configuration of departures cannot be completely interlaced. For an individual flight, there are generally three possibilities: departure i operated by an airline l may have either two, one or zero neighboring departures offered by a competing airline l; such departures are referred to as 'unfriendly neighbors', while we call two neighboring flights operated by one and the same airline 'friendly neighbors'. The assumption of uniform pricing for all flights per airline is retained. Thus, each airline sets one and the same price for all its tickets, i.e., there is no price differentiation between departures of one firm. While it can be argued that airlines do differentiate prices in reality, this seems to be related to passenger types more than to departure characteristics (Doganis, 1991; Tretheway and Oum, 1992). The expression for the market boundary t_b depends on the configuration of the departures. With an interlaced configuration, for each departure i the price for both the earlier and the later departure ($i - 1$ and $i + 1$ respectively) is set non-cooperatively by a competing airline. A departure i with two unfriendly neighbors faces market boundaries

$$t_- = -\frac{p_{i-1} - p_i + \theta H}{2\theta} \tag{8.2}$$

$$t_+ = \frac{p_{i+1} - p_i + \theta H}{2\theta} \tag{8.3}$$

from which demand for flight i is derived using equation (7.4). In the following, demand of an individual flight is referred to as q^f, and demand for a flight with two unfriendly neighbors is denoted as q_{cc}^f (completely competitive demand). In the case of a non-competitive flight (with no unfriendly neighbors), demand is derived from the market boundaries

$$-t_- = t_+ = \frac{H}{2} \tag{8.4}$$

because prices are the same for these flights, as they are set by one and the same airline. This type of demand is labeled q_{nc}^f.[71] Note that for any specification of the demand function in (7.4), completely competitive demand is more price sensitive than non-competitive demand.

For the market as a whole, one can now distinguish between two extremes. In a monopoly market, all departures are offered by the same airline; on the other hand, there is the completely interlaced equilibrium, in which all flights have unfriendly neighbors. Of course, there are many possible configurations between these extremes. The range of configurations implies that with multi-product competition, monopoly and oligopoly become relative rather than absolute concepts. Two configurations are considered in Figure 8.1.

The first configuration in the figure is a completely interlaced duopoly. When a duopolist analyzes the effect of a unit increase in departure frequency starting from a symmetric interlaced configuration, he necessarily considers a 'slightly asymmetric' configuration. As is illustrated in Figure 8.1 (b), all non-symmetric duopoly configurations are non-interlaced. An implication of the model structure is that the form of the demand and profit functions in an airline duopoly changes

---

[71] An explicit analysis of demand for the intermediate case of a 'semi-competitive' flight i, i.e., a flight with only one unfriendly neighbor $i - 1$ and one friendly neighbor $i + 1$ is omitted. Note that the number of such flights is always a multiple of 2, so that this type of flight can always be 'decomposed' into one or more pairs of competitive and non-competitive flights. Therefore, demand for two 'semi-competitive' flights is rewritten as the demand for one competitive flight q_{cc} and one non-competitive flight q_{nc}.

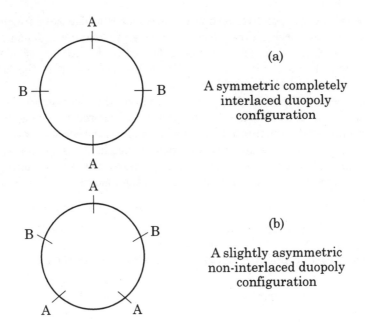

(a)

A symmetric completely
interlaced duopoly
configuration

(b)

A slightly asymmetric
non-interlaced duopoly
configuration

Figure 8.1: Symmetric vs asymmetric departure configurations

at $f_l = f_{-l}$.

Given the possibility of frequency asymmetry in the present duopoly model, an assumption about the configuration type is needed. As mentioned earlier, the assumption used to derive the equilibrium here is that flights are maximally interlaced. That is, a departure of airline A is, if possible, always followed in time by a departure of a competing airline B: clustering of departures operated by one airline in time is minimized. Thus, the types of configuration presented in Figure 8.1 prevail. Given the assumption of maximal interlacing, aggregate demand for services of airline l over all departures, q_l, however, now consists of two parts:

$$q_l = f_l q_{cc}^f \qquad\qquad \text{if} \quad f_l \le f_{-l} \qquad\qquad (8.5)$$

$$q_l = (f_l - f_{-l}) q_{nc}^f + f_{-l} q_{cc}^f \text{ if} \quad f_l > f_{-l} \qquad\qquad (8.6)$$

The demand and profit functions of both duopoly airlines have the exact same form. Clearly, when the first line of the demand function is relevant for one airline, the second is relevant for the other. Only when $f_l = f_{-l}$ do the two parts of the demand function give the same value.

The model analyzes frequency and price decisions as the outcome of a two-stage game in an airline duopoly. In the first stage, each airline chooses a frequency and in the second stage each airline chooses a price given the first frequency choices. As usual in such a model, the solution is derived backwards by calculating the price solution first and using this solution in the calculation of the first-stage, subgame perfect, frequency equilibrium.

As has been outlined in the previous section, the solution to the second-stage price game depends on the configuration of departures: in a symmetric and thus interlaced configuration, pricing is competitive for all departures. In contrast, at least two departures are friendly neighbors in a non-symmetric duopoly configuration. Price competition is analyzed between two airlines 1 and 2 after the carriers have chosen frequencies. In the following, the case of $f_1 \geq f_2$ is considered.

8.3.2   Price equilibrium

First, competition in prices is analyzed. Each airline solves the problem

$$\max_{p_l} \Pi_l\left(p_l, p_{-l}, f_l, f_{-l}\right), \qquad l = 1, 2 \tag{8.7}$$

i.e., each airline maximizes profit Π_l by choosing price p_l given the price choices of the competitor p_{-l} and the first-stage frequency choices. In other words, the solution to (8.7) yields a price reaction function for each firm. For $f_1 \geq f_2$, the reaction functions are

$$\left.\begin{array}{l} R_1(p_2) = p_1^* = \frac{1}{2}\left(c^p + p_2 + \frac{f_1\theta}{f_2(f_1+f_2)}\right) \\[3mm] R_2(p_1) = p_2^* = \frac{1}{2}\left(c^p + p_1 + \frac{\theta}{(f_1+f_2)}\right) \end{array}\right\} \quad f_1 \geq f_2 \tag{8.8}$$

At the Nash equilibrium, prices satisfy

$$p_l^{NE} = R_l\left(p_{-l}^*\right), \qquad l = 1, 2 \tag{8.9}$$

In other words, given that each airline knows the reaction function of the opponent, the profit-maximizing price is chosen contingent on the competitor's profit-maximizing price. The Nash equilibrium prices in the present model are

$$\left.\begin{array}{l} p_1^{NE} = c^p + \frac{(2f_1+f_2)\theta}{3f_2(f_1+f_2)} \\[3mm] p_2^{NE} = c^p + \frac{(f_1+2f_2)\theta}{3f_2(f_1+f_2)} \end{array}\right\} \quad f_1 \geq f_2 \tag{8.10}$$

The difference between the equilibrium price solutions in (8.10) is

$$p_1^{NE} - p_2^{NE} = \frac{(f_1 - f_2)\,\theta}{3f_2\,(f_1 + f_2)}\,, \quad f_1 \geq f_2$$

It can be concluded that the equilibrium prices are equal only in a symmetric frequency solution $f_1 = f_2$. In general, $p_1^{NE} \geq p_2^{NE}$. Furthermore, it is noted that p_1^{NE} increases in f_1.[72] Secondly, with $f_1 \geq f_2$, airline 2's equilibrium price p_2^{NE} of decreases in f_2. This negative frequency effect on the own price of airline 2 is due to increased price competition as a result of the closer spacing between the flights of the two airlines, which more than offsets the increased market share.

Furthermore, it can be shown (see Appendix C) that

$$\frac{dp_1^{NE}}{df_2} < 0$$

$$\frac{dp_2^{NE}}{df_1} < 0$$

$$\frac{dp_1^{NE}}{df_2} > \frac{dp_2^{NE}}{df_1}$$

These expressions state that with inelastic demand, a frequency increase always has a negative effect on the competitor's price, and this effect is, in absolute terms, smaller for a change in the frequency of the high-frequency airline.[73]

8.3.3   Frequency equilibrium

In order to derive an equilibrium, we introduce a restriction on the frequency values that can be chosen. First, with duopoly competition, $f_1 > 0$ and $f_2 > 0$. Secondly, given the 'time length' of the market, an arbitrary minimum frequency $f_{min} > 0$ is introduced, so that frequency choices for both firms lie in the domain $S_l = [f_{min}, \infty)$. If, e.g., we restrict frequency choices to be integers for a particular time length (say 24 hours) of the market, then $f_{min} = 1$. If an airline further decreases frequency, it ceases to operate in the market.

The subgame perfect Nash equilibrium in frequencies is computed as the

---

[72]   The increase of p_1^{NE} is bounded from above. The limit of the price, which may be interpreted as a 'monopoly price', is $\lim_{f_1 \to \infty} p_1^{NE} = \frac{2\theta}{3f_2}$.

[73]   It is noted that at the asymmetric equilibrium prices, positive demand for all flights is not guaranteed. If competing flights i and $i+1$ are operated by airline 1 and 2 respectively and the respective profit-maximizing prices are given by (8.10), t_+ in (8.3) is positive only for $f_1 < 4f_2$. Under the latter condition on the frequency equilibrium, all flights have positive demand. If the condition is not met, some of airline 1's flights may be 'empty': if this situation prevailed in equilibrium, the positive price effect of increasing frequency would apparently make it worthwhile for airline 1 to schedule empty flights.

frequency pair $\{f_l^*, f_{-l}^*\}$ for which

$$\Pi_l \left(f_l^*, f_{-l}^* \right) \geq \Pi_l \left(f_l, f_{-l}^* \right) \; \forall \; f_l \in S_l, \quad l = 1, 2 \tag{8.11}$$

The price solutions found in the previous section are now used to derive the frequency equilibrium. We consider the profit functions of both airlines, given the second-stage price solutions for $f_1 \geq f_2$.

$$\Pi_1 = \frac{D\theta}{9 f_2} \left(2 + \frac{2 f_1^2 - f_2^2}{(f_1 + f_2)^2} \right) - f_1 c^f - F \tag{8.12}$$

$$\Pi_2 = \frac{D\theta}{9 f_2} \left(2 + \frac{2 f_2^2 - f_1^2}{(f_1 + f_2)^2} \right) - f_2 c^f - F \tag{8.13}$$

It can be noted that at a symmetric frequency equilibrium, both firms earn the same profit. In order to derive the frequency equilibrium, the above first-stage profit functions can now be used to derive the best-response functions. However, it should be noted that the profit function of airline 2 strictly decreases in its own flight frequency (see Appendix D), as well as in airline 1's frequency. This implies that for any frequency choice of its opponent, firm 2's best response is a 'minimal' frequency. The explanation for this behavior lies in the effect of scheduling on price competition. The equilibrium price for airline 2 decreases in own frequency, and this negative effect dominates the positive effect on profit of increased market share.

Airline 1 chooses the profit-maximizing frequency given the minimum frequency chosen by airline 2. The profit-maximizing frequency for airline 1 is found by solving

$$\frac{2D \left(2 f_1 + f_{\min} \right) \theta}{9 \left(f_1 + f_{\min} \right)^3} = c^f \tag{8.14}$$

The left-hand side of the above expression decreases in f_1. Evaluating the left-hand side of (8.14) at $f_1 = f_{\min}$, a solution for f_1 exists provided that $\frac{D\theta}{12 \, f_{\min}^2} \geq c^f$. If this solution is denoted f_1^*, $(f_1^*, f_{\min})$ is a duopoly frequency equilibrium only if both firms earn a non-negative profit at these frequency choices. Alternatively, if $\frac{D\theta}{12 \, f_{\min}^2} < c^f$, the solution $(f_{\min}, f_{\min})$ may be an equilibrium, provided that the firm profits are non-negative, which can be checked by substituting the frequency solutions in the profit function (8.12). This gives the parameter condition:

$$\frac{D\theta}{4 \, f_{\min}} - f_{\min} c^f - F \geq 0 \tag{8.15}$$

For the moment, it is assumed that the duopoly profits are non-negative. The above conclusions on the form of the equilibrium indicate that airlines generally choose asymmetric frequencies. Only for relatively high fixed costs is a symmetric frequency equilibrium (f_{min}, f_{min}) a possible equilibrium outcome. In other cases, the Nash equilibrium is asymmetric in frequencies and, therefore, prices and profits. With two identical firms, the equilibrium is not unique: both (f_1^*, f_{min}) and (f_{min}, f_1^*) are equilibria.

The equilibrium pay-offs differ between the two firms: the high-frequency airline 1 earns a higher profit than the low-frequency airline 2. In a symmetric equilibrium both airlines earn the same profit. However, for not too high c^f, an increase in the frequency of airline 1 at (f_{min}, f_{min}) raises its own profit, while it lowers the profit of airline 2. The pay-off structure of the frequency choice game is therefore a variation of the classic game Battle of the Sexes (BoS, see e.g. Osborne and Rubinstein, 1994). Whereas in BoS the players prefer to make the same choice, the preferred pay-offs in this case are not on the diagonal: referring to the pay-off matrix in Figure 8.2, each airline wants to choose 'low' when the competitor chooses 'high' and vice versa, but both would rather have the high frequency. Just as in BoS, there are two pure strategy equilibria, each with an asymmetric pay-off.

Figure 8.2
Pay-off matrix

Airline 2

	Frequency choice	Low	High
Airline 1	Low	(Π_{low}, Π_{low})	(Π_{low}, Π_{high})
	High	(Π_{high}, Π_{low})	(Π_{high}, Π_{high})

Finally, the similarity between the result of (maximal) differentiation in the number of products derived here and that in two-stage models of (mono-product) differentiation is noted. First of all, using quadratic transport costs in the model of two-stage duopoly competition in location and price, d'Aspremont et al. (1979) show that in the unique equilibrium, product (location) differentiation is maximal. Firms move away from each other's location in order to soften price competition. Note that the choice of location does not involve costs for the firm. In a model of vertical product differentiation or quality choice, Shaked and Sutton (1982) derive a maximal differentiation result too (despite the fact that quality is costless to produce); this equilibrium is, however, not unique when firms are identical. These models have in common that the (maximal) differentiation result is driven by the price competition in the second stage.

An alternative interpretation can be given to the model. It may be the case that the profit of firm 2 is negative at the frequency–price equilibrium. In that case, firm 2 would minimize losses by not operating at all, and firm 1 would be a monopolist. In the context of regulatory reform, the model describes a situation in which competition between two former cartel members after regulatory reform forces one of the airlines out of the market, and the monopoly outcome is reinstalled. Stated differently, if firm 2 had a choice, it would not enter the market. It should be noted, however, that there is no predatory behavior in the model. Rather, the model formalizes the effect of strategic interaction under duopoly competition. This interaction is such that price competition is suppressed by the frequency choices. This type of behavior is not unrealistic: firms have an incentive to serve many different parts of the product space on the one hand, while trying to minimize 'encounters' with competing firms. In an extreme case, the monopoly outcome may prevail.

8.3.4 Simulation results

In order to investigate the consequences of allowing for asymmetric frequency choices, duopoly frequency choices are calculated numerically using a simulation model conforming to the analysis for symmetric equilibria in the previous section. The numerical results are calculated using the linear elastic demand specification (8.1), introduced in Section 8.2.3. The numerical solutions for the present model are the Nash equilibria of a bi-matrix frequency choice game. The pay-off matrix of the first-stage frequency choice game is obtained by simulating the profits of both duopolists for each frequency pair, using the second-stage Nash price solutions. The strategy spaces consisting of the possible frequency choices have been restricted to integer values in the set $S = [1, 2, ..., f_{max}]$; f_{max} has been set at some 'large' value so that it does not influence the equilibrium choices.

Equilibria in frequencies and prices are computed for the markets operated by two airlines before and, according to the symmetric simulations, after regulatory reform, using the same calibrated parameters as in the simulations for symmetric equilibria. The results can be compared with results for the symmetric model, in order to assess the sensitivity of the results obtained there.[74] Table 8.5 presents the results for the case of asymmetric competition in terms of the resulting equilibrium and the changes in frequency, price, passengers and loadfactor with respect to the monopoly equilibrium.

Table 8.5 shows that competition in the present model results in asymmetric equilibria.[75] The equilibria show that the high-frequency airline has the high price; the low-frequency airline chooses the low price. Furthermore, frequencies and fares under competition are generally higher and lower, respectively, than under monopoly, as in the case of symmetric competition.[76] It is noteworthy,

---

[74] It is noted, however, that the outcomes computed for the asymmetric model are short-run results in the sense that the number of firms has been fixed at two.

[75] As discussed in the previous subsection, a second asymmetric equilibrium is present. Denoting the two equilibria by superscripts 1 and 2, the second equilibrium mirrors the first equilibrium: $f_1^1 = f_2^2, f_1^2 = f_2^1, p_1^1 = p_2^2$ and $p_1^2 = p_2^1$. Only the first of these two equilibria is presented in the table.

[76] An interesting case is the Milan–Frankfurt market, which is characterized by very high

however, that with asymmetric equilibria, the effects are mitigated in comparison with symmetric competition. This can be seen by comparing the frequency and price changes reported in Table 8.5 with the changes in Table 8.3 (for ease of comparison, the average changes for the symmetric equilibria have been included in the last row of Table 8.5). As a consequence, the effects on passenger number are smaller too. The effect on loadfactor is larger here, because the frequency change is much smaller compared with the change in passenger number.

Table 8.5
Airline liberalization in EU duopoly markets:
simulation results: elastic demand, asymmetric equilibria

Duopoly	Equilibrium		Changes (%)				
	Freq.	Prices	Freq.	Price		Pass.	Lf
	$\{f_1, f_2\}$	$\{p_1, p_2\}$		p_1	p_2		
Athens–Bruss.	{14,8}	{308,266}	38	−32	−41	43	6
Barcln–Bruss.	{20,10}	{291,242}	37	−32	−43	43	7
Madrid–Bruss.	{23,13}	{341,293}	33	−33	−43	47	9
Milan–Bruss.	{36,15}	{254,198}	38	−42	−54	56	15
Milan–Frankf.	{22,21}	{186,186}	−20	−34	−34	32	65
Milan–Lisbon	{8,4}	{392,329}	20	−28	−39	41	15
Stockh.–Bruss.	{15,9}	{414,368}	33	−22	−30	37	2
Stockh.–Frankf.	{22,14}	{330,294}	33	−29	−37	43	6
Vienna–Bruss.	{11,7}	{348,310}	39	−30	−38	45	3
Average			28	−31	−40	43	14
Symm. eq. avg			58	−49	−49	55	4

Welfare effects of introducing competition are presented in Table 8.6. Given the conclusions on the equilibrium choices, it is not surprising that the welfare effects have the same sign but lower absolute values than the effects calculated for symmetric equilibria. A comparison with the results for the symmetric case, given in the last row of Table 8.6, indicates that, on average, the percentage profit decrease is only half the value for the symmetric case. Similarly, the increase in consumer surplus is only some three-quarters of the symmetric case value.

The intuition for these results is that allowing for asymmetry enables airlines to avoid complete interlacing, with price competition between all flights. Because of the two-stage structure, airlines take the effect of their frequency choices on the

---

density. Therefore, lowering the number of flights is relatively costly, because of the loss of demand. This loss has to be traded off against the gain of less intense price competition. Whereas the latter effect was shown to dominate in the case of inelastic demand, the former effect apparently dominates in the present case of 'high' demand density and elastic demand, as a nearly symmetric equilibrium is found. However, at (near) symmetric configurations, an increase in frequency lowers prices. Therefore, the equilibrium has a relatively low number of departures and high loadfactors.

second-stage price equilibrium into account. In other words, the present model offers the airlines ways to mitigate competition. These features cause the resulting equilibrium to be much less competitive, and therefore profits are higher and consumer surplus lower compared with strictly symmetric equilibria. Because of the lower frequency increase, the environmental cost per passenger is lower than in the symmetric case too. The result that non-interlaced configurations cause higher price equilibria is in line with Nero (1998), who finds that temporal segmentation of the market leads to significantly higher prices in European airline markets.

Table 8.6
Airline liberalization in EU duopoly markets:
welfare results: elastic demand, asymmetric equilibria

Duopoly	Consumer surplus		Profits		Env. costs
	(%)	(ECU/ pass.)	(%)	(ECU/ pass.)	(med. val., ECU/pass.)
Athens–Brussels	87	163	−35	−58	7
Barcelona–Brussels	88	153	−36	−54	8
Madrid–Brussels	89	183	−32	−64	8
Milan–Brussels	114	176	−36	−72	3
Milan–Frankfurt	73	86	−15	−25	3
Milan–Lisbon	74	168	−27	−49	2
Stockholm–Brussels	61	149	−34	−44	7
Stockholm–Frankfurt	78	156	−30	−51	6
Vienna–Brussels	82	173	−62	−60	7
Average					
Simple	83	156	−34	−53	6
Weighted	85	146	−30	−50	5
Symmetric equilibrium	128	204	−59	−88	8

According to the above results, the net consumer gains due to airline liberalization are positive but lower than in the case of symmetric equilibria. Therefore, when airlines are able to circumvent head-to-head competition by choosing asymmetric equilibria, the consumer gains of liberalization may be lower than those predicted by the symmetric model. The above results show that even when airlines are identical in cost and demand characteristics, they have an incentive to choose asymmetric, less competitive, solutions; this tendency is even stronger when competitors are less equal. Clearly, this affects the division of gains from airline reform and is therefore of interest in competition policy: in order to preserve consumer gains, competition authorities should seek to ensure route-level competition between competitors of equal strength. However, the qualitative conclusions with respect to the overall net welfare effect of introducing competition are not altered by the previous results: the average absolute net effect is positive in both the asymmetric and the symmetric case, with per passenger gains of 97 and 108 respectively.

8.4   Conclusion

Some empirical applications of frequency competition in airline markets have been addressed. The first application considered numerical results for the models of frequency determination discussed in Chapter 7. Characteristics of these models are inelastic aggregate demand and symmetry of the equilibria. The results were calculated for the symmetric multi-departure equilibrium (SSME) using empirical parameters for a set of 21 regulated European interstate routes in 1990. The analysis addressed the changes in market equilibria and resulting welfare effects due to the introduction of competition in these markets. It is concluded that consumer benefits increase significantly due to frequency increase and fare decreases after regulatory reform, both for elastic and for inelastic demand. In the case of inelastic demand, the change in the sum of producer and consumer surplus is negative. However, with elastic demand the aggregate welfare effect is positive: in this case new travelers are attracted by lower prices and lower schedule delay costs, resulting in a consumer surplus increase that more than offsets the negative effect on profits. In fact, the positive effect on consumer welfare is so large that it also compensates for the increase in environmental costs.

Asymmetric frequency competition was investigated as an extension with respect to the basic model. Given a fixed number of firms, competition in frequency and prices is modeled as a two-stage game: in the first stage, airlines choose frequencies; in the second stage they choose prices. A second modification is that the analysis allows for asymmetric, non-interlaced frequency equilibria. Due to the dynamic set-up of the model, airlines may choose frequency equilibria such that price competition is avoided. This feature is most pronounced in the case of inelastic demand, for which a maximal differentiation result is derived. Maximal differentiation does not hold in the case of elastic (linear) demand. However, in the elastic demand case asymmetric equilibria do frequently occur. When competing airlines are not identical, asymmetric equilibria are particularly relevant. The effect of introducing competition in a monopoly market is studied using a simulation model. The model allows for an analysis of the welfare effects of airline deregulation for various types of post-deregulation entry. The size and distribution of the welfare effects prove to depend on the type of entry. Low-cost entry results in the highest welfare gains, both as a result of price decreases and of frequency increases. In all cases, however, the gain in consumer benefits more than compensates the profit loss.

The use of the above analyses and simulation experiments for policy evaluation is straightforward. Welfare effects of bilateral airline liberalization in European markets are found to be positive in all cases investigated, even when allowing for the less competitive asymmetric equilibria. An important finding in the context of the entire study is that incremental environmental costs appear to form only a small part of the welfare change. It can therefore be concluded that the introduction of competition in these airline markets is socially beneficial. Furthermore, the methods used here can be applied to study similar policy questions for other regions, and even other transport markets.

Looking ahead, a related policy concern presents itself: given that the introduction of competition increases social welfare, how can the benefits of competition be preserved? Issues of spatial market concentration have received a lot of attention following US airline deregulation, and research has shown that having competition both at the route level and at the nodes in aviation networks is important for maintaining the benefits of liberalization. Therefore, re-emergence and possible abuse of monopoly power should be checked carefully in order to maintain the gains in social welfare.

Chapter 9
Airline Liberalization in Networks

9.1 Introduction

Airline behavior in a small airline network, under monopoly and duopoly competition, is investigated in this chapter. The analysis is restricted to situations where at least one of the firms in the market operates a hub-and-spoke (HS) system. Consumer demand is affected by price, schedule delay and transfer time, while the latter two are determined by the airlines' frequency decisions. The difference in decision flexibility between frequency and price is accounted for by modeling airline competition as a two-stage game: in the first stage, airlines choose schedules, i.e. flight frequencies for each link in their network, while in the second stage, having observed the respective first-stage choices, they choose prices. The equilibrium is thus computed as the subgame perfect Nash solution in schedules. A central policy issue addressed by the model is the welfare effect induced by airline deregulation, defined as the introduction of competition in (a part of) the network.

A number of articles in the large literature on airline (network) competition and deregulation are particularly relevant here. The model has the same two-stage structure as the network design model in Lederer (1993), but differs in two ways. First, customer demand is distributed with respect to preferred departure times, so that there is not one least-price 'path' per origin–destination (OD) market and more than one firm provides transport between OD markets in equilibrium. Secondly, demand in each market is elastic with respect to both frequency and price.[77] Brueckner and Spiller (1991) use a model of quantity-setting duopoly competition in a network; they conclude that with returns to density or cost complementarities in a network, competition in a part of the network may result in an overall welfare decrease because of the negative externalities imposed on the other passengers in the system. Using a similar model Nero (1996) concludes that airline deregulation unambiguously improves welfare in the network when returns to density are absent. The present chapter analyzes the introduction of competition in a simple network using the two-stage schedule competition model outlined above. A limitation is that the problem is investigated by computer simulation, which limits the generality of the results.

The model is introduced and calibrated in the next section, and some of its properties are discussed. Then simulated market outcomes are considered

---

[77] Furthermore, passengers are assumed not to 'bundle' flights, i.e., not to switch between airlines when making a transfer. Lederer (1993) shows that such bundling may lead to non-existence of the price equilibrium.

under monopoly and duopoly competition for a number of different competitive situations in simple networks. Direct and leg competition are discussed for a one-hub and a two-hub network. For all of these cases, welfare effects resulting from the introduction of competition are discussed.

9.2 The model

9.2.1 Demand

A base assumption of the model is that at least one airline operates an HS system. Therefore, passengers fly either directly to their destination (local passengers) or have to transfer to a connecting flight (connecting passengers). Connecting passengers are assumed to use the services of one airline only during their trip. Furthermore, demand for which more than one transfer is necessary is not considered, so that connecting passengers are on two flights during their trip, passing through two spokes or legs s via a hub. Passengers make one-way trips between nodes (cities) in the network, so that the market m for transport between cities Y and Z represents two one-way markets $m_{Y \to Z}$ and $m_{Z \to Y}$.

As in the other models discussed in this and the previous chapter, a traveler derives gross utility $\bar{v}$ from making a trip, and faces a price p. Furthermore, a consumer suffers a linear schedule delay cost $\theta_1 x$ when the flight leaves at a time distance $x = |t_{dep} - t_{pref}|$ from his or her preferred departure time, and a linear travel time cost $\theta_2 d$, where d is the duration of the trip. Given the network layout, trip duration in the model is fixed for local passengers, whereas it depends on the departure frequency on the second spoke traveled during the trip for connecting passengers. When the gross valuation exceeds the sum of price, schedule delay cost and travel time cost, the traveler buys a ticket. It is noted that the schedule delay of a connecting passenger is determined by the departure time of the first of his two flights, whereas his travel time is partly determined by the departure time of the second flight.[78]

The representation of consumer preferences in the context of a circular market follows the discussion in Chapter 7, Section 7.2. Only the representation of the choice between two flights i and $i + 1$ differs slightly: potential passengers derive the following net utilities or consumer surplus from the two options:

$$\begin{aligned} v_i &= \bar{v} - p_i - \theta_1 x - \theta_2 d \\ v_{i+1} &= \bar{v} - p_{i+1} - \theta(H - x) - \theta_2 d \end{aligned} \tag{9.1}$$

Clearly, a consumer will choose the flight belonging to the larger of the above

---

[78] Alternatively, one could assume that consumer utility is determined by arrival times at the destination airport.

expressions and buy a ticket if the net utility is positive. For the moment, it is assumed that the travel time of the two options is equal. Aggregate demand for flight i is calculated as the sum of direct passengers and connecting passengers who choose the flight on the first leg of their journey.

The demand for travel in a one-way market $m_{Y \to Z}$ is considered, which is either a direct market for local passengers on spoke s or a transfer market for which s is the first spoke to be traveled. Aggregate demand for market $m_{Y \to Z}$ is found by summing $q_{m_{Y \to Z}, i}$ over all flights. Thus, for an airline l operating a departure frequency $f_{l,s}$ in spoke s, demand $Q_{l, m_{Y \to Z}}$ is

$$Q_{l, m_{Y \to Z}} = \sum_{i=1}^{f_{l,s}} q_i \left(p_i, p_{i-1}, p_{i+1}, H, d \right) \tag{9.2}$$

Finally, total demand for city-pair market YZ is the sum of the demand in the two one-way markets $m_{Y \to Z}$ and $m_{Z \to Y}$ respectively.

9.2.2   Cost and profit

For each flight, the costs consist of a (major) fixed part c^f and a marginal cost c^p per passenger. The model assumes that each airline l charges a single ticket price for each city-pair market $m, m = 1, ..., M_l$ it operates. Furthermore, airlines decide on the flight schedule, i.e., the departure frequency for each spoke $s, s = 1, ..., S_l$ in their network. Thus, airline behavior is represented by the vectors $\bar{p}_l = \{p_{l1}, ..., p_{lM_l}\}$ and $\bar{f}_l = \{f_{l1}, ..., f_{lS_l}\}$. Using (9.2), profits of airline l facing a competitor $-l$ in one or more of the markets in its network are

$$\Pi_l = \sum_{m=1}^{M_l} (p_m - c^p) Q_{l,m} \left(\bar{f}_l, \bar{p}_l, \bar{f}_{-l}, \bar{p}_{-l} \right) - 2 \sum_{s=1}^{S_l} f_{l,s} c^f \tag{9.3}$$

9.2.3   Calibration

For the calibration of the model the procedure in Norman and Strandenes (1994) is followed, namely, solving for the demand parameters using price, frequency, cost and demand observations for a base monopoly situation in combination with the monopolist's first-order conditions (see also Appendix B). Again, a linear demand function $g(.)$ is imposed:

$$g \left(p + \theta_1 x + \theta_2 d \right) = \alpha - p - \theta_1 x - \theta_2 d \tag{9.4}$$

Monopoly demand per flight is then derived as

$$q = D \int_{x_-}^{x_+} g\left(.\right) dx = D\left(-x_- + x_+\right)\left(\alpha - p - \theta_1 \frac{x_b}{2} - \theta_2 d\right) \qquad (9.5)$$

Data are available for a non-stop monopoly route only.[79] It is noted that for such a trip, the monopolist's first-order conditions only refer to price and frequency on the leg. Adding the demand equation, a system of three equations is obtained, which allows one to solve for the three demand parameters $D, \widehat{\alpha}$ and θ_1, with $\widehat{\alpha} = \alpha - \theta_2 d$. The data thus do not enable one directly to infer a value for θ_2, which represents the common value of travel time. Morrison and Winston (1990) report estimated values of travel and transfer time to be much higher (a factor of 10 and 20, respectively) than the value of schedule delay. The relative values seem to depend on the type of traveler. As indicated by Morrison and Winston, business travelers are likely to have a much higher relative value of θ_1 than other travelers. Dobson and Lederer (1993) use a value of schedule delay higher than the value of travel time in their simulation model, while Berechman and de Wit (1996) use a single value of time to calculate utility as a function of flight frequency for local and connecting passengers.[80] Given the scarcity of evidence and the difficulty of comparing parameter values between rather different models, a fixed value is not assigned to θ_2 here. Rather, the sensitivity of the results to changes in the relative value is investigated.

As indicated above, for local passengers, the utility loss caused by the time involved in the trip is represented by the parameter $\widehat{\alpha} = \alpha - \theta_2 d$. For connecting passengers, the calculation differs on three accounts. First, the trip consists of two-leg flights. Secondly, the connecting passengers have to wait for a connecting flight. Thirdly, the gross trip valuation may differ between non-stop and one-stop travel. In order to simplify the calculations, we have assumed the following. For connecting passengers, gross trip valuation is higher than for local passengers, e.g., because of the larger travel distance. However, the difference in trip valuation is exactly matched by the utility loss derived from the incremental travel time. Therefore, the parameter $\widehat{\alpha}$ has the same value for both passenger types. The difference between the demand functions, however, stems from the waiting time of the connecting passengers, which depends on the frequency of the airline on the second leg of the trip. For connecting passengers

$$d_c = \mu H_{leg2} = \mu \frac{L}{F_{leg2}} \qquad (9.6)$$

where μ is a parameter indicating proportion of the headway time on the second

---

[79]   Data refer to the pre-deregulation Tel Aviv–Eilat monopoly, and consist of price, frequency and passenger observations. Furthermore, passenger and per flight cost data were available.
[80]   They do, however, distinguish between business and non-business passengers.

leg which the passenger has to wait, with $0 \leq \mu \leq 1$. Thus, even at a low frequency on the second leg, the waiting time can be small when arrival and departure times of connecting flights are close. An arbitrary value of $\mu = 0.5$ is chosen in the calculations. The base set of parameters is presented in Table 9.1, with all monetary equivalents in US$.

Table 9.1
Base simulation coefficients

Calibrated parameters	
D	0.5
$\hat{a}$ (\$)	174.5
θ_1 (\$)	131.6
Imposed parameter	
μ	0.5
Cost parameters (\$)	
c^p	5
c^f	1500

Using these parameter values, frequency and price decisions in network markets have been simulated. The simulation results are presented and discussed in the next sections.

9.3   A one-hub network

In this section, the effects of introducing competition in a simple network consisting of one hub and two spokes, as depicted in Figure 9.1, are considered. It is assumed that the network is symmetric in the sense that legs 1 and 2 have the same length, and that all markets have the same density. Using the same type of aircraft on both legs, the demand and cost characteristics are equal on non-stop flights.

9.3.1   Monopoly

The schedule choice of a monopolist operating an HS system in the above network is considered first. As the monopolist does not have to take into account the possible actions of an opponent, the problem is simply

$$\max_{\bar{f},\bar{p}} \Pi = \sum_{m=1}^{M} \left(p_m - c^p\right) Q_m \left(\bar{f}, \bar{p}\right) - 2 \sum_{s=1}^{S} f_s c^f \qquad (9.7)$$

where M is the number of markets and S the number of spokes. Clearly, the number of spokes is two, so that $\bar{f} = \{f_1, f_2\}$. Three city-pair markets are

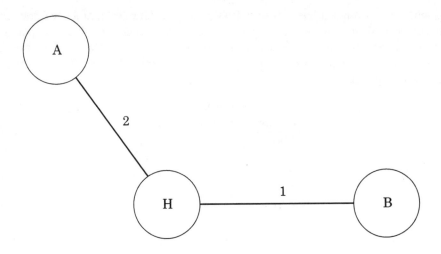

Figure 9.1: A one-hub network

distinguished, namely, the local markets AH and HB, and the connecting market AB, so that $\bar{p} = \{p_{AH}, p_{HB}, p_{AB}\}$.

The price solution of the monopolist is considered first. Using (8.1), the monopoly price solution for a given market is derived as

$$p^*_{mon} = \frac{c^p + \alpha - \theta_1 \frac{x_l}{2} - \theta_2 d}{2} \qquad (9.8)$$

It is concluded that, for given flight frequency, the profit-maximizing monopoly price decreases in both θ_1 and θ_2, and so, given (8.1), revenues decrease in both parameters. Similarly, an expression for the frequency decision of the monopolist can be derived. Considering a non-stop market for simplicity, the profit-maximizing solution is

$$f^*_{mon} = \sqrt{\frac{(p - c^p)\theta_1 L}{4c^f}} \qquad (9.9)$$

Next, the simultaneous solution to the monopoly network problem (9.7) is analyzed. Using the parameters in Table 9.1, profit-maximizing frequencies and prices for a range of values of θ_2 are calculated. The results are presented in Figure 9.2, which only shows results for one of the two identical local markets and legs.

As Figure 9.2 illustrates, the price in the connecting market decreases in θ_2, as the travel time costs increase. The profit-maximizing frequency is concave in θ_2, which can be understood as follows: when θ_2 rises from 'low' to 'intermediate' values, the monopolist can counteract the negative demand effect by increasing the departure frequency in the legs (which has a small positive effect on the price in the direct market). However, for 'too high' levels of θ_2, the marginal revenue of the added flights becomes too low and, therefore, the profit-maximizing frequency falls.

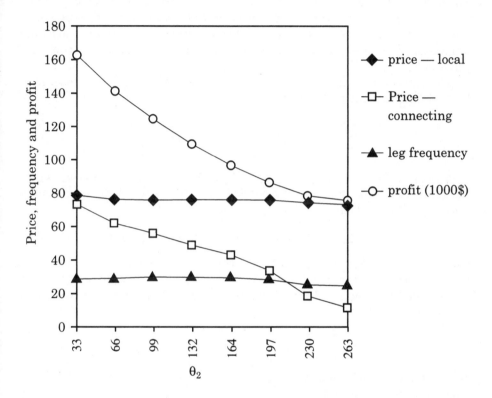

Figure 9.2: **Monopoly solutions**

Clearly, the overall effect of an increase in θ_2 on profit is negative. From this conclusion, a restriction on the value of θ_2 can be derived. From the calibration data, the profit in a single-leg market is known. A monopolist will choose an HS network whenever the profit of such a network is larger than the profit in a fully connected (FC) network. Therefore, from the assumption that the monopolist operates an HS network, a maximum value for θ_2 follows, namely, the value of $\theta_2 = \hat{\theta}_2$ for which the profits of both network types are equal. Put differently, values of θ_2 have to be consistent with the choice of the network type. In the following simulations, the maximum value of θ_2 consistent with the HS network type is used, namely, $\theta_2 = 0.8 * \theta_1$.[81]

9.3.2   Leg competition

In this subsection, the introduction of competition in leg 1 of the network in Figure 9.1 is analyzed. One can think of the entry of a small airline only serving the local market between H and B. An important asymmetry is thus present in the competition in market 1. The incumbent, airline 1, carries both local and connecting passengers on leg 1, while the entrant, airline 2, only carries local passengers.

The outcome of the following two-stage frequency and price game is considered. Both airlines face the profit function

$$\Pi_l = \sum_{m=1}^{M_l} \left(p_m - c^p \right) Q_m \left(\bar{f}_l, \bar{p}_l, \bar{f}_{-l}, \bar{p}_{-l} \right) - 2 \sum_{s=1}^{S_l} f_{l,s} c^f \qquad (9.10)$$

with $M_1 = 3, M_2 = 1$ and $S_1 = 2, S_2 = 1$. The equilibrium is found by solving the game backwards: for each pair of schedules $\{\bar{f}_1, \bar{f}_2\}$ the Nash equilibrium in prices $\{\bar{p}_1^*, \bar{p}_2^*\}$ is calculated as the set of prices at which

$$\Pi_l \left(\bar{p}_l^*, \bar{p}_{-l}^*, \bar{f}_l, \bar{f}_{-l} \right) > \Pi_l \left(\bar{p}_l, \bar{p}_{-l}^*, \bar{f}_l, \bar{f}_{-l} \right), \quad \forall\, \bar{p}_l, \; l = 1, 2 \qquad (9.11)$$

(Note that for airline 2, the problem is confined to finding a single departure frequency and a single price.) Given the second-stage price equilibria, the first-stage Nash equilibrium in flight schedules is calculated as the set of schedules for which

$$\Pi_l \left(\bar{f}_l^*, \bar{f}_{-l}^*, \bar{p}_l^*, \bar{p}_{-l}^* \right) > \Pi_l \left(\bar{f}_l, \bar{f}_{-l}^*, \bar{p}_l^*, \bar{p}_{-l}^* \right), \quad \forall\, \bar{f}_l, \; l = 1, 2 \qquad (9.12)$$

The first-stage equilibrium choices and market outcomes are compared with the monopoly solution in Table 9.2.

A few interesting characteristics of the equilibrium are noted. As explained in Section 3 of Chapter 8, asymmetric frequency choices result in non-interlaced configurations of departures. This confers the monopoly power to the airline with the higher number of departures, which explains the asymmetry in pricing. Clearly, the schedule asymmetry is determined by the network asymmetry: for airline 1, the marginal flight has a higher profitability because it serves both the local duopoly market and the monopoly market for connecting passengers.

The overall conclusion is that leg competition raises welfare. Not surprisingly, a reallocation of surplus from producers to consumers takes place. Aggregate consumer surplus increases by some 23 percent, which represents a gain for

---

[81]   The choice of this 'maximum' can be defended by referring to the relatively high empirical values reported in Morrison and Winston (1990).

local travelers in market 1 (60 percent) and a loss for connecting passengers (–6 percent), while nothing changes for local passengers in market 2. Note that the welfare loss for connecting passengers caused by airline 1's frequency decrease in leg 1 is partly compensated by the lower ticket price. This conclusion is partly in line with the conclusion by Brueckner and Spiller (1991). In their model, leg competition raises welfare for local passengers in market 1 and hurts connecting passengers too. The reason for this negative welfare effect is, however, the existence of negative cost externalities between markets, which also causes a welfare reduction for local passengers in market 2. In the present model, connecting passengers are affected through the higher costs of schedule delay and travel time, not through an increase in price (marginal cost). Therefore, local passengers in market 2 are not affected, while local passengers in market 1 benefit from both higher flight frequencies and lower prices. Note that the two-stage character of the model gives both airlines an incentive not to choose symmetric frequencies: with a symmetric, interlaced configuration of departures, price competition is more intense and second-stage prices are lower than in a non-symmetric equilibrium. Finally, it is noted that the model outcomes represent a slight S-curve effect, i.e., airline 1 carries a share of the passengers traveling on leg 1 that is higher than its share of departures. The effect is a result of the connecting travel carried by airline 1 while having a lower than proportional share of the local traffic, as a result of the high price in market 1.

Table 9.2
Market equilibria: a one-hub network

	Monopoly	Leg competition
Schedules	$\{29, 29\}$	$\{26, 29\}, \{13\}$
Prices	$\{76, 76, 54\}$	$\{66, 76, 52\}, \{57\}$
Passengers	$\{1673, 1673, 1161\}$	$\{1673, 1673, 1161\}, \{820\}$
CS ('000)	$\{62.4, 62.4, 31.5\}$	$\{99.9, 62.4, 29.6\}$
CS total	156326	191952
Profit	121221	87410, 16944
Welfare		
Absolute value	277547	296307
% change		6.8

9.4   A two-hub network

The solution of firms to the network frequency–price problem is investigated for a slightly more complex network under regimes of monopoly and competition. The network under consideration now consists of two hubs and three spokes or legs, as depicted in Figure 9.3.

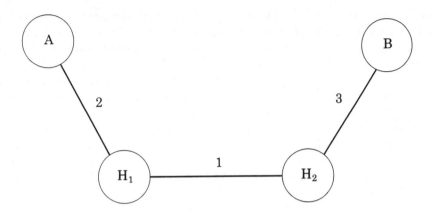

Figure 9.3: A two-hub network

9.4.1 Monopoly

The monopoly network problem has the same general form as for the one-hub network presented in (9.7). In this case, however, $S = 3$ and we distinguish $M = 5$ city-pair markets, namely, three markets for local passengers AH_1, H_1H_2 and H_2B, and two markets for connecting passengers AH_2 and H_1B.[82] The monopoly network problem can be interpreted either as the scheduling problem of a single airline operating two hubs or as the problem of two airlines maximizing joint profits. In the latter interpretation, local market H_1H_2 may represent a route market between hubs of flag carriers before deregulation in the European Union, which until recently were governed by restrictive bilaterals, while the other markets can be thought of as hinterland monopoly markets in the absence of cabotage, e.g., as in Nero (1996).

Using the same parameters as in the one-hub system, the (base) solution to the monopoly scheduling problem is

$$\bar{f} = \{f_1, f_2, f_3\} = \{36, 29, 29\} \tag{9.13}$$

and

$$\bar{p} = \{p_{H_1H_2}, p_{AH_1}, p_{H_2B}, p_{AH_2}, p_{H_1B}\} = \{79, 76, 76, 58, 58\} \tag{9.14}$$

As before, $\theta_2 = 0.8 * \theta_1$, a value at which the HS system is slightly more profitable than the FC system. As before, equilibrium profit decreases in θ_2.

---

[82] As indicated before, we do not consider trips for which more than one transfer is necessary.

9.4.2 Hub competition

The case of competition on the local market H_1H_2 is now considered. The situation can be interpreted as an example of partial deregulation, in the sense that a collusive bilateral containing capacity and fare restrictions is abolished for the international route H_1H_2, while carriers continue to operate monopoly routes within their respective countries. The model assumes that two identical airlines with identical hinterland markets compete on H_1H_2. In the following, airline 1 operates the monopoly markets AH_1 and AH_2, and airline 2 operates monopoly markets H_2B and H_1B. The results of the base simulation are compared with the monopoly regime in Table 9.3.

A basic characteristic of the equilibrium is the asymmetric frequency choice on leg 1. This result is due to the second-stage price competition: airlines have an incentive to avoid symmetry, as this results in lower equilibrium prices (see Chapter 8, Section 8.3). In equilibrium, airline 1 operates three more flights than does airline 2, which enables it to charge a higher price in the duopoly market H_1H_2. The higher frequency of airline 1 in leg 1 also lowers schedule delay and travel time for its transfer passengers relative to those of airline 2, so that the price in market AH_2 is higher than in airline 2's transfer market H_1B.

Table 9.3
Market equilibria: a two-hub network

	Monopoly	Hub competition	
		Airline 1	Airline 2
Schedule	$\{36, 29, 29\}$	$\{24, 28\}$	$\{21, 28\}$
Prices	$\{79, 76, 76, 58, 58\}$	$\{54, 76, 50\}$	$\{52, 76, 47\}$
Passengers	$\{1735, 1673,$	$\{1265, 1661, 1059\}$	$\{1171, 1661, 987\}$
	$1673, 1242, 1242\}$		

A comparison of the monopoly and hub competition regimes shows that the individual duopoly airlines have a lower flight frequency on each leg than the monopolist. On legs 2 and 3, the difference is quite small. On leg 1, however, the individual flight frequencies are much lower with competition, while the combined flight frequency on this leg is much higher. As it has been assumed that connecting passengers never transfer to a flight operated by another airline, the connecting passengers suffer from longer travel times as a result of the decrease in airline flight frequency. This decrease in utility is reflected by the lower transfer demand and the much lower prices in the transfer markets of both airlines. The local passengers in duopoly market H_1H_2 do benefit, both from increased flight frequency and lower prices, because of price competition. In this market, there is a significant increase in passengers.

In Table 9.4, welfare results of both regimes are compared, where the welfare total is defined as the sum of consumer surplus in all markets plus industry profit. A first result of deregulation in market H_1H_2 is a dramatic decrease in industry profit. Secondly, there is an increase in total consumer surplus. The table shows that the aggregate increase is the sum of a gain for local passengers (in market H_1H_2) and losses for connecting passengers. The result of these opposing changes is a net decrease in the welfare sum.[83]

Table 9.4
Welfare results: a two-hub model

	Monopoly	Hub competition
Industry profit	215016	138545
CS ('000) per market	$\{66, 62, 62, 40, 40\}$	$\{127, 62, 62, 28, 31\}$
CS total	269875	309454
Welfare		
Absolute value	484891	447999
% change		−7.6

The general welfare result above is qualitatively in line with earlier work on the effect of deregulation in network markets. Nero (1996), using a similar HS network, concludes that for particular parameter combinations in his model, welfare (the sum of consumer surplus and profits) over all markets in the network is higher under monopoly (after an airline merger) than under competition. Brueckner and Spiller (1991) reach a similar conclusion for leg competition. In these papers, the form of the cost function drives the results. In particular, the cost function reflects increasing returns to traffic density; i.e., marginal passenger costs are decreasing.

In the present model, marginal passenger costs are constant, so that network externalities take the form of demand rather than cost complementarities. This difference, which follows from the model specification, has a number of implications. As indicated in the previous section (leg competition), the introduction of competition in a local market does not result in higher marginal costs and prices for connecting passengers in our model. Rather, prices decrease for connecting passengers as their net trip utility decreases in travel time. However, consumer surplus for connecting passengers still decreases, as the price decrease does not compensate for the travel time increase. Similarly, the marginal passenger cost of local passengers, e.g. in market AH_1, is constant, so that demand, price and consumer surplus changes, if any, are due to changes in the flight frequency on leg 2. The consumer surplus change is still positive, but is

---

[83] In a number of simulations, the sensitivity of the welfare results with respect to the value of travel time parameter θ_2 has been investigated for parameters in the range $0.2\theta_1 \leq \theta_2 \leq \theta_1$. As expected, the negative welfare effect of deregulation increases in θ_2; the qualitative conclusions remain, however, unchanged.

smaller than the profit decrease, so that the overall welfare effect is negative in the two-hub model.

Finally, it is noted that external costs have not been taken into account in the analysis. However, one can expect increased environmental costs in the network, e.g. taking the form of noise and emissions, after deregulation. The effects are not evenly spread over the network. Whereas there is a slight decrease in aircraft movements at airports A and B, there is a significant net increase at the hub airports.

9.5   Conclusion

A model of schedule competition in simple airline networks has been presented in this chapter as an extension of the models developed in the previous two chapters. Again, airline competition in frequencies and prices is modeled as a two-stage game, for a fixed number of competitors: in the first stage, airlines choose frequencies on the legs in their network; in the second stage they choose prices for direct and connecting markets. Profit-maximizing schedule solutions are calculated for two types of networks, and monopoly solutions are compared with solutions under competition in part of the network. The numerical results indicate that for both types of networks, the introduction of competition in part of the network has a positive effect on aggregate consumer welfare. However, consumers in transfer markets lose because, under the assumption that they do not transfer to a competing airline's flight, their schedule delay and travel time costs increase. Furthermore, industry profit decreases. In the case of leg competition in a one-hub model, the positive consumer surplus effect dominates the profit loss, resulting in an increase in overall social surplus. In the case of hub competition, the profit loss dominates, so that there is a net welfare decrease. The network analysis agrees qualitatively with the results of the previous two simulation models as far as aggregate consumer benefits and profits are concerned. The negative effect on consumer welfare in a part of the network is added, however. Furthermore, the analysis shows that the profit decrease may outweigh the gain to consumers.

The welfare conclusions of the above analyses are less straightforward than those reached in the previous chapters. The analysis of the two-hub network shows that liberalization may decrease rather than increase social welfare. It should be noted, however, that travelers still gain in all cases studied. Therefore, the conclusions about liberalization do not change qualitatively for policy makers aiming to secure consumer benefits. However, given that the possibility of 'unexpected' welfare conclusions has been raised in other types of network analysis, it is clear that the topic deserves more attention, both in modeling efforts and in empirical application. The network system that has emerged historically, and present tendencies towards increased concentration in Europe, underline the need for policy makers to understand the effects of policy in a network context.

Chapter 10
Welfare Effects of European Airline Liberalization

10.1 Introduction

A short history of reforms in aviation policy in a number of countries and regions has been presented in Chapter 2. Consequences of regulatory reform in airline markets have been analyzed theoretically in other chapters. In this chapter, the effects of reform on market equilibria and consumer welfare are investigated empirically for a set of European interstate airline markets.

As described in Chapter 2, the process of multilateral regulatory reform in European aviation was finalized in April 1997, when the restrictions on cabotage were lifted. This step completed a decade of gradual reform towards a 'single aviation market' in the European Union, in the form of the three 'packages' of 1987, 1990 and 1992. Before this multilateral process started, liberalization of bilateral agreements had already been initiated by a small number of EU members in the mid-1980s. The aim of this investigation is to contribute to the empirical evidence on the effects of bilateral reform in European aviation markets using route-level data for the years 1988–92. As the main characteristics and developments in European airline policy have already been discussed, the reader may refer to Chapter 2 for the institutional background to the present analysis.

A number of empirical studies have addressed the effects of airline liberalization. Dresner and Tretheway (1992) analyze the effect of liberalization on pricing on North Atlantic routes, using 1976–81 data, estimating a welfare gain of some 45 (1981) US$ per passenger. Using 1969–89 data, Maillebiau and Hansen (1995) study the welfare effects of bilateral liberalization in North Atlantic routes through the impact on both fares and a quality variable, namely, accessibility; they estimate a welfare gain of 585 (1989) US$ per passenger. Finally, using route- and airline-specific data, Marin (1995) estimates that the liberalization of bilateral agreements has had a significant negative effect on prices in European aviation markets, while any such effect due to the first (1987) EU liberalization package is not observed.

This chapter is organized as follows. In the next section, the theoretical framework used to derive the hypotheses for the empirical estimation is described. Following this description, the econometric model is introduced. In Section 10.4, the sample of routes is described and the estimation results are presented and discussed. Effects of liberalization on consumer welfare and environmental costs are calculated and discussed in Section 10.5.

10.2 A theoretical model

This investigation contributes to the empirical evidence concerning the effects of airline liberalization, using aggregate route-level data on a sample of intra-European routes. The use of route-specific rather than route- and carrier-specific data requires a strong symmetry assumption with respect to airline behavior. As pointed out by Dresner and Tretheway (1992), one has to assume that the individual behavioral equations may be 'averaged' over the firms operating the route, or that market equilibria in terms of pricing and frequency are symmetric. In effect, one assumes that the possibly underlying but unobserved firm heterogeneity does not influence the estimation at the route level. While this approach does not allow the analysis of individual firm behavior, a justification for the use of aggregate data is the fact that there is very little variation in the observed (official) fares. This problem, the absence of variation or choice in published official fares among competitors, has been noted by various authors, e.g. Dresner and Tretheway (1992) for the North Atlantic markets, and Nero (1998) and Jorge-Calderon (1997) for European markets. However, some authors have used carrier-specific price data in supply equations and obtained 'expected' results (Marin, 1995; Nero, 1998). While the adequacy of the assumption of symmetric firm behavior should in principle be tested empirically, the data set does not allow such a test. Therefore, following Dresner and Tretheway, all the equations are specified in terms of route-level variables, analyzing aggregate or average market behavior.

One aim of the analysis is to measure the impact of liberalization in terms of changes in consumer welfare (surplus), which is calculated from the demand function. Demand is assumed to depend on exogenous gravity-type variables such as income and the number of potential passengers on the one hand, and an endogenous ticket-fare variable on the other. Furthermore, the demand effect of the endogenous aggregate flight frequency is investigated. Air transport demand q on route r, measured as the number of passengers, is thus

$$q_r = q\left(\mathbf{z}_r, p_r, f_r\right) \tag{10.1}$$

where $\mathbf{z}_r$ is a vector of exogenous gravity-type demand variables, and p_r and f_r are the price and departure frequency on route r respectively.

Airline behavior, as well as firm behavior in general, can be viewed as a multi-stage process (e.g., Marin, 1995). In the first stage, the airline firm decides whether to enter the industry or not; having entered, airlines may choose, in a second stage, the routes to be operated and the aircraft technology to be used. Next, airlines have to decide on the flight schedule and, finally, to decide on prices, which can be assumed the most flexible variable. The first two decision stages are not considered explicitly in the present analysis. As in the previous chapters, firm behavior with respect to departure frequency and pricing is analyzed.

On route r, a representative airline l maximizes profits

$$\pi_r^l = p_r^l q_r^l - c\left(q_r^l, f_r^l, d_r\right) \qquad (10.2)$$

with respect to price and frequency; $c(.)$ is the cost function and d_r the stage length of the route. Following the analysis in the previous chapters, the effect of liberalization is modeled as a change from collusive behavior to non-collusive oligopoly behavior.

Following Dresner and Tretheway (1992) and Brander and Zhang (1990), the profit-maximizing price of the representative airline is derived from the profit function using a parameter δ, which represents a standard 'conjectural variation' parameter measuring the degree of collusion.[84]

$$p_r^l = \frac{dc_r^l}{dq_r} - q_r^l \frac{dp^l}{dq^l}\left(1 + \delta\right) \qquad (10.3)$$

The parameter δ captures the effect of liberalization, and can be written as

$$\delta = \left(p^{-l} - \frac{dc_r^{-l}}{dq_r^{-l}}\right)\frac{dq^{-l}}{dp^l} > 0 \quad \text{under regulation (collusive price behavior)}$$

$$\delta = 0 \qquad\qquad\qquad \text{after liberalization (non-cooperative behavior)}$$

where the superscript $-l$ refers to airlines other than l. Assuming that restrictive bilaterals result in collusive practices, the airlines take the effect of their price decisions on the profits of the other airlines into account. This has a positive effect on price (Dresner and Tretheway, 1992), so that $\delta > 0$ when a route is regulated, and $\delta = 0$ when the restrictions are lifted. Therefore, the effect of liberalization on the equilibrium price is expected to be negative.

Using the above observations, the (uniform) profit-maximizing price for each route can be written as

$$p_r^* = p(\delta_r, f_r, \mathbf{z}_r) \qquad (10.4)$$

Similarly, frequency choice in the first stage of the game can be either collusive or non-cooperative. When considering a frequency change in a cartel, each airline takes into account both the effect on own profits and the effect on the profits of other cartel members. In order to analyze the effect of collusion on frequency choice, profit of firm l is rewritten as the product of frequency and profit per flight: $\pi^l = f^l \pi^{f,l}$, which holds under a symmetric interlaced equilibrium. It is

---

[84]   The term 'conjectural variation' (CV) refers to the belief or conjecture held by an oligopolist l about the way a rival firm $-l$ will react to changes in the price or quantity chosen by l. The concept of the conjectural variation itself has been subject to debate. The CV has been criticized as an 'ad hoc' assumption about future actions in a static or 'one-shot' model, which should be interpreted as a static approximation rather than a literal expectation of strategic reactions. Brander and Zhang (1990) refer to it as an 'intuitive measure of market conduct', the value of which can be estimated empirically.

noted that $\pi^{f,l} = (p^l - c)\, q^{f,l}$. Considering an airline l and $(n-1)$ other airlines $-l$, the first-order condition for the frequency problem is

$$\frac{\partial \pi^l}{\partial f^l} = \pi^{f,l} + f^l \frac{\partial \pi^l}{\partial f^l} + \delta(n-1) f^l \frac{\partial \pi^{-l}}{\partial f^l} = 0 \qquad (10.5)$$

where the parameter δ again represents collusive behavior. Under competition, δ is zero and the effects on the profits of other airlines are ignored, whereas these effects are taken into account under collusion. Given the symmetry of the airlines, this gives as the profit-maximizing cartel frequency

$$f^l = \frac{\pi^{f,l}}{-\left[(p^* - c)\frac{\partial q^l}{\partial f^l}\left(1 + (n-1)\delta\right)\right]} \qquad (10.6)$$

Again, the parameter conditions are $\delta > 0$ in the collusive situation and $\delta = 0$ under non-cooperative behavior. The effect of δ on frequency is analyzed by taking the total derivative of equation (10.6) with respect to δ. This effect can be written as

$$\frac{df^l}{d\delta} = \frac{\frac{\partial \pi}{\partial p}\frac{\partial p^*}{\partial \delta} + \pi\left[\frac{\partial p^*}{\partial \delta}\frac{\partial q^l}{\partial f^l}\left(1 + (n-1)\delta\right) + (p^* - c)(n-1)\frac{\partial q^l}{\partial f^l}\right]}{M^2} < 0 \qquad (10.7)$$

where M is the denominator in (10.6). The first term in the numerator of (10.7) cancels, because, given the second-stage price equilibrium, $\frac{\partial \pi}{\partial p} = 0$. Both terms in square brackets are negative, because the effect of an increase in flight frequency on the demand for the individual flight, $\frac{\partial q^l}{\partial f^l}$, is negative. With $\pi > 0$, the complete expression is negative. Therefore, a decrease in collusion represented by the parameter δ results in an increase in frequency. The effect may even be stronger when capacity constraints are taken into account. Frequency choice is constrained: if k is plane capacity, frequency has to satisfy $f^l k^l \geq q^l$. Given that the effect on prices is negative, demand is likely to rise after liberalization. Such an increase in demand can be accommodated by a number of means: airlines can either allow loadfactors to increase, increase departure frequency, choose larger aircraft, or a combination of these. These observations can be summarized as:

$$q_r = LF_r \cdot f_r \cdot k_r \qquad (10.8)$$

where LF_r, f_r and k_r denote loadfactor, frequency and aircraft capacity on route r respectively. It is noted that an increase in loadfactor may take place in the very short run, while departure frequency and aircraft type are generally less flexible. Given these observations, there is a potential indirect positive effect of liberalization on frequency through the capacity constraint.

10.3 The econometric model

In this section, an empirical model of the airline market is formulated in order to identify the effects of airline liberalization. First, the demand equation is specified. As outlined in the previous section, it is assumed that demand for air transport depends on price, departure frequency and a vector of exogenous demand variables **z**. This demand specification is quite standard in air transport modeling; see the discussion in Jorge-Calderon (1997). Gravity-type variables are commonly used to control for, e.g., income at the endpoints and the level of social and commercial interactions between them. Following the literature, **z** consists of observations on population, income per capita and trade for the route endpoints, and distance.

The fare variable, representing the money cost of traveling, is standard too. Estimates of price sensitivity of demand, however, may well differ between studies. In a survey of empirical studies of air transport demand, Oum et al. (1992) present a range of (absolute) price elasticities of 0.4 to 4.51, with most estimates falling in the 0.8–2.0 range. The authors discuss the variation in results, which can in part be attributed to sample characteristics (business versus leisure travel) and estimation techniques. For most route markets, multiple fare types or products are available. First, there is the distinction between business and economy (coach) fare. Secondly, one or more discounts with respect to the standard economy tariff may be available. Abbott and Thompson (1991) discuss the generic fare types offered by airlines, noting that in many markets a wider range of fares, subject to *'finely differentiated conditions'*, is available. However, as the data do not allow the identification of the number of passengers per particular tariff or discount rate, demand per product of fare type cannot be estimated. One 'solution' to this problem proposed in the literature is to use only the widely available standard economy fare as an approximate 'average fare'.[85] In the absence of a more elegant solution, this approach is followed. It is noted that, while the economy or Y-fare is an average in the sense that first-class passengers pay more and discount travelers pay less, the use of this fare does not do justice to the huge variation in fares that is observed in reality.

As discussed in previous chapters, a high frequency implies a low average 'schedule delay cost'. A number of studies have found a statistically significant positive correlation between demand and departure frequency (e.g. Jorge-Calderon, 1997). A problem is, however, causality: although it may safely be assumed that travelers prefer a high departure frequency over a low one, the empirical question is whether one can conclude that an increase in service frequency causes an increase in demand when the two variables are statistically correlated. In particular, it is a distinct possibility that airlines adjust their departure frequencies in order to 'accommodate' demand. Therefore, it seems

---

[85] Marin (1995) defends this practice by referring to the high covariance between different fare classes, implying that, e.g., business fares are determined as a mark-up on leisure fares.

appropriate to model the airline demand and departure frequency as a system of simultaneous equations.

The equation to be estimated is then

$$\text{Pass}_{rt} = \varphi_1 \left(\begin{array}{c} \text{Yfare/km}_{rt}, \text{Frequency}_{rt}, \text{Income}_{rt}, \\ \text{Population}_{rt}, \text{Distance}_{rt}, \ \overline{\text{Hub}}_{rt} \end{array} \right) + \varepsilon_{1,rt} \qquad (10.9)$$

where, for each route r and year t,

Pass	=	the number of round-trip passengers carried
Yfare/km	=	the lowest available round-trip economy fare (ECU)
Frequency	=	the number of flights
Income	=	the product of the per capita income of the endpoint regions (ECU)
Population	=	the product of the populations of the endpoint regions
Distance	=	the distance between airports (km)
$\overline{\text{Hub}}$	=	a vector with variables Hub_1 and Hub_2, dummies with value 1 if one (two) of the route endpoints has a share of transfer passengers of 20 percent or more in 1996

and $\varepsilon_{1,rt}$ is an error term. All variables are in logarithms, so that the coefficients can be interpreted as elasticities, and all explanatory variables except Yfare/km are exogenous. It is expected that the coefficients of Yfare/km and Distance are negative; the other coefficients are expected to be positive. The Population and Income variables have been obtained from the Eurostat regional statistics and are measured at the NUTS II (provincial) level. Admittedly, this may produce measurement error, as the region size in the NUTS classification is not uniform across countries. The variables Population and Income are intended to reflect differences between potential passenger populations. The 'catchment' areas to which potential passenger populations belong may well differ, however, from either the NUTS II regions or the entire country. Clearly, the figures are approximations.

Using the considerations in the previous section, summarized in equation (10.3), the fare equation has the following form:

$$\text{Yfare/km}_{rt} = \varphi_2 \left(\begin{array}{c} \text{Pass}_{rt}, \text{Frequency}_{rt}, \overline{\text{LIB}}_{rt}, \text{Cost}_{rt}, \\ \text{Income}_{rt}, \ \text{Distance}_{rt}, \overline{\text{Hub}}_{rt} \end{array} \right) + \varepsilon_{2,rt} \qquad (10.10)$$

where, for route r and year t,

$\overline{\text{LIB}}$ = a vector containing dummy variables
            LIBfull and LIBrestr;
            the dummy variables take on the value 1 in case the route
            is subject to full or restricted liberalization respectively.

Cost = average cost of the main operators (ECU)

Again, the continuous variables are in logarithms, and all variables except Pass are exogenous. The Cost variable represents the average cost level of the main carriers, usually the flag carriers, on the route. The coefficient is expected to be positive. The main variables of interest in the present study measure the impact of liberalization. As discussed earlier, liberalization may be either 'full' or 'restricted'. In order to test the effect of these two types of liberalization, two dummy variables are introduced in equation (10.10), namely, the variables LIBfull and LIBrestr. The LIB variables have a value of 1 for a route when the two endpoint countries have signed a liberal bilateral of the particular type, 0 otherwise. As discussed in Section 10.2, it is expected that the LIB variables have a depressing effect on the equilibrium fare.

The frequency equation is specified as

$$\text{Frequency}_{rt} = \varphi_3 \left(\text{Pass}_{rt}, \text{Aircraftsize}_{rt}, \text{Distance}_{rt}, \overline{\text{LIB}}_{rt}, \text{Operators}_{rt} \right) + \varepsilon_{3,rt}$$
$$(10.11)$$

where, for route r and year t,

Aircraftsize = the average number of seats per flight
Operators   = the number of airline firms offering services

The continuous variables are in logarithms; the passenger variable and aircraft size are endogenous in the model; the other variables are exogenous. It is expected that the coefficient for Pass is positive, and the coefficients for Aircraftsize and Distance are negative. Following the discussion in the previous chapters and in Section 10.2, the sign on the coefficient of both the operator variable and the LIB variables is expected to be positive.

Finally, an equation for the aircraft size is specified as

$$\text{Aircraftsize}_{rt} = \varphi_4 \left(\text{Pass}_{rt}, \text{Distance}_{rt} \right) + \varepsilon_{4,rt} \qquad (10.12)$$

This equation is intended to capture the capacity effect discussed in Section 10.2. Therefore, it is expected that the coefficient of the passenger variable is positive. Further, the effect of distance on size is expected to be positive. This equation is added to the model in order to measure the potential effect of an increased passenger number on environmental damage through an increase in aircraft size.

As indicated earlier, the fare and frequency variables in the passenger equation are treated as endogenous variables, as are the passenger variable in the fare and frequency equation and the frequency variable in the fare equation. The issue of endogeneity has been handled in various ways in the literature. Maillebiau and Hansen (1995) treat the fare variable as exogenous in the demand equation, and estimate both the demand and the fare equation separately using OLS. Dresner and Tretheway (1992) and Nero (1998) treat the passenger variable as endogenous in the fare equation, which they estimate using a two-stage least squares (TSLS) procedure; the fare is not used as an explanatory variable in the passenger equation. Marin (1995) estimates the simultaneous demand and fare equations separately using IV for the endogenous variable in both, but does not consider the frequency variable. In the present analysis, the demand, fare and frequency equations are estimated separately using TSLS for the endogenous passenger, fare and frequency variables.

Furthermore, time and country-pair dummies are included in the model. Systematic time- and space-dependent variation are thus treated as fixed effects in order to control for unobserved heterogeneity between years and country pairs. The relevance of these effects in the model is tested and discussed below. In the analysis, one can choose between fixed route effects and fixed country-pair effects; the specification with fixed country-pair effects has been adopted because this specification saves degrees of freedom. The higher efficiency in estimation shows up in significant coefficients with expected signs in the country-pair specification, while the fixed route dummy model performed much less satisfactorily in this respect. Despite a slightly better fit for the specification with route dummies, therefore, the country dummy specification has been used.

10.4 Estimation and results

10.4.1 Sample

Observations on a sample of 34 European interstate city-pair markets for the period 1988–92 are used. The sample of routes is selected in order to represent various traffic densities and stage lengths. Fourteen routes in the sample connect countries that have signed a 'liberal' bilateral before or during the sample period, while for 20 routes no bilateral liberalization has taken place at all.[86]

In a number of cases, UK bilaterals were negotiated in two stages, with the more liberal terms of agreement, such as double disapproval, arrived at only in a second agreement (e.g. as with the UK–Netherlands and the UK–Ireland bilaterals). In other cases, liberalization remained 'restricted' in some dimensions, e.g., the bilaterals allowed multiple designation but did not introduce 'double disapproval'. Table 10.1 presents an overview of the liberalization of bilaterals

---

[86]   The routes in the latter group have been analyzed in Chapter 8.

relevant to the present empirical analysis, using the distinction between 'full' and 'restricted' liberalization.

In the estimation of the effect of liberalization, routes subject to 'full liberalization' are distinguished from routes subject to 'restricted liberalization' and routes that have not engaged in bilateral liberalization at all. There is no explicit way to represent multilateral liberalization. Therefore, the analysis concentrates on the effect of bilateral liberalization.

Data used in estimation are publicly available. The data on passenger numbers, frequencies, loadfactor and number of operators per route are obtained from the ICAO *Digest of Statistics* (Series TF, traffic by flight stage). Cost data have been compiled from the ICAO *Digest of Statistics* (Series F, financial data commercial air carriers), IATA's *World Air Transport Statistics* and the statistical appendices of the AEA *Yearbooks*, and the fare information is from the OAG *World Airways Guide*. The information on transfer passengers is from the ACI *Yearbook*. As indicated earlier, population and income data are from the Eurostat regional statistics and measured at the NUTS II (provincial) level.

Table 10.1
Bilateral liberalization

Bilateral	Year	Multiple designation	Free capacity choice	Double dis-approval
Full liberalization				
UK–NL	1984/85	Yes	Yes	No/Yes
UK–GER	1984	Yes	Yes	Limited
UK–BEL	1985	Yes	Yes	Yes
UK–IRE	1985/88	Yes	Yes	Yes
Restricted liberalization				
UK–FRA	1985	Limited	Limited	No
UK–SP	1985	Limited	Limited	No
UK–IT	1985	Limited	Limited	No
SP–GER	1989	Limited	Limited	No
FRA–GER	1989	Limited	Limited	No

Sources: Button and Swann (1991); Doganis (1991).

10.4.2 Estimation results

The estimation results for the demand equation (10.9) are given in Table 10.2. Time and country-pair dummies are used, but results for these are omitted from this and the following tables. The model has also been estimated without time and country-pair dummies, but the resulting model is rejected in favor of the model with dummies. The equations are estimated using TSLS. The liberalization status variables, the hub dummy variables, the cost variable and the number of operators have been used as instruments for the endogenous fare and frequency variable, as well as the exogenous variables income, population and distance in the demand equation.

Table 10.2
Demand equation: TSLS results

Dependent variable: Passenger number	Estimated coefficients (t-statistic)	
Variable	Model 1	Model 2
Yfare/km	−1.33	−1.27
	(−2.04)	(−1.94)
Frequency	0.79	0.77
	(7.46)	(7.38)
Income	0.34	0.54
	(0.93)	(1.64)
Population	0.20	0.27
	(1.33)	(2.13)
Distance	−0.72	−0.83
	(−1.53)	(−1.79)
Hub_2	0.24	
	(0.95)	
Adj. R^2	0.96	0.96
Sum squared residuals	10.19	10.32
F-statistic	115.28	118.14
Adj. DW-statistic	1.69	1.67
Included observations	170	170

Two specifications are presented, the first of which (model 1) contains Hub_2 as an explanatory variable, a dummy indicating a route with two hub endpoints. The results show that the Hub_2 variable is not significant, and the same is true for the Hub_1 variable (results of this regression are not presented). This suggests that for the routes studied here, the percentage of transfer passengers is limited. Therefore, the analysis concentrates on the results in model 2. The coefficient on the Yfare/km variable is an estimate of the fare elasticity. The coefficient of the fare variable does not vary much between models 1 and 2, although its significance is somewhat lower in model 2. The respective price elasticities of 1.33 and 1.26 are in the middle of the 0.8–2.0 range presented in the survey of aviation fare elasticities by Oum et al. (1992), but below the elasticity of 1.71 found by

Marin (1995) using another sample of European interstate routes. Frequency has a significant positive effect on demand, with a high elasticity of 0.73. As the overview of air transport demand studies and the estimation results in Jorge-Calderon (1997) shows, however, the estimated frequency elasticity is in line with other analyses. The coefficients on income, population and distance all have the expected signs, but their estimated values and significance are smaller in the first model. Only the coefficient on income is not significant at the 10 percent level in model 2. Finally, the Durbin–Watson statistic has been adjusted to account for the panel structure of the data. Since the observations are stacked in chronological order per route, an adjusted DW statistic, described in, e.g., Florax (1992), should be used.[87] The statistic indicates that the hypothesis of no serial correlation cannot be rejected, but unfortunately the test is not determinate; however, the estimated values of the DW are in the upper end of the indeterminate range.

The estimation results for the fare equation are shown in Table 10.3. Other specifications have been used, but did not lead to different conclusions with respect to the main variables in the model. Again, the liberalization status variables, the hub dummy variables, the cost variable, the number of operators, and income, population and distance have been used as instruments for the endogenous passenger and frequency variable. The main variables of interest in the analysis are the two liberalization dummies. The results indicate that, while restricted liberalization seems to have no significant impact on the standard economy fare, markets with 'full liberalization' have a significantly lower fare. The estimated coefficient of –0.41 translates into a price in 'full liberalization' markets that is some 34 percent lower than in markets without such regulatory reform.[88] The results for the present sample may be compared with the results of Dresner and Tretheway (1992) and Maillebiau and Hansen (1995) for liberalization on the North Atlantic, who estimate fare decreases of 35 percent and 35–45 percent, respectively. The model moreover shows that the passenger variable has a negative but insignificant effect on fares, and frequency has an insignificant positive effect on fares. The significant coefficient on the cost variable (0.29) is an estimate of the cost elasticity of the fare. The value implies that differences in costs are not fully translated into fares. The negative effect of distance on the fare per kilometer is common in the literature, and is interpreted as the decreasing effect of distance on average costs per kilometer. Interestingly, the variable indicating that one of the two endpoints is a hub is negative and significant, which may reflect the fact that price competition is more rather than less intense on non-stop routes that begin or end in a hub. It is noted that this finding contrasts with findings for the United States, e.g., Morrison and Winston (1990), where a positive effect is found. This result suggests that hub domination is less problematic in Europe

---

[87]   The numerator of the corrected DW is calculated by summing the squared differences between errors for subsequent years per route first, and then adding these up over routes.

[88]   This is calculated as $100\% * \left(1 - e^{-0.41}\right)$.

than in the US.

Table 10.3
Fare equation: TSLS results

Dependent variable: Yfare/km	Estimated coefficients (t-statistic)
Variable	
Passenger number	−0.42
	(−1.41)
Frequency	0.39
	(1.26)
LIBfull	−0.41
	(−2.32)
LIBrestr	−0.01
	(−0.12)
Cost	0.29
	(2.12)
Income	0.35
	(1.12)
Distance	−0.40
	(−2.95)
Hub_1	−0.36
	(−2.22)
Adj. R^2	0.83
Sum squared residuals	2.17
F-statistic	26.34
Adj. DW-statistic	1.69
Included observations:	170

The frequency equation is the next to be estimated. Our main interest here is to establish the effects of passenger number on departure frequency and the effect of liberalization on aggregate frequency. As discussed in Section 10.2, an important issue to be resolved is the treatment of the average aircraft size variable as either exogenous or endogenous. A Hausman test rejects the hypothesis of exogeneity of aircraft size in the model, and so aircraft size is treated as endogenous. Instruments for the endogenous passenger and aircraft size variable are the liberalization status variables, the number of operators, and income, population and distance.[89] Two sets of estimates for the frequency equation are

---

[89]   Note that the number of observations is higher here; this is due to the inclusion of data for the year 1993.

presented in Table 10.4.

In both models, the coefficient of the passenger variable indicates that an increase in passenger number leads to a less than proportional increase in departure frequency. Thus, at a constant aircraft size, an increase in passenger number is accommodated partly by a frequency increase and partly by a rise in loadfactor. The endogenous size variable is not significant, nor is the operator number. The dummy variable indicating 'full liberalization' shows a positive and significant effect (at the 10 percent level) on frequency in model 2. The coefficient of 0.31 implies a frequency increase in markets that experienced full liberalization of some 36 percent. However, in model 1, which excludes distance, the effect of full liberalization is not significant.

Table 10.4
Frequency equation: TSLS results

Dependent variable: Frequency	Estimated coefficients (t-statistic)	
Variable	Model 1	Model 2
Passenger number	0.77	0.75
	(5.45)	(5.55)
Aircraft size	−0.18	−0.05
	(−0.23)	(−0.07)
Distance	−0.04	
	(−0.32)	
LIBfull	0.21	0.31
	(0.60)	(1.85)
LIBrestr	0.01	0.2
	(0.09)	(0.12)
Operators	0.07	0.08
	(1.44)	(1.80)
Adj. R^2	0.97	0.97
Sum squared residuals	6.47	8.24
F-statistic	197.98	160.91
DW-statistic	1.69	1.71
Included observations:	204	204

These results can be explained by the correlation between the LIBfull variable and distance: as discussed in Chapter 6, fully liberalized routes have relatively short route distances. As a consequence, it may be that the LIBfull variable 'picks up' the independent effect of distance on frequency in model 2. For example, distance may have a negative effect on frequency because the frequency competition with other transport modes is more intense on shorter distances. Therefore, the LIBfull coefficient is treated with caution, and the estimates of both models are used in the welfare calculations. In model 2, a positive and significant (at the 10 percent level) effect of the number of operators on departure frequency is found, as has been suggested by the theoretical analysis in previous chapters. The dummy variable for restricted liberalization is not significant in either model.

It is noted that the effect of liberalization on departure frequency is twofold. First, there is a direct effect, measured by the LIBfull coefficient in Table 10.4. Secondly, there is an indirect effect through the effect of liberalization on fares (Table 10.3). Using the estimated fare effect and fare elasticity, one can calculate the effect of liberalization on the number of passengers. This change in passenger number results in a less than proportional frequency increase, as the estimate of the coefficient on passenger number in the frequency equation indicates.

Finally, the aircraft size equation (10.12) discussed in Section 10.3 has been estimated. The results (not presented in a separate table) show a significant positive effect of passengers on the aircraft size, with an estimated coefficient of 0.09. Furthermore, there is a significant positive effect of distance on average aircraft size. Given the estimation results for the frequency and the aircraft size equation, it is concluded that airlines accommodate changes in passenger number through both frequency and aircraft size changes.

10.5 Evaluation

The welfare effects of airline liberalization are quantified using the estimated equations in the following. In the measurement of the total welfare change, the change in consumer welfare and the change in environmental costs are taken into account.

10.5.1   The impact on consumer welfare

The estimated demand model has the form

$$q_r\left(p_r, f_r\right) = \alpha_r p_r^{-\epsilon} f_r^{\eta} \tag{10.13}$$

where ϵ is the estimated price elasticity of demand, η is the estimated frequency elasticity of demand and α_r represents the values of the other independent variables in the demand function for route r. Consumer surplus is defined as the area under the general demand function (10.13). Therefore, a change in consumer benefits due to a price change only, say from p_r^0 to p_r^1, is

$$\Delta CS_r = \int_{p_r^0}^{p_r^1} q_r\left(p, f_r\right) dp \tag{10.14}$$

Using the estimated (constant elasticity) demand function, the change in consumer surplus resulting from a change in price due to liberalization, say from p_r^{reg} to p_r^{lib} can be calculated as (Maillebiau and Hansen, 1995)

$$\Delta CS_r = \int_{p_r^{lib}}^{p_r^{reg}} q_r(p, f_r)dp = \alpha_r f_r^\eta \frac{\left(p_r^{reg}\right)^{-\epsilon+1} - \left(p_r^{lib}\right)^{-\epsilon+1}}{-\epsilon+1} \qquad (10.15)$$

When demand is a function of two variables, as is the case here, and liberalization results in a price change and a frequency change from f_r^{reg} to f_r^{lib}, the change in consumer welfare can be written as

$$\begin{aligned}\Delta CS_r &= \int_{p_r^{reg}}^{\infty} q_r(p, f_r^{reg})dp - \int_{p_r^{lib}}^{\infty} q_r(p, f_r^{lib})dp \\ &= \alpha_r \frac{\left(f_r^{reg}\right)^\eta \left(p_r^{reg}\right)^{-\epsilon+1} - \left(f_r^{lib}\right)^\eta \left(p_r^{lib}\right)^{-\epsilon+1}}{-\epsilon+1} \qquad (10.16)\end{aligned}$$

The expression (10.16) can be evaluated using the estimated demand function and the estimated changes on frequency and fares due to liberalization. Given that $\alpha_r > 0$, $\epsilon > 1$, $p_r^{lib} < p_r^{reg}$ and $f_r^{lib} > f_r^{reg}$, the welfare effect in (10.16) is positive. In the calculations presented below, the welfare change is evaluated at the sample median values. First, α_r is calculated, substituting the median of the observed values for the fully liberalized routes in the estimated demand function. Then, using the estimated effects of liberalization on fare and frequency and the observed average fare and frequency for routes that experienced 'full liberalization', one can calculate what the fare and frequency would have been, on average, without liberalization. Substituting these values in (10.16), an estimate of the effect on consumer welfare is obtained. This welfare 'impact' represents the welfare difference between the present welfare sum for the liberalized routes and the welfare sum for these routes in case there would not have been 'full liberalization'.

The consumer welfare results are presented in Table 10.5. Besides the effects measured using the coefficient estimates presented in Section 10.4, a number of sensitivity results with respect to the changes in consumer welfare are provided.

According to the baseline calculation, aggregate welfare in the completely liberalized markets in the sample is 666 million ECU higher than it would have been without 'full' liberalization. The welfare difference or impact per passenger, which has been calculated using the average number of round-trip passengers in liberalized markets, is about 346 ECU. This value falls between the per passenger welfare gain estimates of US\$180 or even US\$585 in the studies of Morrison and Winston (1986) and Maillebiau and Hansen (1995) respectively.[90] However, care should be taken when comparing these absolute figures, as one should take into

---

[90]   These are both 1989 values.

account differences in the trip lengths in the markets concerned: the products in the liberalized markets in the latter two studies are trips on the North Atlantic. Standardizing the values as the welfare gains per passenger per kilometer traveled, the baseline effect measured in the present study is five to seven times higher than the estimates just mentioned.

Results of a number of sensitivity tests are also presented in Table 10.5. First, the sensitivity of the results with respect to the estimated impacts of liberalization has been analyzed. Calculating the welfare gains after lowering the impacts by their estimated standard errors gives the low fare and frequency impacts, respectively. A low fare impact results in a welfare gain that is 15 percent lower than the baseline estimate. A low impact on frequency has a somewhat larger effect: the estimated welfare gain is about 20 percent lower in this case.

Table 10.5
Consumer welfare effects of airline liberalization
(1995 ECU)

Change in:	CS Aggregate (mn)	CS Per passenger	CS Per pass-km
Baseline	666	346	0.41
Low fare impact	569	295	0.35
High fare elasticity	268	139	0.17
Fare impact only	450	233	0.28
Low freq. impact	552	286	0.34
Low freq. elasticity	586	304	0.36
Freq. impact only	366	190	0.23
Fare + direct freq. impact	470	244	0.29
No frequency change	132	68	0.08

Next, the effect of raising the price elasticity and lowering frequency elasticity of demand has been investigated. In both cases, the effect on the welfare result is negative. As noted by Maillebiau and Hansen (1995), with a high price elasticity, fewer people would have been flying under the regulated regime. Therefore, gains accrue to a smaller group of travelers in this case, but the effect of the price decrease itself is larger. In the case of a low frequency elasticity, comparable opposing effects are at work: a higher number of consumers benefit from liberalization, but the gains per person are lower. The net effect in both cases is a decrease in the gains from liberalization. The difference in welfare results between both cases is, however, substantial: compared with the baseline estimate, gains are 60 percent lower with a high fare elasticity; with a low frequency elasticity, the welfare gain is only 12 percent lower.

A further sensitivity result is obtained by lowering the impact coefficients to zero: if only the fare impact is present, welfare gains are 33 percent lower than in the baseline estimate. When the fare impact is zero (frequency impact only), they are 45 percent lower. This difference can be accounted for by the fact that fare changes have two effects in the welfare calculation: first, there is a direct effect on welfare through the price change itself; secondly, there is an indirect effect on welfare through the effect of increased demand on frequency. In the baseline calculation, the direct effect of liberalization on frequency is about 36 percent, while the indirect effect is 33 percent. Because of the indirect frequency effect, the welfare effect is more sensitive to a zero fare impact than to a zero frequency impact.[91] This result is illustrated by the figures in the bottom row of Table 10.5, where the indirect frequency effect has been restricted to zero. In the absence of the indirect frequency effect, i.e., when only the direct frequency effect is present besides the fare impact, the welfare gain is 30 percent lower than in the baseline calculation. Finally, when all frequency effects are restricted to be zero, the welfare gain decreases to only 20 percent of the baseline estimate. Frequency changes, both direct and indirect, clearly have a substantial impact on the welfare gains. In this respect, the results are qualitatively in agreement with the conclusions reached in other studies, e.g., Morrison and Winston (1986) and Oum et al. (1991).

10.5.2   The impact on environmental costs

The calculation of the environmental damage attributable to airline liberalization is based on the environmental cost estimates that were presented in Chapter 6. These costs were estimated per landing and take-off (LTO) and per kilometer of cruise flight. Given the distance flown, the costs per flight can be calculated. In order to apply the available environmental information in the present analysis, information on the aircraft types used on the routes in the sample in 1990 was obtained (see Chapter 6 for a discussion). Using the fleet information and the number of flights in the sample, aggregate noise and emission costs can be calculated per route or subset of routes. The aggregate environmental costs per year in the set of fully liberalized routes, evaluated at the sample mean flight frequency, amounts to some 61 million ECU, according to the intermediate environmental valuation estimates in Chapter 6. As discussed in that chapter, environmental costs are proportional to the number of flights, given flight distance and aircraft type. The effect of airline liberalization on environmental costs is therefore calculated using the effect of liberalization on flight frequency.

---

[91]   This does not show up in a comparison of the 'low impact' results because the parameters are not changed by the same amount in these sensitivity tests: the effect here depends on the difference between the estimated coefficient and its standard error.

The estimation results have shown that bilateral liberalization may have two effects on flight frequency. First, there is a direct effect. According to the results of model 2 in Table 10.4, departure frequency in fully liberalized markets is 36 percent higher than in other markets due to the direct effect.[92] Secondly, there is an indirect effect: the number of passengers increases due to a decrease in prices. As discussed in Section 10.2, airlines accommodate the extra demand in three ways, namely, through an increase in loadfactor, by increasing the number of flights and by increasing the (average) plane size.

The effect of liberalization on environmental costs can now be calculated in two alternative ways. A simple procedure is to apply the environmental costs per flight directly to the estimated frequency changes. Following this procedure, one implicitly assumes that the increase in demand is completely accommodated by an increase in frequency and an increase in loadfactor.[93] In particular, it is assumed that airlines do not respond to demand increases by increasing aircraft size. An alternative procedure is to include the estimated effect of an increase in passenger number on average aircraft size. In this case, given an increase in demand, environmental costs are affected by both changes in the number of departures and a change in aircraft size. Both these procedures are used to evaluate the change in environmental costs.

Following the first procedure, the estimated effect of liberalization on fares (– 34 percent) and the estimated demand elasticity are used to calculate the increase in the number of passengers in fully liberalized markets of 43 percent. These extra passengers have to be accommodated by changes in loadfactor or departure frequency. The estimated elasticity of frequency with respect to passenger number is 0.77, and so departure frequency should increase 33 percent in fully liberalized markets. It is concluded that departure frequency is 33 percent higher in fully liberalized markets if only the indirect effect applies, whereas the frequency increase rises to 69 percent if the direct effect (36 percent) is added. The former corresponds to the 'fare impact only' case in Table 10.5, while the latter is similar to the baseline case.

The change in environmental damage due to airline liberalization is estimated as the amount by which environmental costs would have been lower in the absence of liberalization. The aggregate environmental costs in fully liberalized markets, evaluated at the mean departure frequency in the sample period, amount to 19.3 million ECU, 60.9 million ECU or 332 million ECU, according to the low, intermediate and high valuations respectively. The environmental cost effects of airline liberalization according to the alternative valuation results are presented in Table 10.6. The table presents changes in aggregate costs and in costs per passenger in fully liberalized markets.

---

[92] This is calculated as $100\% * (e^{0.31} - 1)$.

[93] Increases in loadfactors have an impact on environmental costs too, because the weight of the aircraft affects energy use. However, this effect is not considered here.

Additionally, one can take into account the possibility that an increase in passenger trips is accommodated partly through an increase in average aircraft size. The estimated elasticity of aircraft size with respect to the number of passengers is 0.09. Given the estimated increase in passenger number of 43 percent, one can conclude that the average aircraft on fully liberalized routes is about 4 percent larger than would have been the case without such liberalization. Evaluated at the mean aircraft size on liberalized routes, the absolute increase in size is some six seats. Using the environmental cost estimates per aircraft type to estimate the effect of aircraft size on environmental cost per flight, the effect of airline liberalization through larger aircraft size is, according to the intermediate values, about 27 ECU per flight or 1.5 million ECU for the sample mean flight frequency in fully liberalized markets. These figures suggest that the environmental costs due to changes in aircraft size are small compared with the effects through frequency changes.

Table 10.6
Environmental cost effects of airline liberalization
(1995 ECU)

| Effect LIB on: | Change in: | Valuation | | |
		Low	Medium	High
Frequency	Aggr. environmental cost (mn)	7	22	120
Direct: 36%	Cost per passenger	4	11	62
Frequency	Aggr. environmental cost (mn)	6	20	110
Indirect: 33%	Cost per passenger	3	11	57
Frequency	Aggr. environmental cost (mn)	13	42	230
Total: 69%	Cost per passenger	7	22	119

10.6 Conclusion

Welfare effects associated with airline liberalization have been empirically explored in this chapter. To this end, a sample of 34 routes with varying liberalization status has been investigated econometrically for the period 1988–92. The estimated fare and frequency equations showed that standard economy fares and departure frequencies on fully liberalized routes were, on average, 34 percent lower and 36 percent higher, respectively, than on routes without such liberalization. Due to increased demand, frequency was shown to increase by a further 33 percent. Ultimately, welfare calculations based on the estimated demand equation indicated that 'full' bilateral airline liberalization has resulted, for the markets studied, in gains in consumer welfare of 666 million ECU or 346 ECU per passenger.

However, environmental costs have increased too as a result of airline liberalization. The results of the frequency and aircraft size equation have been used to measure the impact of airline liberalization on environmental damage. Following the analysis in Chapter 6, three alternative valuation estimates are used. According to the low, medium and high environmental value estimates, the increase in environmental costs due to airline liberalization amounts to 6 million ECU, 20 million ECU and 111 million ECU respectively, when only the indirect frequency effect is considered. In other words, these are the costs associated with accommodating the increased demand due to lower prices in liberalized markets. When the direct effect of liberalization on frequency is added, the environmental cost estimates rise to 13 million ECU, 42 million ECU and 230 million ECU respectively, while the average cost associated with increased aircraft size is about 1.5 million ECU.

Welfare conclusions based on the above analysis should be qualified as changes in producer surplus are not analyzed. The analysis in Chapters 8 and 9 has shown that profits decline in all cases where monopoly solutions are replaced by competition.[94] Therefore, such a negative welfare component is not quantified in this chapter. Restricting the analysis to consumer gains and environmental costs here, the results in this chapter indicate that the net welfare effect of liberalizing interstate airline markets in Europe has been positive. The positive effect on consumer welfare is so large that the conclusion about the net welfare change is qualitatively insensitive to the parameter changes analyzed. In particular, the conclusion does not alter when high environmental valuation estimates are applied. For the baseline estimate, the ratio of consumer benefits to environmental costs is 16 using the medium values, and about three when the high values are used. It may be noted that the conclusion about net consumer benefits is qualitatively similar to that reached in Chapter 8; however, the ratio of consumer benefits to environmental costs is lower here. It can thus be concluded that the increase in environmental costs due to liberalization in airline markets is compensated by the increase in consumer welfare.

---

[94] Part of the fare changes may have been compensated by cost reductions. Further, recent developments in the European airline industry indicate that airlines react to changing competitive conditions by forming alliances in order to lower costs and improve services (Button et al., 1998).

Chapter 11
Conclusion

Regulatory reform and environmental externalities represent two major areas in contemporary air transport analysis and policy. Although regulatory change and environmental problems are not confined to air transport markets, public policy attention with respect to both regulation and environmental pressure in aviation has been intense in recent years, particularly in the European Union. Moreover, these themes have a significant bearing on welfare and are likely to retain policy relevance in the future.

Until recently, academic attention has focused on market internal effects of changes in airline regulation as part of a wider interest in the functioning of regulatory arrangements. The last three decades have provoked a general change of opinion regarding the merits of regulation in general: in many instances traditional distrust of competition and optimism about the effects of regulatory intervention have been reversed. Economic analyses of regulators' behavior as well as the gains in economic efficiency have played an important part in this change in thinking, not least with respect to airline markets.

The benefits of reform in these economic analyses have generally been framed in terms of welfare changes studied from a market internal perspective. However, a broad range of recent applications of environmental valuation allows for the incorporation of the effects of policy measures on the environment in monetary terms. In this study, the effects of introducing competition in airline markets on economic welfare have been studied from the two perspectives, by paying attention to market internal welfare changes and changes in external costs, in particular those associated with aircraft noise and emissions. The aim of the study has been to compare the size of the changes in the various welfare components affected by regulatory change in aviation. The present chapter summarizes the findings of the analysis and subsequently discusses implications for policy and suggestions for further research.

11.1 Summary

Chapter 2 describes how airline regulation has affected competition in a number of national and international airline markets, and how reform has subsequently been introduced. The institutional arrangements have, in many cases, precluded new entry into airline markets and introduced joint rather than competitive choice of fares and capacities. In such cases, the regulated market structure has the characteristics of a monopoly. The economic motivation for regulation of markets in general is then discussed. Three general types of market failure are highlighted as arguments for government intervention in airline markets; these are externalities, information asymmetries and market power. However, these economic arguments for intervention have not been part of the traditional defense of airline regulation. The intention of regulation may have been to serve the public interest in some cases, but private or rent-seeking motives may well explain its persistence. Many of the regulatory institutions were eventually regarded as inadequate; the shape of subsequent reforms, which were generally designed to introduce competition in airline markets, is discussed as a background to the analysis.

The remainder of the book consists of two parts. In Part I (Chapters 3–6), explicit attention has been devoted to the economic value of the environmental external effects in airline markets. Using these results, the effects of regulatory change on firm behavior, market outcomes and economic welfare have been evaluated in Part II (Chapters 7–10).

Chapter 3 begins with a discussion of the concept of externalities and its relevance in the context of air transport. First, the definition of externalities and their relation to causes of market failure are explored. Next, externalities in air transport markets are examined. Like other transport modes, air transport imposes several types of negative external effects upon society. While the share of aviation in global environmental pollution is currently small, this share is growing steadily due to the high growth rates in airline markets. Furthermore, the environmental pressures of air transport may be very intense locally, as can be illustrated by public debate surrounding airport expansion, which stresses the social relevance of considering resource misallocation associated with environmental externalities in aviation. In order to estimate external costs as a function of output on transport markets, it is necessary to analyze a cause–effect chain that links output to external costs via impacts on ambient conditions. The endpoints of such a chain are goods, e.g., health or quiet, for which a monetary value can be established by means of economic valuation.

Chapters 4 and 5 concern the valuation of endpoints in relation to ambient conditions. Chapter 4 studies the valuation of aircraft noise and reviews the results of two types of valuation studies. A series of noise cost estimates from hedonic price studies is used in a meta-analysis, which explains a measure of the variation in estimates using, among other factors, the timing and specification of the original noise studies. An absolute noise cost is derived and compared with results from noise studies using the contingent valuation method. As expected, noise cost estimates according to the latter type of study are higher than the hedonic price estimates. Chapter 4 thus presents two broad levels of noise costs based on distinct valuation methods, both of which are used as alternatives in the evaluation.

In Chapter 5, two environmental cost pathways related to aircraft emissions are explored. First, the costs associated with the so-called 'greenhouse effect' are assessed. The calculation of marginal greenhouse damages is discussed and recent estimates of these damages are reviewed. This review yields a range of damage estimates with some suggestions for sensitivity analysis. Secondly, the effects of local concentrations of pollutants on human health are studied. In this case, mortality and morbidity are addressed as 'endpoints', for which valuation results are available in the economics literature; the size of physical impacts is obtained from epidemiological studies. The results presented in Chapter 5 allow for the calculation of damage costs for a range of aircraft emissions. As in the case of noise, the range of values is used to derive alternative environmental cost estimates to be used in the evaluation.

Chapter 6 presents calculations of noise and emission damages for a number of aircraft types. In order to accomplish this, the link between ambient noise and air pollution conditions and emissions by these aircraft types is investigated. An average noise cost per landing and take-off cycle is established through the use of a statistical analysis of the relation between the number of noise victims and airport departures for a set of European airports. In addition, based on the relative noise impact of a number of aircraft categories, the noise costs per aircraft type are estimated. The damages per aircraft type associated with local air pollution are calculated for the landing and take-off cycle using aircraft emission data on the one hand, and the relation between ambient concentrations and boundary layer emissions on the other. Estimates of costs associated with accident risk are obtained from the literature. Adding the cost estimates allows one to calculate environmental damages for a number of aircraft types. The results are obtained by combining endpoint valuations with simple representations of the relation between output and ambient conditions. The central estimates and sensitivity analyses provide a measure of environmental damage for each of the aircraft types. The results in Chapter 6 are used as an input to the analyses of regulatory reform in Part II.

Part II concerns the measurement of welfare changes associated with regulatory reform, with an empirical focus on the European Union. In Chapters 7–10, the welfare effect of reform or liberalization is measured as the welfare difference between a competitive oligopoly solution on the one hand and a monopoly (cartel) solution on the other.

In Chapter 7, a basic 'address' model of spatial competition is introduced. The airline market is modeled as a circle on which consumers are distributed uniformly with respect to preferred departure time; thus schedule delay costs are part of the consumer utility function. A model of consumer and firm behavior is subsequently presented, and market equilibria in both prices and departure frequencies are derived. Based on alternative assumptions regarding airline behavior, a number of solutions is investigated in this chapter. In particular, a symmetric mono-departure zero-profit equilibrium and a symmetric multi-departure oligopoly equilibrium are derived. A comparison of results between economic regimes reveals that, since profits are strictly lower under competition than under monopoly, a change from monopoly to competition always results in an increase in departure frequency, implying an increase in environmental costs. Furthermore, parameter conditions for a decrease in equilibrium prices and an increase in consumer surplus are derived. It turns out that a fare decrease is a sufficient condition for an improvement in consumer surplus.

Subsequently, the derivation and substitution of parameters and calculation of welfare differences between regulatory regimes are presented in Chapter 8. Market outcomes under competition are simulated and compared with actual outcomes for a sample of regulated routes. The calculations present an estimate of the welfare effect of introducing competition on these routes, under alternative modeling assumptions and competitive conditions. First, a numerical analysis conforming to the model assumptions in Chapter 7, consumer homogeneity and symmetric equilibria, is performed. The results for the route markets studied indicate that consumer welfare increases significantly due to the introduction of competition. Environmental costs per passenger rise too because of increases in departure frequencies, while producers incur considerable profit losses, which outweigh the gains to consumers in the inelastic demand model. The analysis is extended in order to assess results under alternative assumptions. In the case of elastic demand, the decrease in firm profits is mitigated, and the sum of average profit losses and environmental cost increases is compensated by the increase in consumer welfare. This result is qualitatively insensitive to variations in the environmental cost estimates using the range of values identified in Part I.

Also, asymmetric equilibria are introduced as an extension to the basic symmetric model, reflecting airline strategies to moderate price competition. An analysis of duopoly markets shows that allowing for asymmetry in the frequency equilibrium does not alter the positive conclusion with respect to consumer welfare. However, the negative effects of liberalization on firm profits are smaller in this case.

Finally, the effect of introducing competition in a small airline network is analyzed in Chapter 9. Numerical results indicate that for both types of networks, the introduction of competition in part of the network has a positive effect on aggregate consumer welfare, but that losses are incurred by consumers in transfer markets. Furthermore, industry profit decreases. The one-hub model and the two-hub model differ in aggregate welfare effects of regulatory reform. In the one-hub case the positive consumer surplus effect dominates the profit loss; in the two-hub case the profit loss dominates, so that the result is a net welfare decrease.

Part II concludes with a statistical analysis in Chapter 10. Here, a data set with information on 34 European interstate routes and their endpoints is used to analyze empirically the effect of a change in liberalization status. To this end, a demand equation, a fare equation and a frequency equation are estimated. The fare equation reveals that standard economy fares on routes subject to full bilateral liberalization are 34 percent lower than on routes without such liberalization, while the estimated frequency equation shows that liberalization causes a 'direct' increase of about 36 percent in departures. Furthermore, an indirect effect on frequency of 33 percent is calculated, which is due to the demand increase following the negative effect of liberalization on fares. Using the estimated demand equation, the resulting average change in consumer surplus is estimated at 346 ECU per passenger on the liberalized routes (baseline estimate). In order to estimate the environmental cost, the information on the aircraft types used on the routes and the cost estimates per aircraft type per flight presented in Chapter 6 are used. Based on the estimated changes, both direct and indirect, in departure frequency, the average change in environmental cost due to airline liberalization is an estimated 22 ECU per passenger. This estimate is based on the medium environmental valuation; the sum rises to 119 ECU per passenger for the high variant of the environmental valuation. The welfare analysis in Chapter 10 does not address all welfare changes, since the effects on firm profits have not been taken into account. However, the net effect of the changes in consumer welfare and environmental costs in this empirical study are positive.

In Part II, theoretical models are used to analyze the effects of changes in airline regulation. Reduced-form welfare expressions allow for a comparison of welfare differences in a number of cases. The theoretical analysis was extended and complemented by introducing data for a number of European airline markets. In a sense, such an empirical focus limits the generality of the conclusions that may be drawn. However, it has been shown that the sample represents a variety of route market types. Therefore, keeping in mind the notion that other data would alter the results quantitatively, one may conjecture that the analysis here yields a number of qualitative policy conclusions which are quite general.

11.2 Looking ahead: implications for policy and research

Environmental damage represents one of the failures in airline markets, imposing increasing pressures on society. Although policy makers often encounter the trade-off between market internal benefits of expansion in air transport versus the social costs of noise at the local level in particular, the less directly felt effects of aircraft emissions may result in damages of comparable size. Furthermore, projected growth rates in airline markets suggest that these problems are likely to gain in prominence in the future. It has been argued in this book that in order to deal with these problems in an economically efficient way, policy makers should take into account the costs to society of these environmental pressures in monetary terms.

The application of such monetary values to air transport policy making provides a way towards an economically sensible resource allocation, and may substitute ad-hoc policy rules that often result in acrimonious and protracted public debate. This is the reason why the monetary valuation of environmental externalities has received a prominent place in this study.

Fortunately, scientific progress in a number of disciplines that study the various effects about which knowledge is needed to obtain monetary values allows for the calculation of resource costs at a disaggregate level. Therefore, the data on which economically sound policy could be based are, in principle, available. However, given the often large differences among estimates, one should be aware of the decisions underlying the variation in results in order to choose the appropriate values and policy prescriptions. The issue of choosing between alternative estimates remains largely unresolved in this study. However, by pointing to the decisions involved in deriving the alternative value estimates, the differences between the low, medium and high estimates presented in Chapter 6 are analyzed. With these valuation results in hand, diverse as they may be, it is possible to evaluate the social impact of policies which, directly or indirectly, affect the environment.

In this study, environmental cost estimates are used in an ex-post welfare evaluation of the effects of regulatory reform in aviation. The following conclusions apply. The policy of introducing airline competition in markets where such competition was previously restricted yields consumer benefits of considerable size. The transition from monopoly to competition, however, leads to an expansion of operations in airline markets, representing increased environmental costs. Also, producer surplus decreases as a result of liberalization. The research presented in this book indicates, however, that the welfare gains due to regulatory reform compensate both the increase in noise and emission costs and the lowering of profits that accompany such a transition. Therefore, even in the presence of environmental costs, the introduction of competition in airline markets results in a welfare improvement and is thus desirable from the viewpoint of allocative efficiency.

An important result in Part II is that the welfare conclusions are qualitatively insensitive to the choice of the environmental value estimates. This is a significant finding with respect to the evaluation of airline liberalization: even when all parameters in the valuation pathways considered here are set at their highest – i.e., environmentally most damaging – levels, the welfare conclusion remains positive. In the simple terms of Figure 1.1, the triangle xyz has turned out to be larger than the rectangle $vyzw$.

A different question, beyond the scope of this study, concerns policy in aviation markets once these markets have been liberalized. Does the competitive equilibrium represent a welfare optimum or are improvements possible through economic policy? In particular, one might be interested to know whether the environmental externalities that have been identified and valued can be corrected, e.g. through Pigouvian taxation. The results in Chapter 7 show that the departure frequency under competition is always, even in the absence of environmental costs, higher than the optimal frequency. This conclusion suggests that a positive tax on landings and take-offs would be socially desirable, a policy which is even more recommendable where environmental costs are present.

However, it should be noted that the design of an environmental tax should also take account of the other market failure at hand, namely, market power. Given the existing monopoly or oligopoly power in airline markets, firms produce too little at too high prices. When both market power and externalities are present, an optimal output tax trades off the welfare effects of the two market failures. Whether a positive output tax prevails depends on the demand elasticity and the external cost function. In terms of Figure 1.1, the sign of the tax depends on whether output is socially too high or too low at q_c; in other words, is the sum of externality victims' WTP for a reduction in airline output larger or smaller than the sum of air travelers' WTP for avoiding such a reduction?

It is noted that a large literature concerning this issue exists. An early contribution simply states that, under particular circumstances, environmental charges equal to marginal damage lower welfare when imposed on a monopolist (Buchanan, 1969). Later contributions to the literature on environmental taxation in imperfect markets have concentrated on the welfare optimal adjustments with respect to the basic Pigouvian tax under imperfect competition. For example, the design of a welfare-maximizing tax in the case of a monopolistic polluter is presented in Barnett (1980), who concludes that the second-best optimal tax rate is in general less than marginal damage and may be negative. The general approach has been extended to other forms of imperfect competition, in particular to symmetric Cournot oligopoly, in Ebert (1991) and Katsoulacos and Xepapadeas (1996). A general conclusion emerging from these selected contributions is that the 'simple' Pigouvian output tax (equal to marginal external damages) should be adjusted downwards in the cases of monopoly and fixed-number oligopoly in order to account for the output distortion.[95]

The other market failure addressed in this study is market power. In this area policy may be needed to improve or safeguard (consumer) welfare too. For example, the analysis in Chapter 8 indicates that consumer welfare under free entry is higher than consumer welfare under fixed-number oligopoly solutions, whether they be symmetric or asymmetric departure configurations. Therefore, the supervision of entry conditions by competition authorities as is currently carried out by the European Commission is in the interest of consumers. Also, it has been mentioned that 'symmetry' in frequency competition is better for consumers than 'asymmetry'. Thus, the degree of oligopoly concentration in terms of departures is an important variable determining competitive conditions at the route level.

---

[95] It should be noted, however, that these conclusions depend on the assumption that firms respond to the environmental fee, at least partly, by reducing output. Where only 'waste treatment' is used to abate pollution, the tax should equal marginal environmental damage (e.g. Barnett, 1980; Endres, 1978).

The above issues point to possible directions for further research. One aspect of airline competition which has not been addressed explicitly here is the problem of departure time choice by airlines, particularly in cases where demand is not uniformly distributed.   Given the possibilities for anti-competitive behavior, particularly in network settings, modeling these issues may yield relevant insights for competition policy.   However, it is clear that the extra detail and realism in modeling comes at a cost: as has been shown in certain cases in this book, analytical solutions may not be feasible if realistic details are added to the models. Nevertheless, the use of insights obtained in more abstract models may better clarify the results of simulation experiments based on more elaborate models. For the latter type of approach, powerful programming languages are available and provide a useful extension to the economist's toolbox. Therefore, the combination of relatively simple as well as more complex representations of reality seems worthwhile in future research.

Another area where future research efforts can improve the results is the estimation of external costs in aviation. First, cost calculations presented in Part I are based on ongoing research in various parts of the pathways. In all of these parts of the environmental cost estimation, results may be improved upon by continuing research efforts. In particular, the costs associated with aviation-specific environmental effects at high altitudes deserve detailed attention.

Also, a number of external cost items have not been covered here: since scarce airport capacity is in many cases not priced, congestion problems are often not attended to in airline markets. These intrasectoral external costs could be taken into account in future analysis.   The anti-competitive implications have been discussed briefly here; the general topic deserves detailed treatment as, e.g., in the references concerning the efficient pricing of airport slots mentioned in Chapter 2.

Furthermore, congestion at airports has an indirect effect on other types of external costs: airside congestion adds to noise, fuel use and the emission of pollutants because aircraft fly longer routes, queue on taxiways and circle airports waiting to land. Another issue is road traffic congestion and associated environmental problems like air pollution caused by increased air travel. This problem refers to a more general issue in the design of the present study, which has made use of partial equilibrium analysis only. As the problem of congestion on roads to and from airports makes clear, transport markets are related. Other ways in which markets interact is competition between transport modes, which is relevant on shorter distances. These interactions between markets provide an extensive and interesting area for future research.

The correction of market failure through tax policy has already been highlighted above. A separate issue is the feasibility of optimal taxation, i.e., whether national governments are able to implement an optimal tax.   When governments do not coordinate tax policy at a supranational level, the optimal tax is not likely to be arrived at. Also, the effectiveness of economic instruments should be compared with current quantitative restrictions such as night curfews and measures such as government noise insulation schemes.

The list of interesting topics relevant to the subject but not addressed here is undoubtedly longer than the one suggested. It is hoped that the analysis and results in this book shed some light on the questions posed in Chapter 1, and meanwhile, through the unanswered questions, stimulate future research in an area which is highly relevant, both to science and society.

Appendix A
Proof of the Positive Frequency Effect

From the first part of (7.30), $\Pi^m > \Pi^{SSME}$, one can derive the parameter condition:

$$D > d_1 = \frac{1}{2}\left(a^2 + 2b + a\sqrt{a^2 + 4b}\right) \tag{A.1}$$

where

$$a = \left(\sqrt{\frac{n}{n-1}} - \sqrt{\frac{n-1}{n}}\right)\frac{2\sqrt{\theta}c^f}{\bar{v} - c^p} \tag{A.2}$$

and

$$b = \frac{2\theta c^f}{(\bar{v} - c^p)^2} \tag{A.3}$$

Further, it can be shown that the condition on the frequency difference $f^{SSME} - f^m > 0$ holds for

$$D > d_2 = \frac{n}{n-1}\frac{\theta}{c^f(\bar{v} - c^p)^2} \tag{A.4}$$

Thus, given (A.1), (A.4) holds if $d_1 - d_2 > 0$. It can now be shown that

$$d_1 - d_2 = \frac{2\theta c^f}{(\bar{v} - c^p)^2}\left[1 + \left(z^2 + z\sqrt{(z^2 + 2)}\right) - \frac{n}{2(n-1)c^f}\right] \tag{A.5}$$

where

$$z = \sqrt{\frac{n}{n-1}} - \sqrt{\frac{n-1}{n}} \tag{A.6}$$

Consider the three terms in square brackets in (A.5). The third term tends to zero for large c^f and $n \geq 2$. The second term is close to -0.62 for $n = 2$, and increases in n. The complete expression in square brackets in (A.5) is therefore positive, and so is the term outside the square brackets. Therefore, $d_1 - d_2 > 0$, and thus $f^{SSME} - f^m > 0$, QED.

Appendix B
Data and Calibration

The numerical analysis aims to evaluate the policy process of regulatory reform in aviation. To this end, the welfare expressions belonging to each of the competitive regimes are compared with welfare in the regulated (monopoly) regime. As shown in Chapter 7, a set of seven parameters is needed in order to perform the evaluation. The procedure is similar to that used by Norman and Strandenes (1994). First, the demand parameters are calibrated using observations and the equilibrium choice expressions derived in Chapter 7. In the present analysis, 1990 data for a set of regulated European interstate routes are used. These routes are a subset from the sample used in Chapters 6 and 10; the complete sample has been selected in order to represent various traffic densities, stage lengths and regulatory status in European interstate aviation. Data on the regulated routes are presented in Table A.1.[96] The three relevant demand parameters for the inelastic demand case are density D, gross valuation $\bar{v}$ and schedule delay cost θ.[97]

These routes are considered regulated routes, because they had not been subject to bilateral liberalization, while the block exemptions with respect to joint capacity planning, revenue sharing and fare consultations had not yet been eliminated by 1990 (see Chapter 2). Therefore, the data are considered to represent a (joint) monopoly equilibrium. The three demand parameters can now be solved. Using the fact that the whole market is covered under monopoly, the total number of passengers is equal to density D. Further, by substituting the data in Table A.1 in the equations representing the monopoly price and frequency equilibrium choices (see Section 7.3) and solving for the two remaining unknowns $\bar{v}$ and θ, the three parameters are obtained for each route.

Secondly, four parameters concerning the cost side are needed, namely, passenger costs c^p, departure costs c^f, fixed route costs F and environmental costs per flight ε. These cost parameters are derived using a second set of data concerning the aircraft types used on the routes. On most routes, more than one type of aircraft is used; e.g., on the first route, Athens–Brussels, Boeings 727-200, 737-200 and 737-300 were flown. The different aircraft represent both varying operating costs and, as shown in Chapter 6, varying noise and emission costs. Furthermore, the different aircraft sizes represent different seat capacities. Using

---

[96] Data are from the OAG *World Airways Guide* and ICAO *Digest of Statistics* (series TF). Here and in the following, only scheduled traffic is analyzed. All figures concern one-way transport from the indicated origin to the destination. The weekly figures have been obtained by dividing the yearly figures by 52. Furthermore, it has been assumed that origin–destination traffic equals destination–origin traffic.

[97] The 'length' or perimeter of the circular market L is still equal to 1. Here, L is taken to represent a period of one week, implying that all time-related variables such as frequency are expressed relative to this period.

the share of each type in total operations per route, a weighted average of aircraft capacity was constructed for each route.

The environmental cost parameters are obtained using the estimates in Chapter 6. Taking into account the flight distance and aircraft types used, (average) environmental costs per flight could be calculated for each route. The market internal cost parameters per route are derived from airline-specific cost figures from ICAO and IATA publications (IATA, 1990; ICAO, 1990). From these figures, the average total operating expenses per available ton-kilometer (ATK) per route for the operators for which 1990 data were available were obtained. From this figure, the total operating cost per route was obtained by using information on the aircraft types used on the route, the route distance and the number of operations.

Table A.1
Sample of EU interstate routes (1990)

Routes		Pass/ week	Departures/ week	Y-fare (ECU)
1	Athens–Brussels	1357	16	374
2	Athens–Frankfurt	2677	23	335
3	Athens–Lisbon	176	2	438
4	Athens–London	4463	26	417
5	Barcelona–Brussels	1201	22	353
6	Barcelona–Lisbon	510	7	255
7	Madrid–Brussels	1596	27	422
8	Madrid–Lisbon	3156	36	175
9	Milan–Brussels	2624	37	359
10	Milan–Frankfurt	4206	54	235
11	Milan–Lisbon	907	10	448
12	Paris–Brussels	3756	73	165
13	Paris–Lisbon	2659	20	466
14	Stockholm–Brussels	834	18	436
15	Stockholm–Frankfurt	1752	27	386
16	Stockholm–Lisbon	134	2	702
17	Stockholm–London	4721	60	406
18	Vienna–Brussels	642	13	413
19	Vienna–Frankfurt	4661	60	272
20	Vienna–Lisbon	67	1	693
21	Vienna–London	3400	40	435

Total operating costs (TOC) represent a range of cost items, which for present purposes should be categorized as fixed (F), frequency dependent (c^f) or passenger dependent (c^p). In order to allocate the total operating expenses to the three cost categories, the British Airways breakdown of cost items (Doganis, 1991) is used. In this breakdown (for 1988), the categories Indirect Operating Costs (IOC), Fixed Direct Operating Costs (FDOC) and Variable Direct Operating Costs (VDOC) are distinguished. These categories differ in the 'escapability' of costs, i.e., the time period needed before a particular cost can be avoided, and can therefore be used to fit the time structure in the simulation models. IOC include station and ground expenses, general and administrative costs, sales, ticketing and promotion costs. These costs (41.5 percent of TOC) are fixed in the medium and short term and a part of them represents the fixed costs associated with route entry. Two issues have to be addressed when translating indirect costs to the parameter F. First, there are two principal ways to treat the IOC: they can be allocated either fully or partly to each route entry. In the former case, it is assumed that marginal IOC are equal to average IOC for each route; in the latter case marginal route IOC are lower than average IOC. An argument for allocating only part of the IOC is that a number of IOC items, e.g. 'general and administrative costs' and 'station and ground expenses', are associated with entry into the industry rather than with route entry. On the other hand, returns to network size have been demonstrated to be constant in empirical studies (Caves et al., 1984), a finding that has been explained by the presence of considerable fixed route entry expenses when a route is added to a network (Tretheway and Oum, 1992). Based on the two arguments, IOC items are allocated for 50 percent to the parameter F. Furthermore, many IOC items such as ground expenses and administrative costs may be assumed not to vary much with route distance or capacity. However, because the cost data are in ATK terms, the IOC cost totals differ over routes. In order not to let this affect the results, it is assumed that the fixed route costs are equal across routes. In conclusion, the parameter F has been calculated as the average over all routes of 50 percent of the estimated aggregate IOC on these routes.

FDOC are operating costs that depend on airlines' schedules, and are therefore only escapable in the medium term, i.e., through a change in schedules. Because of the relation with schedules, this category of costs is part of the frequency-dependent costs. A number of items from the VDOC also fits into this category, namely, flight and cabin crew variable expenses, fuel costs and airport charges. Together, these cost items correspond to the flight-related costs represented by the parameter c^f, which amounts to 50 percent of TOC. Thirdly, passenger-related costs are meals, handling fees and other passenger expenses. This category, corresponding to the parameter c^p, amounts to 8.5 percent of TOC. In order to derive the absolute cost figures needed in the calculations, the TOC per route was allocated to the fixed route costs, flight-related costs and passenger-related costs using the indicated shares. Consequently, F corresponds to the total for the first category, while c^f and c^p are calculated as the averages for the second and third category respectively.

Appendix C
Sign of the Frequency–Price Derivatives

Consider the second-stage price solutions in equation (8.10). Taking derivatives and simplifying, the derivatives of the second-stage Nash price solutions with respect to the own and competitor's frequency choice for firm 1 and 2 are, respectively

$$\frac{\partial p_1^*}{\partial f_1} = \frac{\theta}{3(f_1 + f_2)^2} > 0 \tag{C.1}$$

$$\tag{C.2}$$

$$\frac{\partial p_1^*}{\partial f_2} = -\frac{2f_1^2 + 4f_1 f_2 + f_2^2}{3f_2^2(f_1 + f_2)^2} < 0 \tag{C.3}$$

$$\tag{C.4}$$

$$\frac{\partial p_2^*}{\partial f_2} = -\frac{\theta}{3(f_1 + f_2)^2} < 0 \tag{C.5}$$

$$\tag{C.6}$$

$$\frac{\partial p_2^*}{\partial f_1} = -\frac{f_1^2 + 2f_1 f_2 + 2f_2^2}{3f_2^2(f_1 + f_2)^2} < 0 \tag{C.7}$$

Therefore, observing that $f_1 \geq f_2$, we conclude that

$$\frac{\partial p_1^*}{\partial f_2} < \frac{\partial p_2^*}{\partial f_1} \tag{C.8}$$

Appendix D
Sign of Airline 2's Profit Derivative

Using the profit function of airline 2, after substitution of the second-stage price solutions, one can derive

$$\frac{\partial \Pi_2}{\partial f_2} = -\frac{D \left(f_1^3 + 3f_1^2 f_2 + 4f_1 f_2^2 + 4f_2^3 \right) \theta}{9f_2^2 (f_1 + f_2)^3} - c^f < 0 \qquad \text{(D.1)}$$

Bibliography

Abbott, K. and D. Thompson (1991), De-regulating European aviation: the impact of bilateral liberalisation. *International Journal of Industrial Organization*, 9, 125–140.

Abelson, P.W. (1979), Property prices and the value of amenities. *Journal of Environmental Economics and Management*, 6 (March), 11–28.

ACI (1997), *Yearbook.* Airports Council International, Brussels.

AEA (1988–1993), *Yearbook, Statistical Appendices.* Association of European Airlines, Brussels.

Anderson, S.P., A. de Palma and J.-F. Thisse (1992), *Discrete Choice Theory of Product Differentiation.* Cambridge, MA, MIT Press.

Archer, L.J. (1993), *Aircraft Emissions and the Environment: CO_x, SO_x, HO_x & NO_x.* Oxford Institute for Energy Studies.

Azar, C. and T. Sterner (1996), Discounting and distributional considerations in the context of global warming. *Ecological Economics*, 19, 169–184.

Baarsma, B. (2000), *Monetary Valuation of Environmental Goods: Alternatives to Contingent Valuation.* Universiteit van Amsterdam/Tinbergen Instituut, Thesis Publishers, Amsterdam.

Bailey, Elizabeth and J. Panzar (1981), The contestability of airline markets during the transition to deregulation. *Law and Contemporary Problems*, 44, 125–145.

Banister, D. and K.J. Button (1991, eds), *Transport in a Free Market Economy.* Macmillan, London.

Barnett, A.H. (1980), The Pigouvian tax rule under monopoly. *American Economic Review*, 70, 1037–1041.

Barrett, S.D. (1992), Barriers to contestability in the deregulated European aviation market. *Transportation Research*, 26A(2), 159–165.

Baumol, William J. (1982), Contestable markets: an uprising in the theory of industry structure. *American Economic Review*, 72(1), 1–15.

Baumol, W.J. and W.E. Oates (1988), *The Theory of Environmental Policy.* Cambridge University Press.

Beesley, M.E. (1986), Commitment, sunk costs, and entry to the airline industry. *Journal of Transport Economics and Policy*, May, 173–190.

Bensaid, B. and A. de Palma (1994), *Spatial Multiproduct Oligopoly.* University of Geneva, Technical Report 1994.8.

Berechman, J. and J. de Wit (1996), An analysis of the effects of European aviation deregulation on an airline's network structure and choice of a primary West European hub airport. *Journal of Transport Economics and Policy*, 30(3), 251–274.

Berechman, J., S. Poddar and O. Shy (1995), *Network Structure and Entry in the Deregulated Airline Industry.* CORE Discussion Paper 9464, Louvain-la-

Neuve.

Van den Bergh, J. and K.J. Button (1997), Meta-analysis of environmental issues in regional, urban and transport economics. *Urban Studies*, 34(5–6), 927–944.

Blaylock, J. (1977), *Airport Noise and Housing Values: An Investigation into the Hedonic Theory of Housing and the Value of Quiet*. Ph.D. thesis, Texas A&M University.

Bleijenberg, A.N., M.D. Davidson and R.C.N. Wit (1998), *The Price of Pollution*. Centre for Energy Conservation and Environmental Technology, Delft.

Bleijenberg, A.N. and R.C.N. Wit (1997), *A European Environmental Aviation Charge: Feasibility Study*. Centre for Energy Conservation and Environmental Technology, Delft.

Bleijenberg, A.N., W.J. van den Berg and G. de Wit (1994), *Maatschappelijke Kosten van het Verkeer: Literatuuroverzicht*. Centre for Energy Conservation and Environmental Technology, Delft.

Borenstein, S. (1992), The evolution of US airline competition. *Journal of Economic Perspectives*, 6(2), 45–73.

Brander, J.A. and A. Zhang (1990), Market conduct in the airline industry: an empirical investigation. *Rand Journal of Economics*, 21(4), 567–583.

Brouwer, R., I. Langford, I. Bateman, T. Crowards and R. Turner (1997), *A Meta-analysis of Wetland Contingent Valuation Studies*. CSERGE Working Paper GEC 97-20.

Brueckner, J.K. and P.T. Spiller (1991), Competition and mergers in airline networks. *International Journal of Industrial Organization*, 9, 323–342.

Bryson, B. (1994), *Made in America*. Minerva, London.

Buchanan, J.M. (1969), External diseconomies, corrective taxes, and market structure. *American Economic Review*, 59, 174–177.

Button, K.J. (1999), The usefulness of current air transport statistics. *Journal of Transportation and Statistics*, May, 71–89.

Button, K.J. (1994), Privatisation and deregulation, its implications for negative transport externalities. *The Annals of Regional Science*, 28, 125–138.

Button, K.J. (1993), *Transport, the Environment and Economic Policy*. Edward Elgar, Aldershot.

Button, K.J. (1991, ed.), *Airline Deregulation: International Experiences*. David Fulton Publishers, London.

Button, K.J. (1990), Environmental externalities and transport policy. *Oxford Review of Economic Policy*, 6(2), 61–75.

Button, K.J. and D. Swann (1991), Aviation policy in Europe. In K.J. Button (ed.), *Airline Deregulation, International Experiences*, David Fulton, London.

Button, K.J. and D. Swann (1989), European Community airlines – deregulation and its problems. *Journal of Common Market Studies*, 27(4), 259–282.

Button, K.J., K. Haynes and R. Stough (1998), *Flying into the Future: Air*

Transport Policy in the European Union. Edward Elgar, Cheltenham.

Card, D. and A. Krueger (1995), Time-series minimum-wage studies: a meta-analysis. *American Economic Review*, 85(2), 238–243.

Caves, Douglas W., Laurits R. Christensen and Michael W. Tretheway (1984), Economies of density versus economies of scale: why trunk and local service airline costs differ. *Rand Journal of Economics*, 15(4), 471–489.

Chestnut, L.G., B.D. Ostro and N. Vichit-Vadakan (1997), Transferability of air pollution control health benefits estimates from the United States to developing countries: evidence from the Bangkok study. *American Journal of Agricultural Economics*, 79(5), 1630–1635.

Cline, W.R. (1992), *The Economics of Global Warming.* Institute for International Economics, Washington DC.

Coase, R.H. (1960), The problem of social cost. *Journal of Law and Economics*, 3, 1–44.

d'Aspremont, C., J. Gabszewicz and J.-F. Thisse (1979), On Hotelling's stability in competition. *Econometrica*, 47, 1045–1050.

Dameris, M., V. Grewe, I. Köhler, R. Sausen, C. Brühl, J.-U. Grooß and B. Steil (1998a), Impact of aircraft NO_x emissions on tropospheric and stratospheric ozone. Part II: 3-D model results. *Atmospheric Environment*, 32(19), 3185–3199.

Dameris, M., V. Grewe, R. Hein and C. Schnadt (1998b), Assessment of the future development of the ozone layer. *Geophysical Research Letters*, 25(19), 3579–3582.

De Vany, A.S. (1976), An economic model of airport noise pollution in an urban environment. In S.A.Y. Lin (ed.), *Theory and Measurement of Economic Externalities.* Academic Press, New York.

Diamond, P.A. and J. Hausman (1994), Contingent valuation: is some number better than no number? *Journal of Economic Perspectives*, 8(4), 45–64.

Dobson, G. and P.J. Lederer (1993), Airline scheduling and routing in a hub-and-spoke system. *Transportation Science*, 27(3), 281–297.

Dodgson, J.S. (1994), Competition policy and the liberalisation of European aviation. *Transportation*, 21, 335–370.

Dodgson, J.S., Y. Katsoulacos and C.R. Newton (1993), An application of the economic modelling approach to the investigation of predation. *Journal of Transport Economics and Policy*, 27(2), 153–170.

Doganis, R. (1991), *Flying Off Course: The Economics of International Airlines.* Routledge, New York.

Dorland, K. and X. Olsthoorn (1998), *Environmental Costs of Transport. The ExternE Methodology Applied in Dutch Case Studies.* Mimeo, Institute for Environmental Studies, Vrije Universiteit Amsterdam.

Dresner, M. and M.W. Tretheway (1992), Modelling and testing the effect of market structure on price: the case of international air transport. *Journal of Transport Economics and Policy*, 26(2), 171–184.

Dygert, P.K. (1973), *Estimation of the Cost of Aircraft Noise to Residual Activities.* Unpublished Ph.D. dissertation, University of Michigan.

Ebert, U. (1991), Pigouvian tax and market structure. *FinanzArchiv*, 49(2), 154–166.

Economides, N. (1989), Symmetric equilibrium existence and optimality in differentiated product markets. *Journal of Economic Theory*, 47, 178–194.

Emerson, F.C. (1972), Valuation of residential amenities: an econometric approach. *Appraisal Journal*, 40, 268–278.

Encaoua, D., M. Moreaux and A. Perrot (1996), Compatibility and competition in airlines – demand side network effects. *International Journal of Industrial Organization*, 14, 701–726.

Endres, A. (1978), Monopoly-power as a means for pollution-control? *Journal of Industrial Economics*, 27(2), 185–187.

European Commission (EC, 1999), *ExternE: Externalities of Energy, Methodology.* EC, DGXII, Science, Research and Development/JOULE, Luxembourg.

European Commission (EC, 1995), *ExternE: Externalities of Energy, Vol. 2, Methodology.* EC, DGXII, Science, Research and Development/JOULE, Luxembourg.

Eurostat (1998), *EU Transport in Figures, Statistical Pocketbook.* Office for Official Publications of the European Communities, Luxembourg.

Evans, A. (1987), A theoretical comparison of competition with other economic regimes for bus services. *Journal of Transport Economics and Policy*, 21(1), 7–36.

van Ewijk, C. (1997), Luchtvaart en welvaart. In Project Toekomstige Nederlandse Luchtvaart Infrastructuur, *Hoeveel Ruimte geeft Nederland aan de Luchtvaart, deel 2: Economie en Procedure.* TNLI, Den Haag.

Eyre, N.J., E. Ozdemiroglu, D.W. Pearce and P. Steele (1997), Fuel and location effects on the damage costs of transport emissions. *Journal of Transport Economics and Policy*, 31(1), 5–24.

Fankhauser, S. (1992), *Global Warming Damage Costs: Some Monetary Estimates*, working paper GEC 92, CSERGE, London/Norwich.

Feitelson, E.I., R.E. Hurd and R.R. Mudge (1996), The impact of aircraft noise on willingness to pay for residences. *Transportation Research*, 1D(1), 1–14.

Florax, R. (1992), *The University: A Regional Booster?* Avebury, Aldershot.

Forsyth, P. (1991), The regulation and deregulation of Australia's domestic airline industry. In K.J. Button (ed.), *Airline Deregulation: International Experiences.* David Fulton, London.

FPC (1998), *Emission Charges and Taxes in Aviation.* Report of the Focal Point on Charges, prepared for CAEP/4. Ministry of Transport, The Hague.

Freeman, A.M. III (1997), Externalities, prices and taxes: second best issues in transportation. In D.L. Greene, D.W. Jones and M.A. Delucchi (eds), *The Full Costs and Benefits of Transportation. Contributions to Theory, Method and Measurement.* Springer-Verlag, Berlin.

Freeman, A.M. III (1993), *The Measurement of Environmental and Resource Values: Theory and Method.* Resources for the Future, Washington, DC.

Friedman, J.W. (1983), *Oligopoly Theory.* Cambridge University Press, Cambridge.

Gibbons, R. (1992), *A Primer in Game Theory.* Harvester Wheatsheaf, Hemel Hempstead.

Gravelle, H. and R. Rees (1992), *Microeconomics.* Longman, New York.

Greene, D.L., D.W. Jones and M.A. Delucchi (1997, eds), *The Full Costs and Benefits of Transportation. Contributions to Theory, Method and Measurement.* Springer-Verlag, Berlin.

Greenhut, J., G. Norman and M.L. Greenhut (1991), Financial economic aspects of airline deregulation. *International Journal of Transport Economics*, 18(1), 3–30.

Greenhut, M.L., G. Norman and C.-S. Hung (1987), *The Economics of Imperfect Competition: A Spatial Approach.* Cambridge University Press, Cambridge.

Grossman, G.M. and E. Helpman (1994), Protection for sale. *American Economic Review*, 84(4), 833–850.

Hanemann, W.M. (1994), Valuing the environment through contingent valuation. *Journal of Economic Perspectives*, 8(4), 19–43.

Heaver, T. (1991), Transportation deregulation and privatisation in Canada: the forces for change. In D. Banister and K.J. Button (eds), *Transport in a Free Market Economy.* Macmillan, London.

Hedges, L.V. and I. Olkin (1985), *Statistical Methods for Meta-Analysis.* Academic Press, Orlando.

Heller, W.P. and D.A. Starret (1976), On the nature of externalities. In S.A.Y. Lin (ed.), *Theory and Measurement of Economic Externalities.* New York, Academic Press.

Hensher, D.A. (1997), Behavioral value of travel time savings in personal and commercial automobile travel. In D.L. Greene, D.W. Jones and M.A. Delucchi (eds), *The Full Costs and Benefits of Transportation. Contributions to Theory, Method and Measurement.* Springer-Verlag, Berlin.

Hoevenagel, R. (1994), *The Contingent Valuation Method: Scope and Validity.* Ph.D. thesis, Vrije Universiteit/IVM, Amsterdam.

IATA (1988–1993), *World Air Transport Statistics.* International Air Transport Association, Geneva.

ICAO (1988–1993), *Digest of Statistics, Financial Data, Series F.* International Civil Aviation Organization, Montreal.

ICAO (1988–1994), *Digest of Statistics, Traffic by Flight Stage.* International Civil Aviation Organization, Montreal.

ICAO (1974–1997), *Digest of Statistics, Airport Traffic.* International Civil Aviation Organization, Montreal.

IMF (1996, 1997), *Yearbook of Financial Statistics.* International Monetary

Fund, Washington, DC.

Janic, M. (1999), Aviation and externalities: the accomplishments and problems. *Transportation Research*, 4D, 159–180.

Janssen, M. (1996), *Meeting Targets: Tools to Support Integrated Assessment Modelling of Global Change*. Ph.D. thesis, Universiteit Maastricht.

Johansson, P.-O. (1991), *An Introduction to Modern Welfare Economics*. Cambridge University Press, Cambridge.

Johansson, P.-O. (1987), *The Economic Theory and Measurement of Environmental Benefits*. Cambridge University Press, Cambridge.

Jones-Lee, M.W. (1985), The value of safety: results from a national sample survey. *Economic Journal*, 95, 49–72.

Jorge-Calderon, J.D. (1997), A demand model for scheduled airline services on international European routes. *Journal of Air Transport Management*, 3(1), 23–35.

Kågeson, P. (1993), *Getting the Prices Right, A European Scheme for Making Transport Pay its True Costs*. European Federation for Transport and Environment, Brussels.

Kahn, A. (1988), Surprises of airline deregulation. *American Economic Review*, 78(2), papers and proceedings, 316–322.

Katsoulacos, Y. and A. Xepapadeas (1996), Emission taxes and market structure. In C. Carraro, Y. Katsoulacos and A. Xepapadeas (eds), *Environmental Policy and Market Structure*, Kluwer Academic Publishers, Dordrecht.

Katsoulacos, Y. and A. Xepapadeas (1995), Environmental policy under oligopoly with endogenous market structure. *Scandinavian Journal of Economics*, 97(3), 411–420.

Kaufman, H. (1996), *No Plane, Big Gain: Airport Noise and Residential Property Values in the Reno-Sparks Area*. MSc. thesis, University of Nevada, Reno.

Kay, J. and D. Thompson (1991), Regulatory reform in the United Kingdom: principles and application. In D. Banister and K.J. Button (eds), *Transport in a Free Market Economy*. Macmillan, London.

Kay, J. and J. Vickers (1988), Regulatory reform in Britain. *Economic Policy*, 7 (October), 286–351.

Krupnick, A.J., R.D. Rowe and C.M. Lang (1997), Transportation and air pollution: the environmental damages. In D.L. Greene, D.W. Jones and M.A. Delucchi (eds), *The Full Costs and Benefits of Transportation. Contributions to Theory, Method and Measurement*. Springer-Verlag, Berlin.

Laffont, J.J. and J. Tirole (1991), The politics of government decision-making: a theory of regulatory capture. *Quarterly Journal of Economics*, November, 1089–1127.

Lederer, P.J. (1993), A competitive network design problem with pricing. *Transportation Science*, 27(1), 25–38.

Levesque, T. (1994), Modeling the effects of airport noise on residential housing markets: a case study of Winnipeg International Airport. *Journal of Transport Economics and Policy*, 28, 199–210.

Levin, D. (1985), Taxation within Cournot oligopoly. *Journal of Public Economics*, 27, 281–290.

Levine, M.E. (1987), Airline competition in deregulated markets: theory, firm strategy, and public policy. *Yale Journal on Regulation*, 4, 393–494.

Levine, M.E. (1981), Revisionism revised? Airline deregulation and the public interest. *Law and Contemporary Problems*, 44(1), 179–195.

Levinson, D.M., D. Gillen and A. Kanafani (1998), The social costs of intercity transportation: a review and comparison of air and highway. *Transport Reviews*, 18, 215–240.

Lindsey, R. and E. Tomaszewska (1998), *Schedule Competition, Fare Competition and Predation in a Duopoly Airline Market*. Working paper, Department of Economics, University of Alberta.

Maddison, D. (1995), A cost benefit analysis of slowing climate change. *Energy Policy*, 23(4–5), 337–346.

Maddison, D., D. Pearce, O. Johansson, E. Calthrop, T. Litman and E. Verhoef (1996), *Blueprint 5: The True Costs of Road Transport*. CSERGE/Earthscan, London.

Maillebiau, E. and M. Hansen (1995), Demand and consumer welfare impacts of international airline liberalisation: The Case of the North Atlantic. *Journal of Tranport Economics and Policy*, 29(2), 115–136.

Mankiw, N.G. and M.D. Whinston (1986), Free entry and social inefficiency. *Rand Journal of Economics*, 17(1), 48–58.

Marin, P.L. (1995), Competition in European aviation: pricing policy and market structure. *Journal of Industrial Economics*, 43(2), 141–159.

Markandya, A. (1998), *Summary of Developments in the Area of Health Impacts*. Discussion paper, University of Bath.

Markandya, A. (1994), *Externalities of Fuel Cycles, Economic Valuation*. ExternE project, working document no. 9, Metroeconomica, Dorset.

Martin, Stephen (1993), *Advanced Industrial Economics*. Blackwell, Oxford.

Maser, S.M., W.H. Riker and R.N. Rossett (1977), The effects of zoning and externalities on the price of land: an empirical analysis of Monroe County, New York. *Journal of Law and Economics*, 20 (April), 111–132.

McGowan, F. and P. Seabright (1989), Deregulating European airlines. *Economic Policy*, October, 283–344.

McMillan, M.L., B.G. Reid and D.W. Gillen (1980), An extension of the hedonic approach for estimating the value of quiet. *Land Economics*, 56(3), 315–328.

Mieskowski, P. and A.M. Saper (1978), An estimate of the effects of airport noise on property values. *Journal of Urban Economics*, 5 (October), 425–440.

Miller, T.R. (1997), Societal costs of transportation crashes. In D.L. Greene, D.W. Jones and M.A. Delucchi (eds), *The Full Costs and Benefits of Transporta-*

tion. Contributions to Theory, Method and Measurement. Springer-Verlag, Berlin.

Mishan, E.J. (1971), The postwar literature on externalities: an interpretative essay. *Journal of Economic Literature*, 9, 1–28.

Morey, M. (1990), The effects of aircraft noise at Williams Air Force Base auxiliary field on residential property values. Working paper, Economics and Law Section, Argonne National Laboratory, Illinois.

Morrison, S.A. (1994), Review of: Why airplanes crash: aviation safety in a changing world. *Journal of Economic Literature*, 32(1), 164–166.

Morrison, S.A. and C. Winston (1990), The dynamics of airline pricing and competition. *American Economic Review (Papers and Proceedings)*, 80(2), 389–393.

Morrison, S.A. and C. Winston (1989), Enhancing the performance of the deregulated air transportation system. *Brookings Papers on Economic Activity; Microeconomics*, 61–123. Brookings Institution, Washington, DC.

Morrison, S.A. and C. Winston (1987), Empirical implications and tests of the contestability hypothesis. *Journal of Law and Economics*, 30(1), 53–66.

Morrison, S.A. and C. Winston (1986), *The Economic Effects of Airline Deregulation.* The Brookings Institution, Washington, DC.

Morrissette, S.E. (1996), A survey of environmental issues in the civilian aviation industry. *Journal of Air Transport World Wide*, 1, 22–38.

Moses, L.N. and I. Savage (1990), Aviation deregulation and safety, theory and evidence. *Journal of Transport Economics and Policy*, 24, 171–188.

Myles, G.D. (1995), *Public Economics.* Cambridge University Press, Cambridge.

Nelson, J.P. (1981), Measuring benefits of environmental improvements: aircraft noise and hedonic prices. In V.K. Smith (ed.), *Advances in Applied Microeconomics*, Vol. 1. JAI Press, Greenwich.

Nelson, J.P. (1980), Airports and property values: a survey of recent evidence. *Journal of Transport Economics and Policy*, 14(1), 37–52.

Nelson, J.P. (1978), *Economic Analysis of Transportation Noise Abatement.* Ballinger, Cambridge, MA.

Nero, G. (1998), Spatial multiproduct pricing: empirical evidence on intra-European duopoly airline markets. *Applied Economics*, 30, 465–475.

Nero, G. (1996), A structural model of intra European Union duopoly airline competition. *Journal of Transport Economics and Policy*, 30(2), 137–155.

Nero, G. and J.A. Black (1998), Hub-and-spoke networks and the inclusion of environmental costs on airport pricing. *Transportation Research*, 3D(5), 275–296.

NLR (1997), TNLI, Vliegtuiggebonden Gegevens. In Project Toekomstige Nederlandse Luchtvaart Infrastructuur, *Hoeveel Ruimte geeft Nederland aan de Luchtvaart, deel 6: Achtergronddocumentatie.* TNLI, Den Haag.

Nordhaus, W.D. (1993), Rolling the 'DICE': an optimal transition path for controlling greenhouse gases. *Resource and Energy Economics*, 15, 27–50.

Nordhaus, W.D. (1991), To slow or not to slow: the economics of the greenhouse effect. *Economic Journal*, 101, 920–937.

Norman, G. and J.-F. Thisse (1996), Product variety and welfare under tough and soft pricing regimes. *Economic Journal*, 106, 76–91.

Norman, V.D. and S.P. Strandenes (1994), Deregulation of Scandinavian airlines: a case study of the Oslo–Stockholm route. In P. Krugman and A. Smith (eds), *Empirical Studies of Strategic Trade Policy*. NBER/CEPR, The University of Chicago Press, Chicago.

Novshek, W. (1980), Equilibrium in simple spatial (or differentiated product) models. *Journal of Economic Theory*, 22, 313–326.

Oates, W.E. and D.L. Strassman (1984), Effluent fees and market structure. *Journal of Public Economics*, 24, 29–46.

O'Byrne, P.H., J.P. Nelson and J.J. Seneca (1985), Housing values, census estimates, disequilibrium, and the environmental costs of airport noise: a case study of Atlanta. *Journal of Environmental Economics and Management*, 12, 169–178.

Olivier, J.G.J. (1995), *Scenarios for Global Emissions from Air Traffic*. National Institute of Public Health and Environmental Protection, Bilthoven, The Netherlands.

Olivier, J.G.J. (1991), *Inventory of Aircraft Emissions: A Review of Recent Literature*. National Institute of Public Health and Environmental Protection, Bilthoven, The Netherlands.

Opschoor, J.B. and H.M.A. Jansen (1973), Waardering van de Invloed van het Vliegtuiglawaai op Woongebied rond de Potentiële Locaties van de Tweede Nationale Luchthaven. Part I, II, and Appendices, Instituut voor Milieuvraagstukken, Vrije Universiteit, Amsterdam.

Organization for Economic Cooperation and Development (1997), *Environmental Data Compendium 1997*. OECD, Paris.

Organization for Economic Cooperation and Development (1994), *Project and Policy Appraisal: Integrating Economics and the Environment*. OECD, Paris.

Organization for Economic Cooperation and Development (1993), *Environmental Data Compendium 1993*. OECD, Paris.

Organization for Economic Cooperation and Development (1991), *Fighting Noise*. OECD, Paris.

Organization for Economic Cooperation and Development (1988), *Deregulation and Airline Competition*. OECD, Paris.

Organization for Economic Cooperation and Development (1987), *Environmental Data Compendium 1987*. OECD, Paris.

Osborne, M. and A. Rubinstein (1994), *A Course in Game Theory*. The MIT Press, Cambridge, MA.

Oum, T.H., W.T. Stanbury and M.W. Tretheway (1991), Airline deregulation in Canada and its economic effects. *Transportation Journal*, 30(4), 4–22.

Oum, T.H. and M.W. Tretheway (1984), Reforming Canadian airline regulation. *The Logistics and Transportation Review*, 20(3), 261–284.

Oum, T.H., W.G. Waters II and J.-S. Yong (1992), Concepts of price elasticities of transport demand and recent empirical estimates: an interpretative survey. *Journal of Transport Economics and Policy*, 26(2), 139–154.

Oum, T.H., A. Zhang and Y. Zhang (1995), Airline network rivalry. *Canadian Journal of Economics*, 28(4), 836–857.

Oum, T.H., A. Zhang and Y. Zhang (1993), Inter-firm rivalry and firm-specific price elasticities in deregulated airline markets. *Journal of Transport Economics and Policy*, 27(2), 171–192.

Palmer, R.R. and J. Colton (1983), *A History of the Modern World*. A.A. Knopf, New York.

Palmquist, R.B. (1992), Valuing localized externalities. *Journal of Urban Economics*, 31, 59–68.

Palmquist, R.B. (1991), Hedonic methods. In J.B. Braden and C.D. Kolstad (eds), *Measuring the Demand for Environmental Quality*. North-Holland, Amsterdam.

Panzar, J.C. (1979), Equilibrium and welfare in unregulated airline markets. *American Economic Review (Papers and Proceedings)* 69, 92–95.

Pearce, D.W. (1978), Noise valuation. In D.W. Pearce (ed.), *The Valuation of Social Cost*. George Allen and Unwin, London.

Pearce, D.W. and A. Markandya (1989), *Environmental Policy Benefits: Monetary Valuation*. OECD, Paris.

Pelkmans, J. (1991), The internal EC market for air transport: issues after 1992. In D. Banister and K.J. Button (eds), *Transport in a Free Market Economy*. Macmillan, London.

Pels, E., P. Nijkamp and P. Rietveld (1997), Substitution and complementarity in aviation: airports vs airlines. *Transportation Research*, 33D(4), 275–286.

Peltzman, S. (1989), The economic theory of regulation after a decade of deregulation. *Brookings Papers on Economic Activity; Microeconomics*, 1–59.

Pennington, G., N. Topham and R. Ward (1990), Aircraft noise and residential property values adjacent to Manchester International Airport. *Journal of Transport Economics and Policy*, 24(1), 49–59.

Perl, A., J. Patterson and M. Perez (1997), Pricing aircraft emissions at Lyon-Satolas airport. *Transportation Research*, 2D(2), 89–105.

Pickrell, D. (1991), The regulation and deregulation of US airlines. In K.J. Button (ed.), *Airline Deregulation: International Experiences*. David Fulton, London.

Plowden, S.P.C. (1971), *The Cost of Noise*, Metra.

Price, I. (1974), *The Social Cost of Airport Noise as Measured by Rental Changes: The Case of Logan Airport*. Unpublished Ph.D. dissertation, Boston University, Boston.

Pryke, R. (1991), American deregulation and European liberalisation. In D.

Banister and K.J. Button (eds), *Transport in a Free Market Economy.* Macmillan, London.

Raubitschek, R.S. (1987), A model of product proliferation with multiproduct firms. *Journal of Industrial Economics,* 35(3), 269–279.

Rietveld, P. and F. Bruinsma (1998), *Is Transport Infrastructure Effective?* Springer-Verlag, Berlin.

Roos, J.H.J., A.N. Bleijenberg and W.J. Dijkstra (1997), *Energy and Emission Profiles of Aircraft and Other Modes of Passenger Transport over European Distances.* Centre for Energy Conservation and Environmental Technology, Delft.

Rothengatter, W. (1993), Externalities of transport. In J. Polak and A. Heertje (eds), *European Transport Economics.* Blackwell, Oxford.

Rowe, R.D., C.M. Lang, L.G. Chestnut, D. Latimer, D. Rae, S.M. Bernow and D. White (1995), *The New York State Environmental Externalities Cost Study, Vol. I.* Oceana Publications, New York.

Salop, S.C. (1979), Monopolistic competition with outside goods. *Bell Journal of Economics,* 10, 141–156.

Schafer, A. (1998), The global demand for motorized mobility. *Transportation Research,* 32A(6), 455–477.

Schipper, Y., P. Nijkamp and P. Rietveld (1998a), Frequency equilibria in duopoly airline markets. Tinbergen Institute discussion paper, TI 98-080/3.

Schipper, Y., P. Nijkamp and P. Rietveld (1998b), Why do aircraft noise value estimates differ? *Journal of Air Transport Management,* 4, 117–124.

Schipper, Y. and P. Rietveld (1997), Economic and environmental effects of airline deregulation. In P. Rietveld and C. Capinieri (1998, eds), *Networks in Transport and Communications.* Avebury, Aldershot.

Schwartz, J. (1994), Air pollution and daily mortality: a review and meta-analysis. *Environmental Research,* 64, 36–52.

Schwartz, M. (1986), The nature and scope of contestability theory. *Oxford Economic Papers,* 38, Supplement (November), 37–57.

Shaked, A. and J. Sutton (1982), Relaxing price competition through product differentiation. *Review of Economic Studies,* 49, 3–13.

Small, K. and C. Kazimi (1995), On the costs of air pollution from motor vehicles. *Journal of Transport Economics and Policy,* 29(1), 7–32.

Smith, V.K. (1993), Nonmarket valuation of environmental resources: an interpretative appraisal. *Land Economics,* 69(1), 1–26.

Smith, V.K. and J.-C. Huang (1995), Can markets value air quality? A meta-analysis of hedonic property value models. *Journal of Political Economy,* 103(1), 209–227.

Smith, V.K. and Y. Kaoru (1990), What have we learned since Hotelling's letter? A meta-analysis. *Economics Letters,* 32, 267–272.

Sorensen, F. (1991), The changing aviation scene in Europe. In D. Banister and K.J. Button (eds), *Transport in a Free Market Economy.* Macmillan, London.

Spence, M. (1983), Contestable markets and the theory of industry structure: a review article. *Journal of Economic Literature*, 21 (September), 981–990.

Starkie, D.N.M. and D.M. Johnson (1975), *The Economic Value of Peace and Quiet*. Lexington Books, Lexington, MA.

Stasinopoulos, D. (1993), The third phase of liberalisation in community aviation and the need for supplementary measures. *Journal of Transport Economics and Policy*, 27(3), 323–328.

Stasinopoulos, D. (1992), The second aviation package of the European Community. *Journal of Transport Economics and Policy*, 26(1), 83–87.

Stewart, J. (1991), *Econometrics*. Philip Allen, Hemel Hempstead.

Tirole, J. (1988), *The Theory of Industrial Organization*. The MIT Press, Cambridge, MA.

Tol, R.S.J. (1999), The marginal costs of greenhouse emissions. *Energy Journal*, 20(1), 61–81.

Tol, R.S.J. (1997), *A Decision-Analytic Treatise of the Enhanced Greenhouse Effect*. Ph.D. thesis, Vrije Universiteit, Amsterdam.

Tol, R.S.J. and V. Grewe (1999), *Climate-Related External Costs of Nitrogen and Sulphur Emissions*. Mimeo, Institute for Environmental Studies, Amsterdam/DLR, Oberpfaffenhofen.

Tretheway, M.W. and T.H. Oum (1992), *Airline Economics: Foundations for Strategy and Policy*. Centre for Transportation Studies, University of British Columbia.

Uyeno, D., S.W. Hamilton and A. Biggs (1993), Density of residential land use and the impact of airport noise. *Journal of Transport Economics and Policy*, 27(1), 3–18.

Veenstra, D.L., J.P. Beck, T.H.P. The and J.G.J. Olivier (1995), *The Impact of Aircraft Exhaust Emissions on the Atmosphere; Scenario Studies with a Three Dimensional Global Model*. National Institute of Public Health and Environmental Protection, Bilthoven, The Netherlands.

Verhoef, E.T. (1996), *The Economics of Regulating Road Transport*. Edward Elgar, Cheltenham.

Verster, A.C.P. (1997), Kadernotitie Economisch Evaluatie Onderzoek TNLI. In Project Toekomstige Nederlandse Luchtvaart Infrastructuur, *Hoeveel Ruimte geeft Nederland aan de Luchtvaart, deel 2: Economie en Procedure*. TNLI, Den Haag.

Viner, J. (1931), Cost curves and supply curves. *Zeitschrift für Nationalökonomie*, 3, 23–46.

Viscusi, W.K. (1993), The value of risks to life and health. *Journal of Economic Literature*, 31, 1912–1946.

Walters, A.A. (1975), *Noise and Prices*. Clarendon Press, Oxford.

Werkgroep milieuberekeningen TNLI (1997), Zonering en Normstelling Luchtvaartlawaai. Geluidsbelastingcontouren voor Nieuwe Vliegvelden; Quick and Dirty.

In Project Toekomstige Nederlandse Luchtvaart Infrastructuur, *Hoeveel Ruimte geeft Nederland aan de Luchtvaart, deel 5: Ruimtelijke Ordening, Milieu en Ecologie.* TNLI, Den Haag.

Werkgroep LACKS (1997), *LACKS-1: Economische Betekenis en Milieubeslag.* Werkdocument, Schiphol.

Winston, C. (1993), Economic deregulation: days of reckoning for microeconomists. *Journal of Economic Literature*, 31, 1263–1289.

Woodmansey, B.G. and J.G. Patterson (1994), New methodology for modeling annual aircraft emissions at airports. *Journal of Transportation Engineering*, 120(3), 339–357.

World Bank (1995), *World Tables 1995.* Washington, DC.

Yamaguchi, Y. (1996), *Estimating the Cost of Aircraft Noise around Airports in London: a Hedonic Study.* MSc. Thesis, University College, London.

Index